Political Fiction

Political Fiction, The Spirit of the Age, and Allen Drury

Tom Kemme

Bowling Green State University Popular Press
Bowling Green, Ohio 43403

Cover design by Gary Dumm

Library of Congress Catalogue Card No.: 87-71029

ISBN: 0-87972-373-4 Clothbound
        0-87972-374-2 Paperback

To my beloved wife, Marion;

and to my dear children, Tom, Maureen, and John

Acknowledgments

Thanks to all of my teachers and colleagues who have contributed to my learning and study, but a special thanks to the following: Mr. James Leahy, for our numerous conversations about politics, ideology, literature, and style; Sister Clarita Felhoelter, O.S.U., who generously read my manuscript and offered excellent advice at a crucial point of my study; Ms. Marquita Breit and Ms. Rosalind Parnes whose services as librarians were extremely helpful and consistent; Dr. Don Osborn for his insight about serious and popular literature presented in "Reader's Choice," a book review program on television; Dr. Robert Daggy and Dr. Michael Krukones, for insights presented in "Politics in Fiction and Film," an experimental course; and to Ms. Eileen Whalen and Mrs. Pat Allen who have been kind, thoughtful, and extremely competent in the typing of the manuscript.

Contents

Preface

During the sixties tons of political fiction appeared in the market place. For four-hundred and two weeks during the sixties political novels focusing upon Washington or national politics appeared on *The New York Times* Best Seller List. Obviously, there was much profit in publishing political fiction. As one might also expect, the subject of politics appeared in popular fiction with varying degrees of quantity and intensity.

The popularity of political fiction invites a question of genre: on the basis of structure, can we classify some novels as "pure" or elemental political fiction, and can we distinguish "pure" political fiction from fiction which includes the subject of politics but where politics does not shape or inform the structure of the novel in a significant way.

In order to distinguish political novels from novels that are about politics but which treat the subject of politics in a superficial rather than a pervasive way, we have defined a political novel as "a work of prose fiction which primarily focuses upon the exercise of power within the body politic and where political ambition, political plans and political acts permeate and unify the novel through plot and character." Within this context, *Advise and Consent* (1959) is a "pure" or elemental political novel, and Allen Drury serves as the primary novelist in this study of political fiction.

Allen Drury was the most commercially successful political novelist of the sixties. *Advise and Consent* appeared on *The New York Times* Best Seller list for one-hundred and two weeks (August 15, 1959-July 30, 1961); *Capable of Honor* appeared for forty-one weeks (October 2, 1966-July 16, 1967). Not only was Drury the most commercially successful political novelist in the sixties, he was also the most critically acclaimed: *Advise and Consent* was awarded the 1959 Pulitizer Prize. Though Drury can write with exceptional skill, his political fiction is very uneven; nevertheless, even his less aesthetically pleasing fiction—*A Shade of Difference* (1962), *Preserve and Protect* (1966). *Come Nineveh, Comes Tyre* (1973), and *A Promise of Joy* (1975)—was commercially successful, appearing on *The New York Times* Best Seller list for a total of ninety-nine weeks. Although quantity is not an indicator of quality, sometimes popularity and quality coincide. Because the political ideology or philosophy which shapes a political novel sometimes sharply contrasts with that of a reader, the evaluation of political fiction poses some interesting critical problems. Just as Drury's political fiction

1

serves as the primary matter for our critical examination of political fiction as genre, Northrop Frye's definition of fiction and his categories of *novel, anatomy, romance, and confession* function as our analytical instrument.

In "pure" political fiction there is an aesthetic wholeness formed by plot, character, theme, and setting. An essential element of the setting is the Spirit of the Age. Just as Machiavelli warns that a prince must perceive, identify, understand, and merge with the temper of the times if he is to be successful, so likewise must the political novelist create a Spirit of the Age within his or her fiction if that fiction is to generate "a willing suspension of disbelief" in a popular audience. Although the Spirit of the Age is not always immediately identifiable in political fiction, the Spirit of the Age integrates and vitalizes plot, character, and theme. The sixties and the seventies were decades of extraordinary conflict and change in the American body politic. The Civil Rights Movement, the Vietnam War, and the Watergate break-in and cover-up were historical events with political significance, and these events were frequently reported directly to the American public through television. These events significantly reflected and shaped the Spirit of the Age, and consequently some knowledge of them is essential for an understanding of popular political fiction during the sixties and the seventies. To understand Drury's popularity and his literary achievement—to write "pure," popular, and serious political fiction is no trivial accomplishment— Drury's political fiction must be viewed in the context of the times, as well as against the background of his competition: the best selling political fiction of the sixties and the seventies.

In *The Defense of Poetry* Shelley advises us that literature both reflects and shapes the spirit of the age. Drury's popular political fiction reflected the conflicts and the agony of the American body politic during the sixties and seventies. It also reflected a conservative voice as a part of an evolving conservative movement in the American body politic. Although Senator Barry Goldwater was soundly defeated by President Lyndon Johnson in the 1964 election and the future of the conservative segment of the Republican Party appeared very dim at that time, the ideological battle between liberals and conservatives continued, and Ronald Reagan, a conservative, eventually emerged as the leader of the Republican Party and as a twice-elected President of the United States. In a *Time* magazine article in November, 1975, Ronald Reagan identifies Allen Drury as one of his two favorite authors. Thus my study in genre.

Chapter I
"Pure" and Serious Political Fiction
Some Problems of Definition

Although politics is interesting, and many interesting novels have been written about politics, and several critical works have been written about politics in fiction, the definition of "a political novel," a "pure" political novel, remains elusive. Since the problem of definition is so challenging, there is a tendency to trivialize the task of definition, as well as to trivialize those critics who attempt to define "a political novel." Irving Howe, for example, in the *Politics and the Novel*, is not too much concerned with "labels, categories, and definitions;" some minds, he observes, "called perhaps a little too easily, the academic mind, insist upon exhaustive rights of classification" (18). Gordon Milne in *The American Political Novel* also trivializes the value of definition: "Efforts to create rigid Classifications to distinguish the political novel from the economic, the social, the proletarian, and other types," he warns, "are likely not only to be unsuccessful but to detract from an understanding of the development of the novel rather than to add to it" (5). Despite such disclaimers, both Howe and Milne attempt to describe or to define a political novel, but neither do so as directly as Edmund Speare does in *The Political Novel*.

To Speare, a political novel "is a work of prose fiction which leans rather to 'ideas' than to 'emotions': which deals rather with the machinery of law making or with a theory about public conduct than with the merits of any given legislation; and where the main purpose of the writer is partly propaganda, or exposition of the lives of the personages who maintain government, or the forces which constitute governments. In this exposition the drawing room is frequently used as a medium for presenting the inside life of politics" (ix). Although Speare's definition is compact, it is rather lengthy. More importantly, Speare's definition deemphasizes the aesthetic component in the political novel. According to Speare, the primary purpose of the political novelist is not to entertain, nor to produce an art object for aesthetic purposes. To Speare, "the main purpose of the writer is partly propaganda, public reform, or the exposition of the lives of personages who maintain government, or the forces which constitute governments."

The element of aesthetics quite naturally suggests the question of when "popular" political fiction crosses the boundary into "serious" political fiction.[1] Although Howe is rather "loose" in his definition of the political novel, he is very precise in his definition of a "serious" novel.[2] "Ideas,"

3

Howe believes, "be they in free isolation or hooped into formal systems, are indispensable to the serious novel" (xiii). To Speare, the political novel "leans rather to 'ideas' than to 'emotions;' " to Howe, ideas are the essential element in political fiction. "By a political novel," Howe writes in his Preface, "I mean a novel in which political ideas play a dominant role or in which the political milieu is the dominant setting" (21). When Howe offers another definition of the political novel, the focus is upon the ideas and ideology rather than upon the political milieu. In the first chapter of *Politics and the Novel* we are advised that a political novel is "the kind in which the idea of society, as distinct from the mere unquestioned workings of society, has penetrated the consciousness of the characters in all its problematic aspects, so that it is to be observed in their behavior, and they are themselves often aware of, some political loyalty or ideological identification. They now think in terms of supporting or opposing society as such; they rally to one or another embattled segment of society; and they do so in the name of, and under prompting from, an ideology" (21). Such a definition, as Howe indicates in a footnote, makes it often "impossible or not very useful to draw a sharp distinction between the political and social novels as I have described them" (21). Perhaps more useful distinctions can be made if we define "power" as the operative word in the definition of a "pure" political novel and view the political novel as one kind of a social novel.

Although William Blotner observes that "a political novel is hard to define," he grapples with the problem in both *The Political Novel* (1955) and *The Modern American Political Novel* (1966).[3] Blotner, like Howe, provides a "loose" rather than a "tight" definition, a definition which "is wide and inclusive." According to Blotner a political novel must "portray political acts, so many of them that they form the novels main theme, or *in some cases*, a major theme" (Italics added.). The "prime material" of the political novel is not ideas or ideology as Howe suggests, but rather "the politician at work: legislating, campaigning, mending political fences, building his career." Major characters "must carry out political acts or move in a political environment;" a political novel is taken to mean a book which *directly* describes, interprets or analyzes political phenomena where the political element is in the foreground" (Italics added.). On the other hand, political acts "are not always obvious ones" (1-2). In *The Modern American Political Novel* (1966) we are advised that political novels have politics as the primary subject; they "deal with the overt, institutionalized politics of the office holder, the candidate, the party official, or the individual who performs political acts;" political novels "deal primarily with political processes and actions."[4] Such description is helpful, but there are two "loose" or soft spots in Blotner's definition: politics and political acts. The term *politics* is "defined in a very literal and functional sense" and the term *political acts* refers to political acts "as they are conventionally understood"

(8). *Politics* and *political acts* can mean different things to different people. Like beauty, politics is sometimes found only in the eye of the beholder.

A political novel, then, according to Speare, Howe and Blotner is rather loosely defined; a political novel is one that includes the subject of politics and politics can appear in the novel in several ways or forms, including purpose (education or propaganda); setting (a legislative body, that is, a federal state or local government); social events, (for example, as Speare suggests "the drawing room is frequently used as a medium for presenting the inside life of politics"); plot and character (professional politicians engaged in political acts). In some novels which include the subject of politics, politics might penetrate the novel in each of these ways; in other novels which include the subject of politics, the political dimension might appear in only one or two forms, and the politics in such novels may be superficial and have very little shaping effect upon the vital or organic quality of the novel. Is a "tighter" definition possible, a definition which will enable us to make sharper distinctions about the quality and quantity of political content in a novel, as well as the shaping effect of the political content upon the novel when the novel is viewed as an art object or as an aesthetic whole? Is it possible to make sharper distinctions between the terms "a political novel" and "a novel about politics" and to discern "pure" forms of the political novel? Let us try.

A political novel might be defined as *a work of prose fiction which primarily focuses upon the exercise of political power within the body politic and where political ambition, political plans, and political acts permeate and unify the novel through both plot and character.* Power, within this context, is the ability to influence people and events in the political arena; it is the ability to make things happen within the body politic.[5] Because of its examination of the phenomenon of power—the desire to influence or control people or events—political fiction has the potential to present universal experiences, predispositions of personality or character which transcend time and place: man's desire for power (political ambition); his pursuit of power (plans and actions which enable him to influence events in the body politic, directly or indirectly); his acquisition of power (actions and personality traits necessary for winning or obtaining an elected office); and the implementation of power (how to govern effectively when elected or appointed to office). This definition of the political novel, *"a work of prose fiction which primarily focuses upon the exercise of political power within the body politic and where political ambition, political plans, and political acts permeate and unify the novel through both plot and character"* includes "the political environment," "political acts," and political ideology, as has been suggested by Speare, Blotner, and Howe; however, something more has been added: the examination and the presentation of political power as the unifying or fusing element in "pure" political fiction.

Obviously, power and the exercise of power are subjects of much complexity; so also is the concept of the body politic, the political environment where the politician or the political activist exercises power. The American body politic is both a process (a government in action) and a product (a government which was created as a result of a process and which is sustained as a result of that process). When a group of people agree to form a government, a body politic is created. To put it another way, the American body politic is a group of individuals who *voluntarily* enter into a system of agreements (laws) which include the pursuit of a common purpose, the delegation of authority, the subordination of individual desires and interests to the desires and interests of the group in accordance with the structure and the policy of the group, and an agreement to act in concern, that is, not as individuals but as a group or unit.[6] The structure of the national American body politic—the Executive, Legislative, and Judicial branches of government, as well as the citizens who actively or passively participate in government by voting or non-voting—are necessarily a part of the setting or "political environment" of politics and political fiction (Tussman 3-11). In political fiction, dramatic political activity occurs when there is a clash of opinions, ideology, or self-interest concerning elections or policies (domestic or foreign) and individuals act for the purposes of obtaining office and/or influencing policy. The word *politics*, one might say, denotes those processes or activities whereby conflicts involving the interest of the individual citizen and the common good are initiated, sustained, and frequently, though not always, resolved. This resolution, or the lack of resolution always involves the exercise of influence or power. The terms "power" and "the body politic" are abstractions; it is the challenging task of the political novelist to make them concrete and vital through the creation of plot and character.

II

If readers are not conversant with or interested in government and the processes of government, if they lack a political information base, the political novelist will have difficulty engaging the reader's interest in a "pure" political novel. What Marianne Moore wrote about poetry is also true of political fiction: "that we do not admire what we cannot understand." At bottom, "pure" political fiction is cerebral; it deals with political systems and ideas, and ideas are a part of the spirit of the age: the social, intellectual, political, and economic milieu. Through techniques of realism, political novelists can make a political novel come to life, that is, in Coleridge's words, to induce "a willing suspension of disbelief" in the mind of the reader. The techniques of realism, however, though they significantly contribute to the creation of verisimilitude, are not enough by themselves to be totally convincing in political fiction. More is needed. In order to engage the sympathetic imagination of an audience, authors must also create the spirit of the age and an aura of ideological credibility. Before we turn to the ideological component of political fiction, however, let us turn briefly to the techniques of realism as they appeared in both fictional and non-fictional prose in the sixties and seventies and view these techniques as part of the novelist's craft which enables the writer to induce "a willing suspension of disbelief" in the mind of the reader and create a fictional world in the imagination.

As a result of the author's creative gift and the craft of fiction, attentive readers should vicariously experience "the sight, sound, and feel of the political experience" (Blotner 12). Political novels should present political realities and political truths. From this perspective, when political fiction presents "real" politicians as "real people" within the context of a "real" body politic in a "real" society, we are viewing a work of political fiction, adopting Northrop Frye's terminology, as a novel. In *The Anatomy of Criticism*, Frye views fiction not as something "unreal", but as "something made for its own sake," thereby suggesting that a work of fiction created strictly for commercial or propaganda purposes is somewhat inferior to a work of fiction created primarily for aesthetic purposes although this may not always necessarily be so. For Frye, the strictly defined novel which "deals with real people" in a "real" society is only one of four forms of fiction: novel, anatomy, romance, and autobiography (Frye 303-314). How is it, through what means, we might ask, does a literary artist create in political fiction enough verisimilitude to induce "a willing suspension of disbelief" in a reader's mind so that politician's become "real" people in a "real" world in the reader's imagination?[7]

Much of the "willing suspension of disbelief" or the absorbing quality of a novel can be traced to the effective implementation of what Tom Wolfe calls "the techniques of realism": scene by scene development, the minimalization of historical narrative, dialogue, the third person point of view, and the presentation of details (*The New Journalism* 31-34). What scenes, what dialogues, what details should be selected to convince the reader of the "truth" of the political characters? How does a politician talk? What does he talk about? What does he do? How does he do it? Why does he do it? In the real, nonfictional world, most readers learn about politics and politicians in several ways: through formal education, through media (radio, television, newspapers, magazines), through books, through personal contact during election campaigns, and for some, through professional and social contact in professional activities and at social events. In the real non-fictional world, there are thousands and thousands of politicians and each is significantly different; yet in their quest for an implementation of power, the overwhelming majority are essentially the same, and this "sameness" is recorded in the memory bank of the citizens who constitute the reading public. When the political novelist creates plots and characters and selects details, he or she must tap the storehouse of information and experience stored in the conscious and the unconscious memory of his or her readers. By an author's judicious selection of detail, readers will "know" or "recognize" the authenticity of political characters, as well as the authenticity of the political landscape or setting. In *The New Journalism* Tom Wolfe writes knowingly about the selection of detail and its importance in the creation of vitality in fiction:

This is the recording of everyday gestures, habits, manners, customs, style of furniture, clothing, decoration, styles of traveling, eating, keeping house, modes of behaving toward children, servants, superiors, inferiors, peers, plus the various looks, glances, poses, styles of walking and other symbolic details that might exist within a scene. Symbolic of what? Symbolic, generally, of people's *status life*, using that term in the *broad* sense of the entire pattern of behavior and possessions through which people express their position in the world or what they think it is or what they hope it to be (32).

In the sixties and seventies novelists and journalists quite effectively merged the selection of detail with the other techniques of realism to blur the distinctions between fact and fiction. For example, Truman Capote wrote *In Cold Blood*, a true life account of murder and murderers which many viewed and still view as a non-fictional novel. In *The Final Days* through the mastery of point of view, scene, detail, and dialogue, Carl Bernstein and Robert Woodward, Pulitzer Prize winning journalists of the *Washington Post*, created a similar impression of fiction. The facts of history, graphically and sometimes imaginatively presented in *The Final Days*, make President Nixon's last days in office read with the immediacy and vitality of fiction. Bernstein and Woodward imaginatively recreate the details and conversations in scenes which depict actual events, and the journalists present those events through the consciousness of the historical figures who were intimately observing President Nixon's *Final Days*. The two journalists recorded political history by using the techniques of realism; ironically, (William Faulkner had warned in 1962 that political fiction risked being ephemeral because political fiction has a tendency to become journalistic) Bernstein and Woodward's combination of journalism, history and imagination created a non-fictional novel which will outlast most of the political fiction written in the seventies (Blotner, 361).

One approach which minimizes the political novelist's risk of creating short lived or ephemeral fiction is the integration of ideas and ideology within the novel; however, such an integration of ideas and ideology within the political novel involves a significant aesthetic risk. Although the inclusion of ideas and ideology contributes to the durability of political fiction, ideas and ideology also possess the potential of destroying a novel's vitality. Ideas and ideologies can take on a life of their own; as Irving Howe suggests, ideas and ideologies can stir "characters into passionate gestures and sacrifices;" they can even "seem to become active characters in the political novel;" however, as Howe so aptly cautions. "When the armoured columns of ideology troop *en masse* they do imperil a novel's life and liveliness" (23,22). More than a few political novels have been aesthetically destroyed by an immersion of ideas and ideologies, and this is certainly true of *Come Nineveh, Come Tyre* and *A Promise of Joy*, the concluding novels in Allen Drury's political series. On the other hand, the third novel in the political series, *Capable of Honor*, is saturated with ideas and ideologies—liberalism and conservatism—which not only motivate and stir characters, but which also seem to take on a life of their own in such characters as "Wonderful Walter" Dobius (Do Be Us who are *dubious*) a "liberal" and Orrin Knox (*Ore in Knox*) a "conservative." When an author introduces ideology into a novel, he runs the risk that what the author perceives to be knowledge or truth (the way the world really is) will be viewed by some readers as a shallow understanding of reality, as a failure of intellectual vision. As a result, for some initially interested readers—the effective use of details, dialogue, and point of view can create compelling reading—the fragile fabric of the novel which induces "a willing suspension of disbelief" will eventually be jeopardized and shattered. Unlike the overtly propagandistic *Come Nineveh, Come Tyre* and *The Promise of Joy*, the conservative ideology in *Advise and Consent* is moderate and unobtrusive; or perhaps it only seems so because *Advise* reflects the ideas and emotions—militant anti-Communism and a fear that America and Russia will engage in an armed conflict— that were a significant component of the spirit of the age in the fifties and sixties and were therefore easily and comfortably processed and absorbed into the imaginations of millions of readers.

In serious political fiction, if that serious political fiction is to become truly alive, it is not enough that the techniques of realism be mastered in order to create verisimilitude. Ideological *respectability* and credibility are also essential for inducing into readers "a willing suspension of disbelief." However, even sophisticated readers sometimes possess intellectual blind spots: prejudices and emotional blocks. In terms of ideology, a political novelist cannot be all things to all people and still maintain his or her intellectual vision and integrity. Consequently, the serious political novel provides a very severe test to both the writer who wishes the broadest possible audience for his novel and for the reader who not only wishes to be entertained but who also desires to have his or her intellectual vision and emotional commitments reinforced. Irving Howe clearly defines the problem:

For both the writer and the reader, the political novel provides a particularly severe test: politics rakes our passions as nothing else, and whatever we may consent to overlook in a novel, we react with an almost demonic rapidity to a detested political opinion. For the writer the great test is, how much truth can he force through the sieve of his opinions. For the reader the great test is, how much of the truth can he accept though it jostles *his* opinions? (26)

And we might add, how much "truth" can a reader accept without eroding interest and destroying the fictional world created by the imagination? For example, few would doubt that readers ideologically and temperamentally inclined toward a "conservative" disposition would tend to find more enjoyment in Drury's fiction than those of a more "liberal" ideological bent. Although there are significant universal elements in the Pulitzer Prize winning *Advise and Consent*, it would be an unusual Russian Communist indeed who could sustain "a willing suspension of disbelief" in the presence of Drury's novel. The ideological conflict between American Capitalistic Democracy and Russian imperialistic Communism is continued in *A Shade of Difference* and *Capable of Honor* at a much more strident and obtrusive level, thereby ideologically and emotionally limiting its appeal not only to Russian readers, but also American. Although many readers of *Capable* were and are unsympathetic to the conservative ideas, attitudes, opinions, and judgements presented in *A Shade* and *Capable* about Russia, America, the anti-Vietnam War Movement, and the "liberal" media, sophisticated readers would recognize that Drury's conservative vision was one that vitally existed in the American body politic, a political vision and philosophy that was evolving and becoming more articulate, and as a result, becoming a significant influence in shaping the spirit of the age, that is the political, intellectual, social and economic milieu.[8] The following themes or perceptions, views which many American liberals could not take seriously, permeate *Capable of Honor* and are woven into the texture of Drury's political fiction:

There are only two major ideological groups in America: Liberals and Conservatives.
Liberals control the media.
The liberal media significantly influences the thoughts and emotions of the American
     voter to support Liberals and oppose Conservatives.
Liberals are intellectually shallow, especially in their understanding of the nature
     of Communism, its methods and goals.
Liberals, though not always deliberately or consciously, destroy patriotism by attacking
     the ideals, the goals, and the accomplishments of America.
Liberals perceive that Communism is changing for the better and that Communism
     becomes more civilized as Communist ideology matures.
American power and influence is decreasing and America is becoming less confident
     about protecting her interest in foreign countries.
Conversely, Communist power and influence is increasing through the world.

Liberals believe that the best American foreign policy is one of accommodation with
    Communism.
There is a growing fear of atomic war in America and many Americans would prefer
    a Communist America than risk atomic destruction of America and the world.
The media—newspapers, magazines, radio, and television—uncritically adopts the
    liberal views of the most successful commentators and columnists ("pack"
    journalism).
Anyone who expresses views opposite to those of the liberal media will have their
    views misrepresented or distorted by the media.
Although Communist imperialism will destroy the emerging African and Asian
    nations without the good will of the United States and the protection of the
    United States and the United Nations, Third World Nations either consciously
    or from ignorance adopt policies which alienate the United States and destroy
    the United Nations.

Whether or not one could agree with Drury's analysis of what "liberals"
believe and do, contemporary readers immediately recognized that Drury
was grappling with ideas and conflicts that were dramatically present in
national and international politics. In the conflict between liberals and
conservatives, Drury was very much attuned to the spirit of the age, those
ideas and emotions that were tearing apart the American body politic and
causing pain to the American psyche in the sixties as a result of the Civil
Rights Movement, the urban riots, and the Vietnam War. During the sixties,
polarization was common in America, and Drury's fiction ideologically
depicted that painful polarization. Both liberals and conservatives
experienced anger, hostility, frustration and betrayal over American's
involvement in the Vietnam War. Drury's fiction depicts what some would
perceive to be the liberal folly of the times from the perspective of a
conservative. Although many sophisticated readers may find Drury's political
vision faulty and his ideology shallow, history dramatically demonstrates
that his fiction was prescient in reading the hearts and minds of the electorate
and the conservative direction of the American body politic, a body politic
that elected a conservative president in landslide elections in 1980 and 1984.
The conservative views of Ronald Reagan—who identified William Buckley
and Allen Drury as his favorite authors in a *Time* Magazine interview ("The
Star Shakes up the Party" 23)—are the anti-Communist sentiments that
permeate Drury's fiction; there can be little doubt that Drury's views,
dramatically expressed in his extremely popular political fiction, helped to
shape and to re-enforce ideas which were already prevalent in the American
body politic, ideas and sentiments that Ronald Reagan had been expressing
years before Allen Drury published *Advise and Concent* in 1959, ideas and
sentiments that were a significant element in the spirit of the age.

III

Drury's militant anti-Communist posture, which is at the core of his least aesthetically pleasing fiction, has ideological parallels with the anti-Communist rhetoric expressed by Ronald Reagan as an actor, as President of the Actor's Union, and as a lecturer for General Electric.[9] When Ronald Reagan examined the spirit of the age in 1961 during a frequently delivered speech, he found it to be sick with the "evil" of Communism and he sounded a warning. The United States and the Soviet Union were in a "declared war," a death struggle. Karl Marx, Reagan told his audiences,

established the cardinal principle that Communism and Capitalism cannot co-exist in the world together. Our way of life, our system, must be totally destroyed; then the world communist state will be erected on the ruins. In interpreting Marx, Lenin said, "It is inconceivable that the Soviet Republic should continue to exist for a long period side by side with imperialistic states. Ultimately, one or the other must conquer" (Reagan 677).

Despite the words of Marx and Lenin, Reagan noted that many government officials and members of the press were not alert to the danger. Obviously, such was not the case with Ronald Reagan who had direct experience with Communism in the movie industry. "On direct orders from the Kremlin," Reagan reported, "hard core organizers infiltrated the movie industry with the intention of gaining economic control and subverting our screens through the dissemination of Communist propaganda" (677). Communist organizers duped "well meaning but misguided people" who sometimes became members of Communist cells or Communist front organizations. The Communists, Reagan said, were confident of victory. In 1923 Lenin had spoken of world domination: first Eastern Europe, then Asia, then America. But Lenin believed that the takeover of America would be easy. According to Lenin, "that last bastion of Capitalism will not have to be taken. It will fall into our outstretched hands like over-ripe fruit" (677). The Communist believe, Ronald Reagan continued in his frequently delivered speech, that "under the constant pressure of the cold war" Americans will gradually "give up, one by one, our democratic customs and traditions...until one day" we will "have grown so much like the enemy that we no longer (will) have any cause for conflict" (677-678). Such a day, Reagan suggested in his speech, titled "Encroaching Control," was approaching under the guise of liberalism. With the words of Norman Thomas, the Socialist candidate for President, Reagan illustrated his point: "The American people," Thomas said, "would never knowingly vote for Socialism but that under the name of liberalism, they would adopt every fragment of the socialist program" (678). Khruschev, too, had sounded a similar theme: "We can't expect the American people," Reagan quoted the Soviet Premier, "to jump from Capitalism to Communism, but we can assist their elected leaders in giving them small doses of Socialism, until they awaken and find they have

Communism" (678). Socialism, Reagan observed, had already taken root in America: "the federal government owns and operates more than 19,000 businesses" and "the estimated book value of 700 governmental corporations is $260 billion" (679). Because of "the growth of a collection of internal powers and bureaucratic institutions" which are "beyond the reach of Congress and actually capable of dictating policy," the "very essence of totalitarianism" had penetrated America (679). Despite the "Encroaching Control" of government—"one of seven of the nation's work force is on the public payroll"—Reagan told his audiences that the term Socialism is not used (680). In his speech, subtitled "Keep Government Poor and Remain Free," Reagan spoke of liberals. "Liberals" are responsible for increasing government participation in business and in the personal lives of Americans. "Those of 'liberal' persuasion," Reagan reported, "say they 'reject the notion that the least government is the best government' " (680) and they believe that the national debt is without meaning. In Reagan's speech liberals are thus associated with Socialists, and Socialists are associated with Communists. And Communists are in a declared war with America which can only be described as a death struggle which is an immediate threat:

There can only be one end to the war we are in. It won't go away if we simply try to out-wait it. Wars end in Victory or defeat. One of the foremost authorities on Communism in the world today had said we have 10 years. Not ten years to make up our minds but ten years to win or lose—by 1970 the world will be all slave or all free (681).

Twenty-two years later, in a 1983 speech to the National Association of Evangelicals, mixing theology, war, morality, and government, President Reagan bluntly declared his animosity to Soviet Communism. "The focus of evil in the modern world" is Communism, Reagan told the Evangelicals. As he did in 1961, the President declared that there is no room for temporizing or equivocation because the struggle is "between right and wrong, good and evil," and he reminded Americans that we "are enjoined by Scripture and the Lord Jesus to oppose it with all our might." As Americans consider the increase in the military budget and the wisdom of a nuclear freeze, Reagan warned that Americans must not "ignore the facts of history and the aggressive impulse of an evil empire;" "peace," he advised, must be found "through strength." In addition, the Conservative President warned that "simple-minded appeasement or wishful thinking about our adversaries is folly" because "it means the betraying of our past, the squandering of our freedom." To accept Communists "at their word" and to "accommodate ourselves" to Russia's "aggressive impulses," Reagan suggested to his audience, would be to invite disaster (Clines A1,8).

As President, on another public occasion, Reagan vehemently denounced the Soviets. At a 1981 press conference President Reagan expressed views that were shared by many conservatives concerning the nature of totalitarian Communism, its goals, and its methods:

"I know of no leader of the Soviet Union, since the revolution and including the present leadership, that has not more than once repeated in the various Communist congresses they hold, their determination that their goal must be the promotion of world revolution and a one-world socialist or Communist state, whichever word you want to use.

"Now, as long as they do that and as long as they, at the same time, have openly and publicly declared that the only morality they recognize is what will further their cause, meaning they reserve unto themselves the right to commit any crime, to lie to cheat in order to obtain that and that is moral, not immoral, I think when you do business with them...you keep that in mind." (Gwertzman Al).

In Drury's *Come Nineveh, Come Tyre* "liberal" Ted Jason accepts the word of the Communists and accommodates Russia's aggressive impulses; consequently, he squanders America's freedom, and to use President Reagan's terms, America is on the verge of being enslaved by "the evil empire." When America, because of its folly, is confronted with only one path to maintain its freedom—the use of nuclear weapons which risks not only the destruction of Russia, but also the world—America chooses in *Come Nineveh, Come Tyre* not to take the risk. In an interview with *People Magazine* published on December 6, 1983, and published in the official White House compilation of presidential documents, President Reagan spoke about his views concerning Armageddon theology, the belief that the end of the world may be coming soon. When asked about his statement that Russia was an "evil empire," he replied: "Never, in the time between the prophecies and up to now, has there been a time in which so many of the prophecies are coming together. There have been times in the past when people thought the end of the world was coming, and so forth, but never anything like this (Herbers 12). On yet another occasion, President Reagan expressed a similar thought: "I turn back to your ancient prophets in the Old Testament and the signs foretelling Armageddon, and I find myself wondering if, we're the generation that's going to see that come about" (Herbers 12).

To most Americans, such ideas lack immediate active credibility; and when they are integrated into the plots and characters of political fiction, they destroy "a willing suspension of disbelief" beyond repair. Such lack of credibility is certainly true of *Come Nineveh, Come Tyre* and *A Promise of Joy*. The ideological and the religious element, as well as faulty craftsmanship, make *Come Nineveh* and *A Promise* ephemeral fiction. On the other hand, this is not to overlook the fact that for millions of readers who share or shared President Reagan's expressed religious beliefs and perceptions of Communism, these artistically weak novels were both interesting and entertaining. To millions and millions of readers even Drury's least aesthetically pleasing and least artistically crafted political fiction "works" or at least "worked" at the time of publication: it creates or created a vital fictional world in the imagination of the reader. Even those readers, however, who find Drury ideologically unconvincing recognize the reality of the ideological and political conflicts which underly Drury's political series, conflicts which reflected and contributed to the shaping of the spirit of the age, an essential element in political fiction. Before turning to *Advise and Consent* and *Capable of Honor* as examples of serious and "pure" political fiction, let us first observe some of the characteristics of the spirit of the age as it was reflected in the best selling political fiction of the sixties and seventies, the pre-Watergate era.

Chapter II
The Spirit of the Age in
Popular Political Fiction

"One never, of course, asks is it a novel" John Cheever observed in a letter to the *New York Review* of Books, "One asks is it interesting, and interest connotes suspense, emotional involvement, and a sustained claim on one's attention" (Cheever 44). During the sixties and early seventies, the repeated appearance on the *New York Times* Best Seller list of books written by Allen Drury, Fletcher Knebel, Eugene Burdick, Drew Pearson, Gore Vidal, and Irving Wallace provides ample evidence that political fiction involving the president and national politics generated a sustained interest in a large segment of America's reading public. Drury's political fiction, beginning with the Pulitzer Prize winning *Advise and Consent* (1959) and concluding with a sixth book in the series, *The Promise of Joy* (1975), appeared on the *New York Times* Best Seller list for two hundred and thirty-eight weeks.

During the sixties and early seventies such novels as *Seven Days in May, Fail Safe, The Man, The 480, Convention, Vanished, The Night of Camp David, Washington, D.C., The President's Plane Is Missing, The Senator, The President,* and *Dark Horse* also appeared prominently and often on best seller lists. Commenting upon Anthony Trollope, Henry James wrote: "There are two kinds of taste in the appreciation of imaginative literature: the taste for the emotions of surprise, and the taste for the emotions of recognition" (133). There can be little doubt that readers of political fiction had much to recognize in the political novels of the sixties: there are myriad allusions to historical events and public figures; sometimes fictional events are obvious parallels to events which have occurred—or in some prescient instances, will occur—in the actual or real political world. In the generic realm, in the realm of human nature and politics, the abuse and corruption which sometimes accompanies the exercise of power in political fiction, all too often triggers an associative note to one familiar with national politics in the sixties and seventies as a result of watching nightly newscasts dominated by media personalities (Walter Cronkite [CBS], Huntley and Brinkley [NBC]), reading daily newspapers (*New York Times, Washington Post, Chicago Tribune*), and weekly magazines (*Times, Newsweek, Life*).

Obviously, in a vital democracy national events and national politics demand and receive the attention of responsible and educated citizens. Perhaps not surprisingly, two additional subjects appear consistently in popular political fiction which tend to expand the readership base beyond the sophisticated and highly sophisticated reader and which, undoubtedly, tend to increase the marketability and the profit of such books: sex and violence. The prevalence of sex and violence in modern literature has been labeled "violent animalism" in a critique titled *The Trousered Ape: Sick Literature in a Sick Society* by Duncan Williams. In the introduction to *The Trousered Ape*, we are reminded that "literature is not just an isolated thing, anymore than the cinemas, painting or any of the other arts. These are not merely diversions, but true mirrors of preoccupations of the times, in which men not only find what they think amusing or important but also sub-conscious models for their own values and behavior..."(14). The sex and violence in best selling political fiction takes many forms; these forms mirrored life in the real world of the sixties. One dominating form of violence in political fiction is war and the ever present threat of a nuclear holocaust.

For those Americans born in the nineteen-twenties, war has been a fact of life: World War II (1939-1945), The Korean War (1950-1954), and the Vietnam War (1964-1973). Consequently, in political fiction, the creation of a "hot war" or the creation of a threat of a "hot war" has obvious and immediate conscious and subconscious associations. In addition to "hot wars," Americans have lived with a "cold" war of varying intensity since World War II. The Cold War, an ideological conflict between democratic Capitalism and imperialistic Communism, has almost erupted into a "hot" war between the United States and the Soviet Union on numerous occasions. Both America and Russia have practiced brinkmanship and the rattling of nuclear weapons in postures of military confrontation. Violent rebellions against Russian power in Hungary (1956) and Poland (1956), the Russian blockade of Berlin (1948) and the construction of the Berlin Wall (1961), the aborted invasion of Cuba at the Bay of Pigs (1961) by Cubans trained and directed by the CIA, and the Cuban Missile Crisis (1962) were only some of the more extreme moments of national and international anxiety generated by the American and Russian foreign policies. Quite explicitly, John F. Kennedy, expressed the need for vigilance and firmness against the threat of imperialistic Communism in his 1960 inaugural address. President Kennedy's inaugural words are repeated by President Dilman in Irving Wallace's *The Man* as he struggles for the support of the American people in the battle against "Godless communism:" "The free world's security can be endangered not only by a nuclear attack, but also by being nibbled away at the periphery...[by] forces of subversion, infiltration, intimidation, indirect or non-overt aggression, internal revolution, diplomatic blackmail, guerrilla warfare or a series of limited wars." Consequently, President Kennedy idealistically warned, and Irving Wallace repeats that warning, that "every nation" should "know whether it wishes us well or ill, that we shall pay any price, bear any burden, meet any hardship, support any friend, oppose any foe to assure the survival and success of liberty" (Wallace 645-

646). President Kennedy's words were the basis of foreign policy in Vietnam and Cuba. Because of the potential threat of Castro's Cuba to the security of the United States and because the Kennedy Administration believed it desirable to "free" the Cuban people from Communism, Cuban exiles were trained, supplied and sometimes led by CIA personnel as they launched guerrilla raids against Cuba from Miami. This illegal, "secret" war against Cuba, as reported in a CBS Television Special narrated by Bill Moyers, was an "open" secret which was conscientiously unreported by the press (CBS Reports: "The CIA's Secret Army"). "Operation Mongoose," as the CIA's anti-Castro operation was called, involved "six hundred case officers running three thousand Cuban agents, fifty business fronts, and a fleet of planes and ships operating out of the fronts" in Miami (Wills 251-254). In addition to waging a "secret," "illegal" war against Cuba, the CIA also planned the assassination of Fidel Castro—as well as the assassinations of other world rulers. On the day that President Kennedy was assassinated by Lee Harvey Oswald, a Cuban army major was in Paris attempting to obtain a CIA weapon for use in the assassination of Castro. After President Kennedy's assassination, Robert Kennedy "did not want any investigation if it would lead to the plans made against Castro, to his own involvement, and his brothers" (Wills 254).

American history in the sixties is sometimes incredibly bizarre. President Kennedy who campaigned as a practicing Catholic and who projected a dynamic image through the media of a happy and faithful husband was habitually unfaithful to his wife while he was President. Garry Wills, in *The Kennedy Imprisonment*, indicates the perils of John F. Kennedy's promiscuity, a promiscuity which was potentially damaging not only to Kennedy but also to the country:

...a woman a day might help keep the doctor away; but an omnivorous approach to women can compromise the presidential policy as well as reputation. Kennedy had more reason than most people to know this—he was certain, from an early age, that the FBI had at least one set of tapes taken while he made love to a woman suspected of espionage. His father had told him to fear J. Edgar Hoover's use of such tapes. And his grandfather Fitzgerald had been driven from a political campaign by threats to reveal his relationship with a "Toodles" Ryan. Yet, incredibly, John Kennedy continued to make compromising assignations in the White House itself. When he inherited Judith Campbell from Frank Sinatra, he was making love to another woman who might be under investigation—and, as it turned out, was. Overlapping her affair with the candidate, and then with the President, she was intimate with Sam Giancana, who was (a) more or less permanently under investigation for suspected criminal activities, and (b) being approached by the CIA to help assassinate Castro. On several grounds the President's love life was bound to end up in another FBI folder (34).

Obviously, the major concern here is not with President Kennedy's sex life, but rather with its impact or potential impact upon American security and about the vulnerability of the president at a time when Russia, Russian agents, and Russian sympathizers were viewed as dangerous threats to America even by liberals such as President Kennedy. As we have already observed, Ronald Reagan, on the opposite end of the spectrum, shared the same anxiety but perhaps even more so when we consider his rhetoric both as an actor and as a president.

Perhaps not surprisingly then, the conflict between Communism and Democracy provides the tension and suspense in almost all of the Washington-based best-selling political novels: in *Fail Safe*, for instance, there is the immediate threat of the "big" or nuclear war when American Vindicator bombers "accidentally" destroy Moscow; in Drury's novels, the Russian threat is imminent to America and there are "small" wars involving American troops: the "wars of Liberation" in Gorotoland and Panama trigger associations with Vietnam. In Irving Wallace's *The Man*, a Vietnam type conflict erupts in the small, African country of Barazin. Occasionally, political novelists overtly make allusions to the Vietnam War, and in some instances, make comments about the war which are quite perceptive and prophetical. In *The 480*, written by Eugene Burdick in 1964, presidential candidate John Thatcher believes that "were're going to lose in Vietnam" because we are not geared for guerrilla war; Thatcher believes that "the special forces may win a lot of battles, but they'll lose the war" because "wars are won inside the heads of people. We don't understand that yet. Those helicopters go in dropping napalm and napalm is funny . . . it can't tell the difference between a Viet Cong and a six-year-old girl. So it burns them both up." Thatcher would, if elected President, "sit down with the Vietnamese military people and say, 'Boys, the time has come. The Mickey Mouse war is over. Go out there and lead your men or we're getting out. Stop spending all your time in Saigon trying to get in on the next coup. Or we're leaving' "(105-107).

In political fiction the ideological conflict between American Democracy and Russian imperialistic Communism also leads to domestic violence: political assassination, political terrorism, and political riots with racial overtones. For example, in Drury fiction, both President Harley Hudson and Orrin Knox, the party's nominee to succeed him, are assassinated by Communists or by those who are manipulated by the Communists. In *The Man*, black President Dilman survives an assassination attempt by a black member of the Tunerites, a racial, black organization which is financed by Communist money and which is infiltrated by a Communist agent. Political terrorism is a Communist tactic in Drury's *Preserve and Protect*, *Come Nineveh, Come Tyre*, and *The Promise of Joy*. Hal Knox, the son of President Knox has his finger hacked off in *The Promise of Joy* and sent to his father in order to persuade the President to take a soft line against

Communism. Helen-Anne Carew, a "conservative" newspaper columnist in *Capable of Honor*, is assassinated when she discovers that a Communist agent has met secretly with the leaders of NAWAC (The National Anti-War Activities Congress), the political advisors to Governor Ted Jason, the "liberal" presidential candidate. The riots which occur in Drury's fiction are the fruits of Communist propaganda, threats, and political manipulation. Paradoxically, when political riots occur, the "free press" condemns the conservative and patriotic element in the body politic for provoking violence, thereby illustrating a Drury thesis that the press can be manipulated and duped by Communist agents and sympathizers. Such a view is not without ironical overtones: frequently, during the sixties, the press was fed information which was sometimes accurate, sometimes fallacious, about members of Civil Rights organizations and the anti-Vietnam movement for the purpose of discrediting them in the eyes of the public and their followers. Martin Luther King was such a victim. In addition, the CIA sometimes employed foreign American journalists as intelligence agents. Such journalists would plant false or misleading news in the foreign press, and these news stories would eventually be reprinted in American newspapers, thereby misinforming the public about national affairs. (Marchetti and Marks 349-67; Harwood and Pincus, *Courier Journal and Times*, D3; Seib *Washington Post*, 11 June 1976, 27; Seib, *Washington Post*, 14 May 1976).

This manipulation of the press by the CIA and FBI was a reaction against the real or perceived Communist threat to subvert and eventually conquer America. The actual and potential violence of the age, the threat of ultimate nuclear destruction, and the threat of a Communist takeover through the infiltration and the subversion of American values and institutions tended to generate, in political fiction, metaphors suggestive of Yeats' "The Second Coming":

Things fall apart; the center cannot hold;
Mere anarchy is loosed upon the world,
The blood-dimmed tide is loosed, and everywhere
The ceremony of innocence is drowned;
The best lack all conviction, while the worst
Are full of passionate intensity (3-8).

Yeats' images are not Pearson's choice of metaphor in *The Senator* and *The President*; however, the reality behind the metaphor is created in his fiction. Ben Hannaford, the corrupt political protagonist of *The Senator* and *The President*, is perceived by his admirers as "a buffer against something dark and bloody in the national character." That which is "dark and bloody in the national character" is "a tiger," and once "the tiger is out of the cage he's hard to get back in," according to Deever, the narrator of both novels who is Hannaford's special assistant. In *The President* the threat of violence continues. The President is advised that "there is a poison in the body politic,...and poison can have a strange effect on people"; in short, the people may soon "want blood" (*The Senator* 42-43, 438). The President clearly states his views to Secretary of Defense Burke Boswell, an alcoholic: "Sam, you keep quoting scholars and legal experts and constitutional lawyers, as if this country is always guided by reasonable men, who use the past as guide, who try to settle disputes amicably, who believe in laws, and not emotions. Like a lot of my intellectual friends, you are too trusting. There's a lion loose in the streets, and he is in no mood to listen to precedent" (*The President* 221, 276). The inflammatory mood of Pearson's fictional America is fueled by the rhetoric of the presidential campaign. The favorite rallying slogans of Gabe Tutt, Hannaford's opponent, reflect the violent temper of the times: "Nuke the Chink! Vote Upshaw and Tutt" and "I will hang all traitors and hang them high" (24).

In Irving Wallace's *The Man*, the object of America's blood lust is the president. After President Dilman has survived an assassination attempt by a member of the Turnerites, a radical black organization dedicated to improving the quality of life for black people in America, the black president is subjected to racial slurs by a Southern Congressman during the president's impeachment trial. "Kill the Beast," the Congressman exhorts the Senate, "before the Beast kills you" (597). The chaste president is accused of the attempted rape of his social secretary, the daughter of an aging Southern Senator. He is also accused of providing secret information to his girl friend who has Communist affiliations.

The violent temper of the times evolves in stages in Drury's fiction.The "Fatuous Fifties" were followed by "the Sick Sixties" which were, in turn, succeeded by "the Savage Seventies." Predictably, in "the Savage Seventies," everything is out of joint (*Preserve and Protect* 101). Drury categorizes this American sickness, which has been encouraged by "liberal" elements in the media, the universities, and the body politic, as "the Thing"—a force which is out of control. Drury's "Thing" is a demon of anger, hatred, violence, rebellion, and chaos. "The Thing" is the result of the pervading moral, intellectual, and political atmosphere in America. Harley Hudson, the second president in Drury's political novels, identifies the national disease. The major theme in twentieth century America, we learn from President Hudson before he is killed in an airplane crash caused by a Communist saboteur, is "a pointless, insensate rebellion against every thing for no reason, no purpose, no logic, no nothing. Out of the great creeds of liberation, uplift and reform had finally come nihilism—...heartless, pointless, useless" (Drury, *Capable of Honor* 430).

The "tiger," the "lion," and the "thing" are weak metaphors to convey the turmoil and violence of the sixties, but Pearson (or his ghost writer) and Drury cannot be faulted for this. No single metaphor can comprehensively, vividly, and imaginatively capture the deep rooted and extensive turmoil and violence of the sixties. There were riots with racial and economic overtones; there were riots of sheer anger and despair; there were political riots; and there were assassinations of major public figures: John F. Kennedy, Robert Kennedy, Martin Luther King, and Malcolm X. There were murders of Civil Rights organizers in the South and racist bombings, such as the bombing of a black church in Birmingham, Alabama in May, 1963 in which four little girls were killed while , attending Sunday school. All of these violent events were graphically presented on television in news programs and special reports. Through the sixties violent and non-violent protests, demonstrations, and confrontations seemed to make an almost constant appearance on evening news. Such conflicts reflected the expanding and proliferating polarizations which were ripping at the roots of the American soul or psyche: the poor against the rich, the black against the white, the old against the young, the Vietnam "hawks" against the Vietnam "doves," and, in a more general sense in terms which have lost much of their semantic value because of their use as slur and purr words, "the liberals" against "the conservatives."

Even within the Civil Rights Movement itself there were conflicts and polarization between those such as Martin Luther King, who believed that blacks could obtain justice through peaceful, non-violent protest and Malcolm X, who believed that if violence were necessary for blacks to control economic and black power within their black communities, then violence must be employed. In *An American History*, Rebecca Gruber illustrates the contrast between the differing philosophies by presenting the contrasting perspectives of Martin Luther King and Malcolm X, a leader of the Black Muslim Movement who significantly influenced younger black leaders such as Floyd McKissick of CORE and Stokely Carmichael of SNCC when non-violent protest seemed to be ineffective (Gruber 816). Martin Luther King's words seem prompted by universal love, justice, and a need for peaceful protest demonstrations:

You may well ask: 'Why direct action? Why sit-ins, marches, and so forth? Isn't negotiation a better path?' You are quite right in calling for negotiation. Indeed, this is the very purpose of direct action. Nonviolent direct action seeks to create such a crisis and foster such a tension that a community which has constantly refused to negotiate is forced to confront the issue. It seeks so to dramatize the issue that it can no longer be ignored. My citing the creation of tension as part of the work of the nonviolent-resister may sound rather shocking. But I confess that I am not afraid of the word 'tension.' I have earnestly opposed violent tension, but there is a type of constructive, nonviolent tension which is necessary for growth. Just as

Socrates felt that it was necessary to create a tension in the mind so that individuals could rise from the bondage of myths and half-truths to the unfettered realm of creative analysis and objective appraisal, so must we see the need for nonviolent gadflies to create the kind of tension in society that will help men rise from the dark depths of prejudice and racism to the majestic heights of understanding and brotherhood. (1963)

On the other hand Malcolm X's words express a willingness to use violence against whites in order to obtain the long denied Civil Rights of America's blacks:

The seriousness of this situation must be faced up to. You should not feel that I am inciting someone to violence. I'm only warning of a powder-keg situation. You can take it or leave it. If you take the warning perhaps you can still save yourself. But if you ignore it or ridicule it, well, death is already at your doorstep. There are 22,000,000 African-Americans who are ready to fight for independence right here, I don't mean any non-violent fight, or turn-the-other cheek fight. Those days are gone. Those days are over.

If George Washington didn't get independence for this country non-violently, and if Patrick Henry didn't come up with a non-violent statement, and you taught me to look upon them as patriots and heroes, then it's time for you to realize that I have studied your books well...

And the only way without bloodshed that this can be brought about is that the black man has to be given full use of the ballot in every one of the 50 states. But if the black man doesn't get the ballot, then you are going to be faced with another man who forgets the ballot and starts using the bullet. (1964)

The racial polarization that erupted into violence in the American body politic during the sixties was a recurring focus of attention in political fiction, as well as a frequent source of allusion. And a vast resource of allusion it certainly was: in 1963 riots erupted in Birmingham, Chicago, Savannah, Cambridge, and Philadelphia; in 1964 serious riots occurred in Harlem, Brooklyn, Rochester, Jersey City, Elizabeth, Paterson, Chicago, and Philadelphia; in 1965, in the Watts section of Los Angeles, thirty-four people were killed, hundreds injured, and 4,000 were arrested in the worst riot in America since 1943: estimates of property damage ranged from $35 million to $100 million; in 1966, riots again erupted in Harlem and Chicago, as well as in Cleveland; in 1967, forty-one serious civil disorders occurred, including devastating riots in Detroit and Newark.

Early in 1968 the Kerner Commission, a Commission appointed by President Johnson to determine the cause of the riots and to make recommendations to insure against future disorders, made its report. The Commission concluded that there was no Communist conspiracy; the riots were unplanned and a primary cause was "white racism." The report stated that "what white Americans have never fully understood—and what the Negro can never forget—is that white society is deeply implicated in the ghetto. White institutions created it, white institutions maintain it, and white society condones it." Discrimination, segregation, and poverty embittered black youths. Consequently, the Commission recommended improved programs in employment, education, welfare, and housing in order to improve the quality of life for black Americans (Gruber 815; Barck and Blake, *Since 1900: A History of the United States* 677). After the publication of the Kerner Commission Report, in April, 1968, in Memphis, Tennessee, a white escaped convict assassinated Martin Luther King. Rioting again erupted in forty-one American cities. During the sixties there were over one hundred major civil disorders or riots in America's cities.

The Vietnam War and the Vietnam Protest Movement constituted a second extended nightmare in the American body politic, a nightmare which sometimes paralleled the racial turmoil which permeated the cities. Beginning in 1967, massive protests against the war were organized: Martin Luther King joined with the Vietnam protest movement and led a demonstration of 100,000 in New York; 50,000 protested in San Francisco; and, at the Pentagon, in the fall, 100,000 demonstrators marched in a protest which erupted into violence and 647 protesters were arrested (Barck and Blake 170). The anti-war movement had several prominent political spokesmen; two of the more famous were Senators Gene McCarthy and Robert Kennedy, and both campaigned for the democratic presidential nomination on platforms which expressed the belief that America's involvement in the Vietnam War was immoral. Senator Everett Dirkson, the Republican leader in the Senate and one of many public supporters of President Johnson's Vietnam policy, defended America's presence in Vietnam by articulating an extreme variation of the domino theory: if Vietnam falls, Senator Dirksen said, "Then the whole coast of the U.S. is exposed."

Opposition to the war intensified during the Viet Cong's Tet offensive in 1968 when Communist forces attacked one hundred Vietnamese cities. In the process, Communist forces both inflicted and received heavy casualties. According to newspaper reports, reports which may have been apocryphal, one American officer, reflecting on the destruction of a village around him, stated a central paradox of the Vietnam War. Of a village, he said, "We had to destroy it in order to save it." In addition to the assassination of Martin Luther King, rioting in 40 cities, and the Tet offensive, two additional shocks permeated the American body politic in 1968. In June, Senator Robert F. Kennedy was assassinated while he was campaigning for the Presidential nomination; and, during the summer, at the Democratic National Convention in Chicago, a massive political riot occurred after MOB (the Mobilization Committee Against the War) organized a mammoth demonstration at the convention. Although five thousand national guardsmen were mobilized and seven thousand federal troops were flown in from Texas in order to preserve order, massive violence erupted after the protestors chanted "Ho-Ho-Ho-

Chi Minh" in the Chicago streets. In the confrontation between police, national guardsmen, and federal troops, many police and protestors were injured and six hundred demonstrators were arrested. During the political riot, Chicago's Mayor Daley gave police orders to shoot to kill if necessary.

Vietnam psychic shocks continued in 1969. After a determined reporter published a shocking news story, the U.S. Army confirmed that an American platoon had killed one-hundred unarmed men, women, and children in the Vietnamese village of Mai Lai on March 16, 1968, and that there had been an attempted cover-up by the army of the massacre. During 1969, demonstrations against the war continued: 250,000 marchers protested the war in Washington.

After President Nixon began to withdraw troops from Vietnam, protest against the war diminished somewhat in 1969 and 1970. However, when President Nixon announced that American and Vietnamese troops had begun a large search and destroy mission in Cambodia, protest again exploded throughout the country, despite President Nixon's words of explanation. "If when the chips are down," the President explained, "the U.S. acts like a pitiful, helpless giant, the forces of totalitarianism and anarchy will threaten free nations and free institutions throughout the world." Four days after the Cambodian incursion, national guardsmen were provoked by demonstrators at Kent State, and the soldiers fired into the massing students. Two girls and two boys were killed; three other students were critically wounded. Before demonstrations generated by the public outrage at the extension of the war into Cambodia had petered out across the nation, over four hundred colleges and universities had suspended classes; also, in a petition to Washington, thirty-seven college presidents criticized America's Asian policy and 100,000 protesters again gathered in Washington. Quite obviously, not all protesters against the war were committed to non-violence. According to President Nixon, during 1970 there were 3,000 actual bombings and 50,000 bomb threats which had evolved either as a result of the Vietnam Protest Movement or racial animosity. In 1971, as an act of protest against the Vietnam War, the Weathermen, a radical anti-war organization, exploded a bomb in the Senate wing of the Capitol. During a May, 1971 protest demonstration in Washington, 7,000 demonstrators were arrested on the advice of Attorney General Mitchell. Several years after this largest mass arrest in American history, the courts judged the arrests to have been illegal and the government was ordered to pay damages.

In October, 1972, as the presidential election approached, Secretary of State Kissinger declared that "peace is at hand," that "peace was within reach in a matter of weeks or less." However, the most intensive bombing of the war was yet to come. In December, after the re-election of President Nixon and the collapse of the Paris peace talks, American bombers inflicted heavy property damage and casualties in the Hanoi and the Haiphong areas.

During the raids, at least fifteen B-52's, which cost ten million dollars each, were lost, and at least sixty-four crewmen were either killed or captured.[1] A few weeks after the raids, a cease fire was signed. Sixty days later, all American troops had left Vietnamese soil. Although the peace accords included a cease fire between the South Vietnamese and Communist forces, shooting continued intermittently after peace was declared. In April, 1975, after the South Vietnamese army totally collapsed under the pressure of Communist attacks, Saigon and the South Vietnamese government fell victim to the aggression of North Vietnam and the Viet Cong.[2] Within the context of the fall of Saigon, Drury fiction has an extremely credible theme: a country unwilling or unable to defend itself against totalitarian Communism will eventually fall victim to imperialistic Communist aggression. Such reasoning—a commitment of American military forces to prevent a Communist takeover—had motivated President Johnson to send twenty-two thousand marines to the Dominican Government in 1965 after he was informed that Communists had infiltrated the legitimate government (Gruber 809-810). Although Latin Americans and American liberals were furious at American intervention in the Dominican Republic, unlike the tragedy of Vietnam, a Communist takeover was prevented without significant casualties.

II

The theme of violence in much political fiction is frequently depicted in an imaginary world where sexual promiscuity is an acceptable life style among successful politicians and their assistants. As in the actual world, many political characters—candidates and office-holders—consciously conceal from the voters the discrepancy between the image they project to the voters and their habitual sexual activities and sexual ethics. In Gore Vidal's *Washington, D.C.* readers are presented a panoramic perspective of the sex life of potential candidates, Congressmen, and Senators and their active supporters: masturbation (Peter Sanford and Scotty Osborne), fornication (Senator Clay with a variety of partners, sometimes two at a time), incest (Peter Sanford and his sister, Enid), adultery (Senator Clay with a variety of partners; Senator Day with Irene Block; Enid and navy Captain Bailey; Peter Sanford and Diana Thorne), homosexuality (Harold Griffiths, a political journalist is victimized by the police in attempted blackmail; Enid Sanford Clay believes her husband, Senator Clay and her father, a wealthy, influential newspaper publisher and political financier, are lovers), and lesbianism (alleged by gossipers, between Millicent Smith Carhart and Lucy Shattuck).

Although sex is essential to the plot and characterization in *Washington, D.C.* Vidal presents the sexual encounters in the novel with restraint, especially if one compares *Washington, D.C.* to Fletcher Knebel's *Dark Horse.* Eddie Quinn, the political hero—or perhaps anti-hero—of *Dark Horse* has two fixations: sex and cars. While the leaders of his party are examining his credentials in order to determine if he might be a viable presidential candidate, Eddie Quinn is enjoying his fifty-first sexual conquest with Congresswoman Kate Witherspoon—the wife of one of the "kingmakers" at the caucus. Sex in *Dark Horse* is presented with religious imagery— communion, acolyte, celebration of mystery, shrine, celebrant, priest, altar— and erotic detail. For example, the first copulatory union of the presidential candidate and the Congresswoman is graphically described by Knebel, and although some may lament the quality of the prose and the emphasis on the erotic, *Dark Horse* fared well in the marketplace: for nineteen weeks, *Dark Horse* placed on the *New York Times* Best Seller list.[3]

Kate Witherspoon is similar to many women encountered in popular political fiction; she is first viewed as a sex object that is willing, if not eager, to be sexually exploited. In political fiction time and time again, women are sexually used and discarded. However, an interesting reversal of sexual roles occurs in *The President* when an extremely attractive black journalist practices an ingenious form of sexual racism. The promiscuous and talented Miss Varnum punishes white male exploiters by providing them with an ecstasy which can never be repeated. The beautiful Varnum consciously arouses them sexually and beds down with them—one time, and one time only. For the remainder of their lives, Miss Varnum knows, they will always remember and be tortured by the erotic pleasure that will be forever beyond their reach: a uniquely blissful sexual encounter with a liberated, black journalist! Varnum, however, is an exception in popular fiction; most women depicted in the genre are passive creations cast in traditional women's roles: exploited sex objects, wives, helpmates, and mothers. Edna Foster, an anxiety ridden, plain looking and no longer young woman, articulates a traditional view of a woman's role. After the private secretary of *The Man* has received, finally, an offer of marriage, she gushes to George Murdock, a journalist who will exploit her position as the president's private secretary:

I'll make it better than any marriage there's been on earth, George, no bickering like my folks, or bossing around like my girlfriend, Dorothy, did, no unfaithfulness from either of us like the people we know about here—the Arthur Eatons—that kind. You won't have to chase, George, because you'll have no need to, I'll keep a beautiful house, and raise the best-mannered, smartest, children, and give you interesting meals, and help you with your work, and charm your friends so you'll be proud of me. You'd be surprised what I'm really like...(Wallace 426)

For the Edna Fosters of political fiction, there is no concept of, and there will not be, any woman's liberation. Masculine superiority, sex, and violence are deeply engrained in popular political fiction. Such themes are reflections of the social milieu and the historical events of the sixties, and, as such, provided patterns of recognition to the fiction buying public—male and female.

III

More interesting and subtle than the sex and violence which permeate this genre is the recurring cynicism and pessimism of the novels. Paradoxically, much pessimism is generated by the personalities of political "heroes," as well as by their associates or advisors who illustrate in their actions the axiom, "Power corrupts and absolute power corrupts absolutely." Political *hubris*—an overwhelming belief in one's political judgment, even when that judgment suggests actions which contradict traditional moral or ethical principles, established norms, or laws of the body politic—is not an uncommon characteristic of a political "hero." The President, as well as the Vice-President, in Drury's early fiction, illustrates the nature of this moral sickness.

In *Advise and Consent*, after the President has decided to pursue a "softer" policy with the Soviet Union, Robert Leffingwell is nominated to become Secretary of State. Despite indications that Leffingwell was at one time closely affiliated with the Communist party, the President places all of his prestige behind the appointment. A tragedy results when Senator Anderson of Utah learns that the nominee has, in fact, been a member of the Communist party, although Leffingwell has categorically denied this allegation before a Senate sub-committee. Confronted with this allegation, the President expresses a cynical view of human nature. Every man has his price, the President believes, and he asks his advisors what price or prize should be offered to the highly respected, young Senator. A negative reply prompts another question from the President: since everyone holding public office has sordid experiences which, if known by the electorate, could destroy his career, what sordidness or immorality exists in Anderson's life which can provide the grist for blackmail. Homosexuality, the President learns from the Senate Majority Leader, is an Anderson personality flaw. When this information is passed on to an ambitious and opportunistic "liberal" Senator, public exposure of the World War II indiscretion becomes the means of coercing Senator Anderson to withdraw his opposition to the President's nominee. Despite this threat, Senator Anderson forwards his incriminating evidence to a senatorial colleague; however, rather than face public humiliation, and the devastating effect of the revelation upon his wife, his family, and his friends, the "honorable" Senator commits suicide.

As Vice-President, Harley Hudson is appalled by the political ethics of the President who has a long earned reputation as a "wheeler-dealer." Nonetheless, when Harley succeeds the President in office, he, too, learns that a pure political ethic is impossible in a dynamically changing political spectrum. Once a man becomes President, Harley realizes, there are times when he cannot—should not—keep his word even when the word takes the form of a pledge or a promise: "Pledges are broken," he reflects. "Decisions are reserved. Yesterday's absolute becomes today's maybe and tomorrow's negative. History bends Presidents to its will as it bends other men." And Harley also learns that there comes a time in office when "it is literally impossible for the occupant to distinguish any longer between his own interests and the interests of the United States. The White House in time, even for the most determinedly idealistic, gradually obliterates the line between self and service. Presidents after a while—and sometimes a much shorter while than is this case—reach a point where they simply cannot regard themselves objectively anymore" (Drury, *Capable* 309).

Some heroes in political fiction are corrupted by power alone; others—such as Ben Hannaford who is *The Senator* and who becomes *The President*, despite being censured by the Senate for taking a $250,000 bribe—abuse power to satisfy their greed. Hannaford believes that in America "the right things get done for the wrong reasons" and that "controlled greed" is the key to national and world progress. If, incidentally, he becomes richer as a result of a foreign aid bill which will prevent the small Arab country of Djarak from turning Communist, this is little for anyone to become concerned about. If someone does become concerned because of his profiteering, the Senator has the key to rally people behind him:

I will get rich off the bill. My partners will get rich. But at the same time, we'll make ourselves a model country in the Middle East. We'll knock off those communist attacks once and for all! Teach 'em capitalism. A supermarket in every village! Why, we can change that whole part of the world! And you know why. Because they'll be money involved! That's how things get done. Not for virtue, or honor or good will or ideals—but because of *Greed*.

Controlled greed, Walter, that's the answer. I'll admit I want money—but I want money in a good cause! Electric ranges instead of camel dung (Pearson, *The Senator* 271).

Despite his populist appeal, Hannaford's election to the presidency is by a narrow margin. Without rigging the votes of California, a Hannaford victory would have been impossible. To the President, such dishonesty is the "stuff" of history: Kennedy won in 1960 because "every tombstone" in Cook County, Illinois "was voted." Nixon did not complain, Hannaford declares, because his people also juggled votes in California. Kennedy's people, however, "juggled better"(24).

Even when elections are not rigged, the best candidates are not always elected in some political fiction. In Drury fiction, the media engages in advocacy journalism, promoting "liberal" candidates who expose "liberal" positions. "Conservative" candidates, on the other hand, are given weak news coverage and an unflattering slanting of news stories and coverage.

The American voter and the American body politic are victimized by this lack of journalistic professionalism. Ironically, Drury, who lambasts the "Eastern elite" by caricaturing Walter Lippmann as a practitioner of advocacy journalism in *Capable of Honor*, engages in "advocacy" fiction in order to promote a conservative vision of America.

As in Drury fiction, the voters in *The 480* are perceived as persons who can easily be misled or manipulated by candidates and the press. In an Introduction, Burdick expresses his concern about the American voter who, Burdick believes, "has neither the interest nor the information to make a rational decision between the two major presidential candidates." Furthermore, since "candidates often do not say what they believe: and candidates say what they know the people want to hear," new expertise in formulating and conducting polls poses a serious threat to the body politic. Kennedy's 1960 campaign, Burdick believes, was the first extensive use of sophisticated polling techniques which possessed the capability of raising political hypocrisy to a new level (6,7). In *The 480*, not only is the public manipulated by the pollsters, but so also is a presidential candidate. Dr. Devlin, the archmanipulator of the novel, illustrates the potential abuse of psychology and sociology by pollsters and politicians. Dr. Devlin takes "the public temperature" through her polls and learns what "image" the electorate prefers in their candidates; she, then, along with a political colleague, manipulates John Thatcher to conform to the voter's conscious and unconscious expectations. Eventually, John Thatcher, *their* presidential candidate, learns that he has been manipulated and he angrily confronts his political financiers and advisors. His anger at their deceit, however, is short lived. As the novel concludes, the manipulated candidate and the manipulators are anticipating a future campaign for high office.

Frequently in the political fiction of the sixties and early seventies, political heroes and political campaigns reflect a dark side of the body politic, a side that one would prefer to be nonexistent: citizens who are uninterested, uninformed, imperceptive, short sighted, and selfish in fulfilling their responsibilities in the political process; political campaigns which employ "dirty tricks" as a matter of tradition, habit, and expediency, including such "tricks" as counting votes from non-existent people; political candidates and office holders who are mentally ill or who become mentally ill while in office (President Hollenbach in *Night of Camp David*, for instance, and President Jason in *Come Nineveh, Come Tyre*) and political leaders who are corrupted by power and greed.

At times, unfortunately, the created world of pre-Watergate political fiction was depressingly similar to the political world which was, or would become, anchored historical fact. The increased vigilance of the press and Congressional Committees during and after the Watergate burglary and cover-up resulted in bizarre exposés of political *hubris* in the most respected and thought-to-be most trustworthy agencies and offices of the government.

The bold statistics of Watergate charges and convictions can serve *only* as an introduction to the political *hubris* and corruption which permeated Washington in the sixties and early seventies. In addition to the forced resignation of the President, charges stemming from the investigation of the Watergate burglary and cover-up were filed against sixty-nine individuals and twenty corporations. Forty-eight pleaded guilty and thirteen additional persons were convicted at trial; six were acquitted. Twenty-three persons went to prison, including John Mitchell, President Nixon's Attorney General, and Robert Haldeman and John Erlichman, President Nixon's chief advisors and administrative assistants. Still more. Before the Watergate investigations and trials were completed, Attorney General Kleindienst, Acting Director of the FBI Patrick Gray, and the FBI itself, as well as the CIA, would suffer public embarrassment for abusing the responsibilities entrusted to them by the American people. During the Kennedy, Johnson, and Nixon Administrations, too little attention was given to the type of sentiments expressed by Justice Brandeis: "If the government becomes a lawbreaker," Brandeis wrote, "it breeds contempt for law; it invites everyman to become a law unto himself, it invites anarchy."

The original Watergate burglary seemed, on the TV surface, a minor criminal episode, five Miamians and a former CIA agent were arrested while burglarizing the Democratic National Office. One of the participants, however, James McCord, a former CIA agent, was also the Chief Security Agent for CREEP, the Committee to Re-Elect the President; in addition, two of the burglars—Bernard Barker and Eugenio Martinez—were Cuban exiles, veterans of the CIA planned Bay of Pigs invasion, as well as veterans of a CIA financed and directed covert war against Cuba which included guerrilla forays against Cuba from bases in Miami which were analyzed in the CBS report titled "The CIA's Secret Army" in June, 1977. When E. Howard Hunt, a member of the White House Special Investigations Unit known as "the plumbers," approached Barker and Martinez to work with them, it was not their first acquaintance: Hunt, acting as a CIA agent, had recruited Cuban exiles, including Barker, for the Bay of Pigs invasion. Both Barker and Martinez perceived the operation against the Democratic National Committee's office in the same frame of reference as their earlier covert anti-Castro operations, operations which were sanctioned by the Kennedy White House. To find evidence of Castro contributions to the McGovern campaign, they believed, would be a small victory for Cuba and the United States against Castro and Cuban Communism. Prior to Watergate, in September 1971, Barker and Martinez—who were only two of at least one-hundred men recruited by Hunt while acting as a representative of the White House Special Investigations Unit—had broken into a psychiatrist's office, along with Hunt, in order to pilfer the psychiatric records of Daniel Ellsberg, an anti-Vietnam activist who had leaked Pentagon Papers to the press. "The plumbers" reported directly to John Erlichman, the Assistant to the President for Domestic Affairs.

The CIA, then, in the experience of Barker and Martinez, had a White House history of sanctioned operations against Cuban Communists in operations which were covert and illegal. Such operations abused the CIA's government charter. During the sixties, as we have already noted, the CIA planned and attempted the assassinations of foreign leaders as a matter of policy and, on the day President Kennedy was assassinated, another CIA plot to assassinate Castro was initiated. Still more bizarre, on an earlier occasion, the CIA had recruited a mafia boss, Sam Giancana, to help assassinate Castro; incredible as it might seem, Sam Giancana, who was on Attorney General Robert Kennedy's ten most wanted list of organized crime leaders, was the lover of Judith Campbell who was a President Kennedy lover both before and after he became president. Amazingly, after the assassination of President Kennedy, the CIA withheld information from the Warren Commission concerning United States assassination plots against Castro, although a Castro plot to assassinate President Kennedy might have been considered a serious possibility under the circumstances.

The abuses of power by the CIA—assassination plots, assassination attempts, the directing and financing of a covert guerrilla war against Cuba from the coast of Miami, as well as CIA infiltration of the American press working in foreign countries—were revelations which severely damaged the reputation of the CIA and indicated a *hubristic* disease in the national body politic. The FBI, too, in the Kennedy, Johnson, and Nixon Administrations, suffered from an excess of zeal in its war against Communism, Vietnam War protesters, and Civil Rights activists. Too frequently, loyalty was given to government officials instead of allegiance to the FBI charter and the law. The image of the FBI was severely damaged when Acting Director Patrick Gray destroyed evidence taken from Howard Hunt's White House safe which contained material that was pertinent to the Watergate burglary and cover-up. At the suggestion of Erichman, the Presidential Assistant on Domestic Affairs, Gray "deep sixed" a dossier which also contained damaging personal information about Senator Edward Kennedy, information gathered by Hunt to be used for political advantage. There were also "bogus cables fabricated by Hunt to implicate President John F. Kennedy in the 1963 assassination of South Vietnam President Ngo Dinh Diem, and a 'psychological profile' of Daniel Ellsberg." In the words of Erlichman, the revelation of the contents of the dossier " 'could do more damage than the dossier itself' " (Bernstein and Woodward 306).

During the seventies, much more disparaging information was to surface concerning the unethical and illegal activities of the FBI. The FBI, as did the CIA, withheld information pertinent to the investigation of the Kennedy assassination from the Warren Commission. The Warren Commission concluded that Lee Harvey Oswald, *himself assassinated before the American public via live television*, acted alone in the assassination, but many sincere, educated, and intelligent Americans questioned the quality and conclusions of the Commission Report. Although Presidents, Congressmen, and Senators publicly expressed admiration and affection for Edgar Hoover while he was Director of the FBI, their private feelings about him frequently clashed with their public sentiments. By many, Hoover was feared more than he was loved. As *Newsweek* magazine reported, the Director of the FBI gathered derogatory information on members of Congress, federal officials, and "those who simply tried to oppose him," including members of the press. To those who were friendly to the Director, the Hoover files were accessible. Presidents Kennedy and Johnson sometimes employed the Hoover files in order to gain a political advantage. President Johnson, according to one knowledgeable source, "in a close legislative fight,...might call in a key legislator for a chat, planting a stack of FBI folders obtrusively on one corner of the desk" (Goldman and Marro 16-17).

Information and files containing derogatory information—sometimes secured by illegal FBI burglaries and wiretaps—were sometimes employed with less sophistication. Disparaging information about the sexual activities of Civil Rights leader and soon to be assassinated Anti-War Protestor Martin Luther King were "leaked" to Mrs. King in order to destroy King's morale and to destroy his influence with the American people. Files were also kept on "hostile" and "friendly" newspapers. One primary FBI target was the Socialist Party. The FBI actively undermined the Socialist Party by sabotaging its political campaigns and damaging reputations. FBI activity against the Socialist Party included attempts to sow racial dissension among party members and their associates in black activist groups and anti-Vietnam War organizations. Such tactics were effective. Indubitably, many Civil Rights activists, anti-war protestors, and political activists suffered much anxiety in the sixties and manifested signs of paranoia. But, as Secretary of State Henry Kissinger, the winner of a Nobel Peace Prize for planning and negotiating the Vietnam Peace settlement of 1973, reportedly remarked, "...even paranoids sometimes have people after them."

One high government official who had someone after him in the early seventies was Vice-President Agnew. Before his Vice-Presidential resignation which was generated by public allegations of corruption and the threat of prosecution, Vice President Agnew waged an aggressive, verbal attack against "the liberals" in the press, the colleges, and the government in a vigorous attempt to polarize the country. Agnew, while championing the accomplishments of President Nixon and defending his Vietnam policy, developed an extremely loyal following who were responsive to his blunt attacks against Democrats and liberals, attacks divisive in thrust and extremely effective in execution: "...if in questioning we disturb a few people, it is time for them to be disturbed. If in challenging, we polarize the American people, I say it is time for polarization." Agnew's striking adjectives and alliterations—"radic-libs," "spock-marked kids," "hopeless, hysterical, hypochondriacs of history," "troglodylic leftists," and "nattering nabobs of negativism"—were often repeated in the media and contributed to divisiveness in the body politic. Doom was also a popular Agnew theme: "A society which comes to fear its children is effete. A sniveling, hand wringing power structure deserves the violent rebellion it encourages. If my generation doesn't stop cringing, yours will become a lawless society where emotion and muscle displace reason." The Agnew attack against the younger generation was expanded to include intellectuals—college professors, news commentators, and the writers of books—"The student now goes to college to proclaim rather than to learn. The lessons of the past are ignored and obliterated in a contemporary antagonism known as the generation gap. A spirit of national masochism prevails, encouraged by an effete corp of impudent snobs who characterize themselves as intellectuals" ("The Fall of Mr. Law and Order" 27-36). Like Senator Barry Goldwater, the conservative candidate for President in 1964, Vice-President Agnew offered "a choice, not an echo." Like Goldwater, Agnew seemed to indicate "that extremism in defense of liberty is no vice" and that "moderation in pursuit of justice is no virtue." Goldwater's polarization of the body politic was a significant but politically unsuccessful tactic in the 1964 presidential campaign. However, Vice-President Agnew's employment of this aggressive strategy in defense of the Nixon Administration was more successful. Not surprisingly, then, since polarization was a fact of political life in the sixties, polarization between "liberals" and "conservatives" is a recurring theme in political fiction of the sixties.

A second high government official of the sixties and seventies who also had someone after him was John F. Kennedy's former Squadron Leader in the South Pacific during World War II: Attorney General John Mitchell. Mitchell, who was convicted and sent to prison because of his involvement in the Watergate break-in and cover-up, exemplifies the deep polarization and the intense convictions of those who feared Communism and anarchy in America, and the dangers of such convictions to a democracy. Richard Nixon, the Attorney General told the Watergate investigative committee, had to be elected over George McGovern in 1972 for the good of America. He, the Attorney General stated, would do anything to insure Richard Nixon's election, even violate the laws which he had sworn to uphold in his office as Attorney General. In July, 1973, *Newsweek* reported his Watergate testimony:

Mitchell confessed, cheerfully and unrepentantly, that he had placed winning an election above virtually any other consideration—that to this end he had acquiesced in crimes by his silence and had blinkered the President to what was going on.
'All around him' said Georgia's Herman Talmedge incredulously, 'were people involved in crime, perjury, accessory after the fact, and you deliberately refused to tell him that. Would you state that the expediency of the election was more important than that'
'Senator,' Mitchell shot back, 'I think you have put it exactly correct. In my mind, the reelection of Richard Nixon, compared with what was available on the other side, was so much more important that I put it in just that context.'
'Aren't you dead sure in your mind,' Tennessee's Howard Baker pressed next day, 'that that was a mistake, not telling the President'
'No,' said Mitchell—'I still believe that the most important thing to this country was the re-election of Richard Nixon, and I was not about to countenance anything that would stand in the way of that re-election'
'Anything at all' Baker answered, eyebrows soaring ("Mitchell's 'White House Horrors' " 22).

The dichotomy between the projected public and political image of Attorney General Mitchell and his actual philosophy and actions as manifested in his involvement in the Watergate break-in and cover-up represents a profoundly disturbing characteristic of American politics and policy in the sixties and early seventies. The discrepancy between appearance and reality was a dark theme in national and international politics. The resignations of President Nixon, Vice-President Agnew, the prosecution and imprisonment of Attorney-General Mitchell, the unethical and illegal covert activities of the FBI and the CIA, the "secret war" against Cuba, and the surreptitious involvement in and gradual escalation of the Vietnam War into activities in Cambodia were and are reminders to the American voters that frequently our leaders followed the ethic that the ends or goals justify illegal means or methods to obtain those goals. To a very unhealthy and dangerous extent, a Machiavellian element eroded American confidence in the body politic, and this erosion was conducive to cynicism among American citizens: what you see in election campaigns is not what you get. On both a conscious and unconscious level, many Americans came to perceive— correctly or incorrectly—that although candidates and elected officials projected a deep commitment to city, state, and national laws, that in actuality, policy and personal morality were strongly influenced by Machiavellian ethics. In *The Prince* Machiavelli wrote of the "virtue" of the successful political leader:

It is not necessary, then, for a prince really to have all the virtues mentioned above, but it is very necessary to seem to have them. I will even venture to say that they damage a prince who possesses them and always observes them, but if he seems to have them they are useful. I mean that he should *seem* compassionate, trustworthy, humane, honest, and religious, and actually be so; but yet he should have his mind so trained that, when it is necessary not to practice these virtues, he can change to be the opposite, and do it skillfully. It is to be understood that a prince, cannot observe all the things because of which men are considered good, because he is often obliged, if he wishes to maintain his government, to act contrary to faith, contrary to charity, contrary to humanity, contrary to religion. It is therefore necessary that he have a mind capable of turning in whatever directions the winds of fortune and the variations of affairs require, and, as I said above, that he should not depart from what is morally right, if he can observe it, but should know how to adopt what is bad, when he is obliged to (I, 66).

Let us return, now, to the question of what accounts for the marketing success of political fiction in the sixties and seventies and suggest some possible causes before we turn to an intensive examination of Drury's best political fiction: The Pulitzer Prize winning *Advise and Consent*.

Obviously, the political characters, situations, conflicts, tensions, and rhetoric presented in political fiction generate a swift and intense response in many readers, especially those readers who possess an acute political sense and who participate regularly in political processes. Such politically conscious readers have been saturated with political crises, politicians, political profiles, and political commentaries through television, radio, newspapers, and weekly magazines. As a result of such intensive and extensive exposure to the business of politics, many have had little difficulty visualizing political characters and events created in political fiction. In addition, because of the nature and content of political fiction, political novels possess a natural tendency to reflect the spirit of the age, and the informed voter who is frequently a reader of political fiction is very much emotionally attuned to the temper of the time. Consequently, images, rhetoric, events, allusions, and political parallels presented in fiction effortlessly stimulate "a willing suspension of disbelief" and create an "illusion of reality" in a politically sophisticated audience. For the less sophisticated reader of political fiction, there is or was an identification with the political protagonists and political characters who are sexually active and who control or survive the power and violence that is generated by their fictional world. Quite frequently, political protagonists are romantic heroes who walk and talk in a world which is at root a romantic world, a world, that is, where despite pain, suffering, potential catastrophe and catastrophe, all is well at the conclusion of the novel.

There is more that we might observe. If an informed voter is disappointed with his local, state, or national representative, if a political activist is jarred by opposing political philosophies, perceptions of issues, interpretations of events, or polarized political rhetoric, a political novel can be a source of solace and escape, a literary security blanket. We, it would seem, possess a natural tendency to choose political novels which reflect political sympathies similar to our own. To put it another way, it is not entirely coincidental that Allen Drury is or was one of Ronald Reagan's "best liked" authors.

Chapter III
Drury's Political Fiction and A
"Pure" Political Novel: *Advise and Consent*

To appreciate aesthetically Drury's political fiction, it is essential to view it from the perspective of anatomy, as an analysis or dissection of a subject from the perspective of a single, intellectual vision.[1] The subject matter is politics and the central theme is quite clear: Russian imperialistic Communism poses both an internal and external threat to America, and if Americans do not vigilantly oppose the Russians from a position of strength, Russia will conquer America. An introductory note to *Come Nineveh, Come Tyre* identified the pivotal conflict of Drury's political vision: "Running through the first four novels, through this and its successor—as it runs through our times—is the continuing argument between those who use responsible firmness to maintain orderly social progress and oppose Communist imperialism in its drive for world domination; and those who believe in a reluctance to be firm, in permissiveness and in the steady erosion of the law lie the surest path to world peace and a stable society." In addition to presenting a polarizing conservative thesis, Drury's political fiction also presents a systematic depiction of political personalities as they exercise political power within the body politic.

This examination of political power is at the core of Drury's plots and characters. For example, after the President in *Advise and Consent* nominates the "liberal" and controversial Robert A. Leffingwell for Secretary of State, the narrator explicitly presents the effect of this nomination on the minds of all the major and minor political figures in the plot, an effect which permeates and unifies *Advise and Consent*:

It is the events between now and then, the *bargains* to be struck, the *deals* to be made, the *jockeying for power and the maneuvering for position*, which occupy them now...each is aware that the Senate is about to engage in one of the battles of a lifetime; and *each is wondering what it will mean for him in terms of power, reputation, advantage, political fortune, national responsibility, and the integrity of soul* (31 Italics added.).

Again, in *Capable of Honor*, Drury indicates the expanding technique of his novels by presenting how one political mind functions and how ambition possesses the potential of dominating a political personality, even when that politician is a dedicated public servant. When Secretary of State Orrin Knox prepares to meet the influential columnist Walter Dobius to

38

discuss Knox's presidential ambitions and his commitment to the Gorotoland War, a war which parallels the Vietnam War in many significant respects, readers perceive the thoughts and the thought making process of Orrin Knox as he digests the effects of "the slow desperate contest" in Gorotoland where American soldiers are dying:

Underlying compassion, of course, were inevitable thoughts of politics, preferment, the nomination, and the problematic judgments of history. Lifelong politicians possess compartmentalized minds, and all compartments have the ability to function simultaneously; so that while he was deeply concerned about the crisis, emotionally moved by the plight of the fighting men, alertly ready to repel the attacks of his critics, he was also, inescapably, assessing in quite another shrewd and pragmatic place the effect it would all have upon his own political chances. This he could do without in any way sacrificing his integrity or his compassion: it was the Washington habit, ingrained by many years of judging events according to their impact upon the political world, however much they might be affecting one on an emotional level....Through that glass, Gorotoland at the moment seemed to him neither plus nor minus for his own cause (213).

Such multiple perspectives involving the balancing of hierarchies is an essential integrating element of Drury's plots and characters, an integrating element which transcends political ideologies and which has its roots in the real world of Washington politics and personalities.

In recent years psychologists and psychiatrists have been giving increasing attention to the effect of power upon personality. While there are no dramatic new insights about power and personality, professional practitioners and researchers have been reaffirming old truths. Although power does possess the potential to corrupt, this need not be, nor always is, the case. Many people, including successful politicians, enjoy exercising power and retain emotional and mental stability while doing so. On the other hand, there are some people who do not handle power well who might be termed "powerholics," that is, people who are seduced by power and who crave it so much that power becomes an addiction. For such people, "the thrill is in the exercise of power itself" and the exercise of power can be self-destructive (Goleman "Powerholics" are flocking to Washington— and therapists D1,4). Dr. Douglas La Bier, a professional consultant, has noted that political power can be a double edged sword: there are two sides to the lure of power. "On the positive side there's the desire for public service. On the other side is the pull of power *per se*. At its best power goes hand in hand with the sense of a mission. Either without the other is dangerous" (D4). In recent years psychoanalysts have also observed another type or kind of "power" personality, "power groupies" or people who "operate on an illusory, derivative power that depends on some link to an official." Power groupies "relish their titles" and "love the intimacy with those close to the real centers of power'' (D4). Such psychological theories and psychological models are reflected in the concrete, vivid, and memorable characters in Drury's fiction. Plot, we might remember, is character in action. Not surprisingly, the structure of Drury's fiction reflects an emphasis upon political personality. For example, *Advise and Consent* is divided into five books; four of the books are named after Senators (''Bob Munson's Book,'' ''Seab Cooley's Book'' ''Brigham Anderson's Book,'' and ''Orrin Knox's Book'') and the fifth book, ''Advise and Consent,'' is titled after a function of a political body, the Senate, which possesses the responsibility of approving cabinet members nominated by the president. Bob Munson, Seab Cooley, Brigham Anderson, and Orrin Knox are conservatives. In *Advise*, Brig Anderson commits suicide; in *A Shade of Difference* Seab Cooley dies of a heart attack. In the subsequent five books of the series, Bob Munson continues as a senator, but he is no longer a major character in the fiction. Orrin Knox, however, gradually emerges as the political hero of the series; it is his conservative vision which is the ideological base of Drury's fiction. This conservative ideology along with the examination of power shapes the fictional form of the political series as anatomy; however, individual books in the series are not always primarily anatomies, although all do possess a significant ideological component and all do sustain a continuing examination of politics within the context of the spirit of the age.

II

In *The Anatomy of Criticism* Frye reminds us that from an etymological perspective fiction means ''something made for its own sake,'' and he postulates that there are four forms of fiction: confession or autobiography, romance, anatomy, and the novel (303, 303-314). Confessions are first person narratives which select only those events in a person's life that contribute to developing an integrated pattern. Romances deal with heroes, heroines, and villains who are stylized characters rather than ''real'' people. Anatomies deal with abstract ideas (as does the confession) and tend to stylize characters (as does the romance). Anatomies present us with a vision of the world in a single intellectual pattern and characters serve as the mouthpieces of the ideas they represent. On the other hand, novels deal with ''real people'' in a real society. Frye believes that the failure of critics to recognize the generic roots of some fiction has militated against a fair evaluation of some writers and works, especially those authors who have selected the anatomy as the predominant strain of their fiction. Such an author might be Drury.

Although Frye contends that one generic form is usually predominant in fiction, he also recognizes that usually at least two generic forms, and sometimes three, are manifest in almost all works. The best of prose fiction, such as Joyce's *Ulysses*, will incorporate all four forms in a unified manner (313-314). As we have already indicated, if Drury's political fiction is viewed as one entity and the continuing plot is perceived as one extended novel, anatomy is the predominant generic strain. The secondary generic strain is romance. Nevertheless, when the Pulitzer Prize winning *Advise and Consent* is evaluated as an independent work, *Advise* can be properly termed novel.

Advise and Consent presents "real" characters—Senators Bob Munson, Brig Anderson, Seab Cooley, and Orrin Knox—in the political and social setting of Washington, D.C. The political world and the characters in *Advise and Consent* generate their own existence and vitality, harmoniously fusing into an integrated, aesthetic whole. The energy of the novel pivots upon the exercise of senatorial power when the President determines that a more "flexible" Russian policy is necessary; consequently, the President nominates a liberal, Robert Leffingwell (well to the left), for Secretary of State although rumors that he may be too "soft on Communism" will trouble the Senate which must advise and consent to all cabinet appointments. At the conclusion of *Advise and Consent*, Robert Leffingwell is rejected by the Senate, and the President suffers a fatal heart attack. With Orrin Knox as his newly appointed Secretary of State, Harley Hudson, the new President, flies to Geneva to attend a summit conference demanded by the Russians after they have landed a military-scientific expedition on the moon. America's survival is in jeopardy. Because of Drury's conservative thesis and his analysis of politics in action, there is a strong anatomical strain in *Advise*; nevertheless, as a form of fiction *Advise* is primarily a novel since it contains a preponderance of the characteristics which Frye identifies with the novel: rather than being presented as heroes or stylized characters, major characters are presented realistically or naturalistically; they are presented as functioning members in society; there is an exhaustive analysis of human relationships (in a political setting); and *Advise* expands into a fictional approach to history.

Many of the themes of *Advise and Consent* (1959) appear in *A Shade of Difference* (1962) which combines the generic strains of anatomy and romance, but which lacks the vitality of *Advise and Consent*. For the first time, Drury's moral and political vision which clearly differentiates between good and evil, conservative and liberal, and Capitalism and Communism becomes obtrusive and disrupts the illusion of reality which is so essential to the enjoyment of fiction. Through the memory of Secretary of State Orrin Knox readers learn that President Hudson courageously stood firm before the Communist rulers in Geneva when they demanded that America relax its political posture throughout the world or risk an atomic attack from outer space. In *A Shade of Difference* the conflict between Communist imperialism and United States foreign policy shifts to the United Nations in an attempt to persuade readers that the United States should continue in the United Nations despite serious deficiencies in that organization. *A Shade* is also an attempt to persuade America that blacks can best achieve their goals by working legally and non-violently within the established political structure.

At the United Nations "Terrible Terry" Wolowo Ajakje, a Communist trained ruler of Gorotoland, and Felix Labaiya, the Panamanian Ambassador to the United Nations, attempt to embarrass the United States by exploiting racial animosity in America. Although the American delegation is embarrassed by a racial conflict that erupts in South Carolina over school integration, America successfully rebuffs the challenge to her power and prestige because President Hudson plays "political hardball" with foreign aid appropriations and because Senator Frye, the cancer-stricken United Nations Ambassador, heroically exhorts the world body to "love one another." The courage of Hal Frye, his utopian vision, and his optimistic message of love to the United Nations merges the propagandistic and didactic with the romantic. Romantic also are the characterizations. The central characters of *A Shade of Difference*, two blacks ("Terrible Terry" and Congressman Cullee Hamilton of California) and two whites (Felix Labaiya and Senator Frye) lack the vitality of the characters in *Advise and Consent*: they border more on the stylized or the stereotyped than on the "real." *A Shade of Difference* combines the political anatomy with the political romance; it lacks the power to convince which is necessary for a political novel, though at times many of the characters do become "real."

The Communist challenge becomes more aggressive in *Capable of Honor* (1966) and provides Drury with the opportunity to dramatize the belief that despite the extreme ethical pressures of politics and journalism, men and women can perform honorably in those professions. Although Gorotoland is granted independence in *A Shade of Difference* after a United Nation's debate and resolution, the former English colony is beset with severe political and military problems in *Capable of Honor* because the Soviet Union transfers its support from "Terrible Terry" to his cousin who mounts a revolution against the legitimate Gorotoland government. After the Communist trained and supported insurgents kill American missionaries and destroy the property of an American oil company, President Hudson dispatches troops to the troubled third world country, much to the chagrin of the American media. Hudson's policy of "patient and unafraid firmness" is pursued also in Panama when a rebellion erupts against the American presence in the Canal Zone.

Capable of Honor continues the didactic and propagandistic thrust of *A Shade of Difference*; however, these elements are more entertaining than obtrusive because like *Advise and Consent, Capable of Honor* depicts "real characters"—"Wonderful Walter," President Hudson, Senator Knox, and Governor Jason—in a vital political and journalistic setting. Despite biased and inflammatory reporting by the "liberal" news media, "conservative" candidates Harley Hudson and Orrin Knox win their party's nomination for President and Vice-President, but only after a bitter floor fight and violence at the national convention. Much to the relief of the President and the Secretary of State, the platform endorses the administration's foreign policy, a policy which commits American forces to a Vietnam type conflict on the African continent. Unlike *Advise and Consent, Capable* possesses a very effective satirical thrust, a thrust that we might associate with Menippean satire, which Northrop Frye identifies with anatomy. From the perspective of Frye's "Four Forms of Fiction," *Capable* is primarily anatomy: it examines and dissects the exercise of political power in the media and satirizes the flaws of "liberal" journalists and journalism.[2] Instead of ridiculing "the philosophus gloriosus" which is a common occurrence in the anatomy, "the professional liberal" is satirized in the person of a philosopher-journalist who is a symbol of folly (309) in a "loose jointed narrative."[3] Because of the "loose-jointed narrative" and the use of characters as mouthpieces for Drury, *Capable* is more a political anatomy than a political novel.

Preserve and Protect (1968), the fourth book of the series, is a transitional book whose hero, Bill Abbott, is a "Caretaker President" who symbolically represents or reflects the linking function of the novel. Ironically, "the Caretaker President" (so named by the press) is a man of action. When he becomes President after the mysterious crash of Air Force One and the death of Harley Hudson, the former Speaker of the House performs courageously to counter increased Communist aggression: he commits additional troops to Gorotoland in what might be termed in the jargon of the Vietnam War "a protective reaction strike;" he threatens to blockade the Panama Canal so that American "allies" and "enemies" can no longer supply the Communist liberation army which is planning a new and decisive offensive against American and Gorotoland forces; he convenes his party's National Committee to select a presidential nominee to replace the deceased President who had been the nominee of the party; and the "Caretaker President," who has sworn to "preserve and protect" America, sends a "tough" and perhaps unconstitutional anti-riot bill to Congress in an attempt to curb the political violence that threatens America. The conservative heroes of *Preserve and Protect* serve either as mouthpieces or foils to present or to demonstrate two dominant themes: "professional liberals," either consciously or unconsciously, help to implement a Communist, imperialistic plot; and the "liberal" media, through its support of anti-war protestors, has made political violence an acceptable instrument in American politics. This violence is metaphorically presented as a "beast," a beast which is essentially "evil" and uncontrollable once released from its cage, a beast which possesses the potential to destroy America. As an anatomy, *Preserve and Protect* primarily functions to embody and illustrate the potential consequences to America if Drury's moral, intellectual, and political vision is ignored by the press, the voters, and the politicians in contemporary America. Since more and more of the characters become obvious heroes and obvious villains and the plotting becomes more and more episodic, our sense of the "real" becomes strained and we realize that *Preserve and Protect* contains much of the romance along with the anatomy.

At the conclusion of *Preserve and Protect*, the "conservative" Orrin Knox receives his party's presidential nomination, and after extracting a promise from "liberal" governor Jason of California that the governor will repudiate the violent elements who support his presidential bid, Knox selects Jason as his running mate in a pragmatic conservative-liberal alliance which will make possible a Knox victory and a reuniting of an emotionally divided country split by the war issue. As the nominees prepare to make their acceptance speeches, one of the nominees is assassinated. *Come Nineveh, Come Tyre* (1973) explores the national and international consequences of a Knox assassination and the election of a "liberal" president who is "soft on Communism" and who has the enthusiastic support of the media. *The Promise of Joy* (1975), on the other hand, explores the national and international consequences of a Jason assassination and the election of a "conservative" president who is alienated and vilified by the media because he is firm and consistent in his opposition to Communist imperialistic policies. By creating two alternative conclusions to his political series, Drury illustrates the role of God, providence, or fate in the health of the American body politic.

Both *The Promise of Joy* and *Come Nineveh, Come Tyre* are anatomies which continue Drury's analysis of politics and the political process. They present Drury's perception of the spirit of the age and the temper of the times in the sixties and seventies. Almost equally balanced with the anatomical strains in these concluding novels of the series are the elements of romance: Ted Jason, the "liberal," becomes a stylized villain who brings America to the brink of disaster because he does not correctly perceive the "evil" of imperialistic Communism. Orrin Knox, the "conservative" hero, has a perceptive grasp of Communist ideology and tactics; under his guidance, America survives the threat of a nuclear holocaust. After this brief overview of Drury's political fiction, let us now examine *Advise and Consent* as an example of "pure" and serious political fiction.

III

Poetry, Marianne Moore has written, "can present for inspection imaginary gardens with real toads in them." Successful novelists share a similar goal or goals: presenting "imaginary worlds" which become "real" to the reader and creating characters who vividly walk and talk in that "imaginary world," thereby evoking a "willing suspension of disbelief" in the mind of the reader. In *Advise and Consent* Drury creates a vital Washington and peoples the nation's capital with "real" characters whose daily existence involves almost total immersion in the political processes which constitute the life-blood of the American body politic. Although *Advise and Consent* is totally vitalized by political action, the reader's awareness of politics as pure politics seldom obtrudes upon the reader since Drury successfully subordinates or merges the political elements in the plot to the emerging and evolving personalities of his major characters: the President, Senator Munson, Senator Anderson, Senator Cooley, and Senator Knox. Sex, violence, deceit, vindictiveness, ambition, *hubris*, courage, and patriotism stimulate the narrative movement of the novel which is compelling, probable, and even inevitable as it moves toward the suicide of Anderson, the defeat of the Leffingwell nomination, and the fatal heart attack of the President. Unlike the plots in later Drury fiction, especially the loosely structured *The Promise of Joy* and *Come Nineveh, Come Tyre,* the plot of *Advise and Consent* is tight and challenges the intelligence and memory of the reader beyond the realm of pure information and recall.

As the novel begins, the President has decided to shift from a "tough" Russian policy to one which is more conducive to inducing productive Russian-American negotiations. As a result of this shift in policy, the President nominates a "liberal," Robert Leffingwell, to replace his more "conservative" Secretary of State. Predictably, much Senatorial opposition develops, including a vindictive thrust from a seventy-five year old Carolina Senator who is bitterly angry at Leffingwell because he once suggested in a committee that the Senator was a liar. Nevertheless, for the approval of the nomination, normal Senate procedures are initiated. Tom August, the Chairman of the Foreign Relations Committee, appoints Senator Brig Anderson to chair a sub-committee which will hold hearings and make a nomination recommendation to the full committee, which will then decide upon a recommendation to the Senate. The nomination appears in jeopardy when Carolina's Senator Cooley produces a witness who states that Leffingwell had once been a member of a Communist cell while he was teaching at the University of Chicago. Although Leffingwell categorically denies the charge and demonstrates that Herbert Gelman, the witness, had suffered nervous disorders when he was a student at the University and again when he was an employee of the Office of Defense Mobilization, some Senators continue to doubt his integrity, his loyalty to America, and his anti-war philosophy, which is predisposed to be "soft on Communism." The sub-committee, because of such deep-rooted opinions, is unable to reach a consensus; consequently, the sub-committee directs the Chairman to report the results of the sub-committee hearing to the Foreign Relations Committee on the following week.

Before this report is presented, Senator Cooley's experience and political instincts suggest to him the identity of an alleged fourth member of the Communist cell who has used the pseudonym James Morton. While reviewing the transcript of the sub-committee hearings, Senator Cooley shrewdly surmises that since the Director of the Defense Mobilization, Robert Leffingwell, was instrumental in placing Gelman with the Bureau of International Economic Affairs after his last nervous breakdown, that either the Director or the Assistant Secretary of the Bureau might be James Morton since such a favor "would seem to indicate some personal relationship or friendship or knowledge between the nominee and either the Director of the Bureau or the man in over-all charge of it, the Assistant Secretary" (314). Once Senator Cooley recalls from previous, unrelated Senate hearings that the Assistant Secretary was approximately the same age as Leffingwell, and that he had also taught at the University while Leffingwell was teaching, the Senator gambles that a telephone call to "James Morton" might elicit a surprised, shocked and honest response. When, in fact, the Assistant Secretary does confirm the Senator's suspicions, the Senator directs "James Morton" not to publicize his identity; in addition, he advises Morton to telephone Senator Anderson and inform him that Leffingwell lied under oath to the Senate sub-committee. This information, Senator Cooley believes, will be presented to the sub-committee by Anderson despite whatever pressures might be placed upon him by the President, and as a result, the Senator calculates that the Senate will not *advise and consent* to the Leffingwell nomination. Later, just to make certain that the ambitious, responsible, and patriotic Senator will make public the Leffingwell lie, Senator Cooley advises the Senator from Utah that if Anderson does not make public the information at the appropriate moment, Senator Cooley will inform the press that Senator Anderson and the President are collaborating in order to conceal proof of Leffingwell's youthful Communist affiliation from the Senate Foreign Relations Committee.

However, Senator Cooley's plans are shattered by a chain of events set in motion by "liberal" Supreme Court Justice Davis who has lobbied with the "liberal" media to marshal support for the "liberal" Leffingwell. Unknown to Senator Anderson, his "friend" Justice Davis finds a suggestive and therefore potentially damaging war-time photograph of Anderson with a male friend. Subsequently, the Justice, who believes that a Leffingwell confirmation is essential if peaceful co-existence with the Russians is to be achieved, hand delivers the suggestive picture to the Majority Leader who accepts the photograph although he realizes that the photograph is meant for blackmail. Inevitably, the photograph becomes instrumental in the death of Senator Anderson who categorically opposes the nomination when "James Morton" informs him of Leffingwell's breach of integrity before the sub-committee. Although Senator Munson hesitates to provide this compromising picture of his young friend to the President, Munson does so because Justice Davis has anticipated his reluctance and has informed the President that the Majority Leader possesses the potentially damaging picture. After the President has failed in his attempt to persuade Senator

Anderson to withdraw his opposition to Leffingwell, the President assures the Senator that he will withdraw the nomination though he actually has no plans to do so. The departure of Senator Anderson from the secret meeting initiates a painful experience for the Majority Leader. When the President informs Munson that Justice Davis has informed him about the photograph and demands that the Senator produce it, the Majority Leader passes the picture to the President who sends the photograph to "liberal" Senator Ackerman, an American who would "rather crawl on his knees to Moscow than perish under a bomb" (147). Senator Ackerman then traces Anderson's friend in the picture, who reveals their war-time homosexual relationship in return for desperately needed money. On national television Senator Ackerman threatens to reveal Anderson's "secret" if he does not withdraw his opposition to the Leffingwell nomination. After Senator Anderson's wife has received a telegram and an anonymous phone call which shatters his already troubled marriage, Senator Anderson removes a pistol from his desk and drives to his office. Before he commits suicide rather that experience the public disclosure of his homosexual love affair, Senator Anderson writes a detailed Leffingwell report to Senator Knox, a highly respected conservative, personal friend and fellow member of the Foreign Relations Committee.

Since the President persists in his belief that Leffingwell combines the "toughness," duplicity, flexibility, and patriotism necessary to make an excellent Secretary of State who is capable of negotiating with the Russians, Senator Knox reveals Anderson's report to key members of the Senate who band with him to oppose the nomination. After Senator Ackerman is censured by the senate for his public attack and threat upon Senator Anderson, the Senate votes *not* to *advise and consent* to the Leffingwell nomination. This defeat, coupled with a Russian moon landing and renewed Russian threats of war, proves to be too much for the President who suffers from a fatal heart attack. As the novel concludes, the new President, Harley Hudson, is traveling to a summit meeting with the Russians, and readers are left to wonder if President Hudson and Senator Knox, the new Secretary of State, will be "tough" enough to withstand the belligerent Russian demands at Geneva. The plot of *Advise and Consent* is complex, compelling, surprising, and totally political.

The first book of *Advise and Consent* is Bob Munson's book and this permits the readers to perceive political events and the spirit of the age from the perspective of the Majority Leader, one of the principle middlemen in the "eternal bargaining" of Washington politics. After twenty-three years in the Senate, the extremely pleasant and likeable Michigan Senator is highly respected by his peers even though the majority do not share his thematic fears that the "golden age" of America has passed, that a climate of fear exists in America, and that the threat of Communism is "rapidly narrowing to a choice between fight and die now or compromise and die later" (37).

Americans, Bob Munson suspects, are not as alert, perceptive, and courageous as their forefathers, and early in *Advise and Consent* he ponders American problems and reflects Drury's themes while introducing a recurring motif of Drury fiction suggestive of some conservative thought during the late fifties:

> . . . there was just enough of a feeling, just enough to provide a very dangerous potential for appeasement that would be fatal. Faced with an open attack, they would, if they had the time, rouse and fight back as they always had, no matter what the price for America; but make the attack sufficiently intellectual, make the threat sufficiently subtle, give them time to think, let them mull it over and contemplate what would happen if they didn't go along, carry it to the conference table if you liked and be sure you gave them a way to save face as they retreated, and he would not, at this moment, vouch for what her people would allow to be done in America (37).

Despite such views, the Majority Leader works to promote the nomination of a "liberal" who is accused of being "soft on Communism" because his President directs him to do so. As a result of the Leffingwell nomination, the lives of all the significant characters, as well as the minor characters, of *Advise and Consent* are immediately and permanently affected, and from the moment of the nomination everyone involved in political Washington is aware of political repercussions stemming from the potential dramatic conflict between the President and the Senate. This evolving conflict between "liberals" and "conservatives," between those who tend to be "soft on Communism" as opposed to those who tend to be firm in the presence of a Communist threat, provides a dramatic vehicle for Drury to instruct Americans about both the mechanics of power and the abuse of power as it might operate in the Senate.

In the introductory pages of *Advise and Consent*, Senator Munson is the focal point of a scene which establishes the basic conflicts of the novel and which demonstrates Drury's ability to create the illusion of reality with the daily and sometimes boring details of politics. As Bob Munson reads the headline of the *Washington Post*, the reader reads and experiences with him: PRESIDENT NAMES LEFFINGWELL SECRETARY OF STATE. Irritation, anger, hurt feelings, and self-pity attack the Majority Leader before, during, and after he telephones the President who had neglected to consult him about the Leffingwell appointment. Some of the Senator's chagrin is generated by his lack of confidence in Leffingwell's ability to perform competently as Secretary of State; nevertheless, his party responsibility as Majority Leader is to make certain that the "liberal" champion of the media is approved by the Senate. After exchanging information, irritation, and quips about doing "dirty work" for the President, the Senator then begins to make political telephone calls. First, he calls Senator Warren Strickland, the Minority Leader, in order to receive a first hand estimate of the potential strength and intensity of Senatorial opposition to the Leffingwell nomination. When Senator Strickland confirms that the Leffingwell nomination will have serious opposition, the Majority Leader telephones his Majority Whip, Senator Danta, and directs him to canvas the Senate for potential votes and present feelings about the nomination. Additional aggravation besets Munson when Robert Leffingwell refuses to speak with him on the telephone because Leffingwell fears such a conversation might be construed improper. Not easily deterred from his political mission, the Majority Leader then places a call to Senator Seab Cooley, the senior Senator from South Carolina who has been a bitter opponent of Leffingwell for at least thirteen years.

No surprise follows: Senator Cooley vehemently informs the Majority Leader that he "will get that man," a man he does not like "mentally, morally, physically, or Constitutionally," for Senator Cooley does not forget that Leffingwell had called him a liar in a committee meeting thirteen years earlier (19,20). Points of conflict are thus clearly delineated in the opening pages of the novel through the Leffingwell appointment and the telephone calls of the Majority Leader. Through the events which will follow, Senator Munson will come to the realization that he has failed his responsibility to the Senate. His alliance with the President and his activity to gain the confirmation of Leffingwell will reflect a want of judgment and an ethical lapse on his part because he places loyalty to the President and loyalty to his party above his responsibility to the Senate and his country.

This first scene of the novel illustrates Drury's superb ability to construct scenes which vividly establish personalities through interesting dialogue. Through Senator Munson's first reactions to the President's nomination, we observe a politician in action who is intelligent, conscientious, efficient, shrewd, friendly, courteous, and likeable. More insight into the Munson personality is gleaned from a very brief narrative section which is biographical in focus. This structural technique—the narrative biographical sketch—is a staple of Drury fiction. In addition to Bob Munson's relatively short biographical sketch in *Advise and Consent*, more extensive biographical expositions are presented of Senator Cooley, Senator Anderson from Utah, and Senator Knox from Illinois. In each of these biographical narratives Drury depicts early indications of intelligence, sensitivity, sympathy, independence, strong moral character, peer popularity through childhood and adolescence, sexual development, and leadership ability in school, business and community. Such personality traits are woven into descriptions of home and family, expository material which extends over a diversity of regions and cultures, all of which contribute to the formation of unique personalities and have no small bearing on the future success of the potential congressman or senator. Although Drury does not present an intensive in depth psychological portrait of his characters, general psychological profiles of his heroes and villains are presented. Significant, formative, emotional experiences are either narrated or graphically presented in the biographical sections, thereby aiding the reader to perceive the attitudes and the motivations which tend to direct later political decisions and actions. In Drury fiction there is not one political personality or model for political success or failure; there are several, and each evolves from a different region and culture. Senator Munson, a dynamic character in *Advise and Consent,* is from Michigan.

Though he is depicted as a "good," sincere, public servant, as a result of the powerful personality of the President, Senator Munson suffers a lapse of character—the betrayal of his political and social responsibility to the body politic. This transition in character is believable because the Majority Leader engages in politics as the *art of the possible* and as an art which requires bargaining on a daily basis. Such bargaining is sometimes practiced in a highly sophisticated and socially and politically acceptable way, but at the core of such bargaining is the fundamental fact that politics is a "cruel game." This dual aspect of politics—bargaining and cruelty—are crucial to plot and theme and are manifest early in the novel. Senators must "bargain" with potential financial contributors to their election campaigns both past and future. In Book I of *Advise and Consent,* Roy B. Mulholland, the junior Senator from Michigan, is "pressured" by the President of General Motors to vote against the "radical" Leffingwell and reminded that "we're going to be watching Bob Munson closely" on this one (46). Senator Munson, on the other hand, receives pressure from the President of the United Auto Workers to vigorously promote the Leffingwell nomination and to beat the "reactionary bastards." When Senator Munson does not unequivocally agree with the union president, the union president reacts angrily and identifies an unflattering aspect of Munson's political character: "By God," he exclaims, "you're the slipperiest character in seventeen counties. Everytime we think we have you pegged you slip out from under" (54,55). Senator Munson, in turn, applies pressure to work both his and the President's will upon the Senate. During his canvas for the Leffingwell vote, he informs a New Hampshire Senator that "if you'll help us, we'll help you." However, when the New Hampshire Senator demands a firm commitment for an atomic submarine contract for the Portsmouth navy yard, the Majority Leader takes a different tact because it is not politically expedient: too many Senators are listening to their cloakroom conversation, and if the Majority Leader buckles to this demand for *quid pro quo,* he knows he will be asked to make promises to many other Senators. Consequently, Senator Munson expediently takes the high road and purposely speaks in a loud voice so that all present can hear clearly: I will not bargain on a "blackmail basis," he says. Yet later, Senator Whiteside still asks Senator Munson what he will give the Florida Senator in exchange for his vote. Munson, at this point, maintains consistency in this policy by restating that he will not bargain;

however, Senator Whiteside's reply foreshadows the future events of the novel: "You'll bargain Bob,. . . ," he said, "not right now, but you'll bargain. The day's going to come on this one" (93,94,97).

Shortly thereafter, at a party given by Senator Munson's mistress, the Majority Leader does bargain though not with Senators but rather with the present Secretary of State whom the President has forced to resign for alleged "ill health." Although Secretary Sheppard advises Senator Munson emphatically that he will "never" testify in behalf of the nominee to the Foreign Relations Committee, the Senator begins to "bargain." If the Secretary will testify, the Majority Leader and the President have agreed, then the sixty-seven year old Secretary will be made special ambassador to NATO which will be a pleasant way to spend his last years. As an ambassador, Sheppard will receive a "good salary" and have "a good social life." Caught in a dilemma, the Secretary protests that he thought Bob Munson was his friend and that politics need not be such a "brutal" business. In response, the Majority Leader reminds the former Governor of Ohio that the Secretary had practiced brutal politics during his career and that politics is, in fact,

. . .a rough game, underneath the backslaps and the handshakes and the big noble speeches. . .and we all discover it sooner or later. It's a cruel business, sometimes when you're in the big time the way we are, because up here the country is involved and men play for keeps (104).

The "bargaining" is effective. On the following morning the Secretary of State, though he believes the nomination of Leffingwell might be a "mistake," testifies in behalf of Leffingwell in the Foreign Relations sub-committee.

American politics, Munson believes, is far from simple and definately is not "black and white;" however, as he tells a group of diplomats at a party, "there has to come a time on nearly every issue when they are (black and white), when you're either for something or against it, when you're either with somebody or opposing him" (110). This, too, the President knows, and he uses this knowledge for leverage to move Senator Munson in his conflict with Senator Anderson. The President clearly reveals his thinking to the Majority Leader concerning Anderson's opposition to the Leffingwell nomination and what the President believes can and should be done about it. Suggestions that Senator Anderson "be brought" or threatened are not unequivocally denounced by the Majority Leader and the President forces Senator Munson to commit himself on this issue: "Are you with me or against me on this?" (299). Evasive is the Majority Leader's response, thereby signalling to the President that Munson is somewhat "soft" and can be pressured to work his will, whatever the Presidential will may be. Consequently, when the President, the Vice-President, Senator Munson, and Senator Anderson meet privately, and the President communicates to Senator

Anderson that the President will withdraw the nomination because of Leffingwell's breach of integrity, readers are prepared for Munson's silence even though the Senator realizes that the President is being dishonest with Senator Anderson, the Vice-President, and the Majority Leader. Later, then, the Senator's response to the President's demand to see the Senator Anderson picture that suggests Anderson may have been involved in homosexual activities during World War II is predictable:

The Majority Leader felt for one wild second that he should turn and run, that he was so close to the absolute essence of the American Presidency, in the presence of a dedication so severe, so lonely, and so terrible, *so utterly removed from the normal morality that holds society together*, that he should flee from it before the revelation proved too shattering and some great and dreadful damage was done to Brig, to him, to the President, the country, and the world. *But men do not often act on such impulses, which are immediately thwarted by reminders that this is a workaday world*, after all, *and such gestures would be completely irrational*, after all, and what in the hell are they thinking about, after all; and so they do not do them (390 Italics added.).

Not surprising, then, the Senator gives the President the potentially damaging Anderson photograph and thus events are set in motion which will result in the suicide of Senator Anderson.

Two vivid scenes present the painful, guilt-ridden agony which torments Munson as a result of his collusion with the President. The first occurs when Senator Anderson suspects that the President has deceived him, and he visits Munson's office in order to have reassurance from his friend and Leader. The Majority Leader is non-committal and ambiguous; he lacks the courage to tell Anderson that he and the President have betrayed the trust that the Utah Senator has placed in them. The second vivid scene occurs when Senator Knox, a very close friend and long-time colleague, confronts the Majority Leader after Anderson's suicide and Senator Munson declares his intention to withdraw his support for the Leffingwell nomination. On the surface, there appears to be a touch of nobility behind such actions. However, if Senator Munson wishes to regain and then maintain his severely damaged prestige and authority in the Senate, this course of action is the only pragmatic alternative. And an effective alternative it is. After his resignation as Majority Leader, the Senate promptly re-elects him to that position despite his admitted abuse of power; and in his acceptance speech Munson again acknowledges his poor judgment and places in focus for himself, as well as for the Senate, the nature of his role as a Majority Leader: "In the past, perhaps, as is often the case when the Congress and the Presidency are controlled by the same party, I have spoken too much for the White House—to you. From now on...I shall speak for you—to the White House" (542).

Senator Munson appears again and again in every fictional narrative of the political series, but his character is never again depicted with the fullness and vitality possessed in *Advise and Consent*. Although his colleagues are shocked and angered by his role in the destruction of the Senator from Utah, most choose to forget his lapse of integrity because he has recognized and accepted responsibility for his failure, and this failure was the first serious blemish on an outstanding record of many years of service to the Senate and the country. In *Capable of Honor* there is an oblique reference to the ethical dilemma that led to Munson's resignation as Majority Leader. The subject is alluded to by the Speaker of the House during the Gorotoland crisis—a Vietnam parallel—which divides America into two emotional camps: "hawks" and "doves." Although the conversation between the Majority Leader and the Speaker of the House ostensibly has the war in Gorotoland as its focus, both elected representatives understand that the question of Presidential support and loyalty involved in the Gorotoland crisis is similar to that which confronted Senator Munson in the Leffingwell nomination: how much public and private support should Senators and Congressmen give to a President of their own party once the President has firmly committed the country and himself to a position which they believe to be imprudent. While discussing this question, the Speaker observes that Majority Leaders and Speakers of the House resolve such questions "in favor of the man in the White House" largely because their political careers hinge on it and that if the President does not receive their support, then "two other distinguished and able gentlemen would be riding down Pennsylvania Avenue to lunch with the President as Speaker and Majority Leader" (185). Moreover, when Senator Munson explicitly recalls his breach of integrity during the Leffingwell nomination, the Speaker responds, suggesting that there are two kinds of integrity: complete integrity to one's beliefs and a substitute integrity to the body politic. To help relieve the Majority Leader of troublesome feelings concerning the Anderson suicide, Congressman Abbott expresses his belief that as Speaker he has not

...sacrificed much integrity over the years. Look at it this way: the country elects a man President to do certain things. If you help him do this on the hill, then you're helping the country get what it wants. Maybe we have lost our right to eternal challenge that your friend Arly is so fond of, but there's a substitute integrity, you might call it, which is just as valid. The integrity of seeing things through, or getting things done, of having your colleagues know they can trust your word and count on you to deliver the things you promise in return for the support of the man you serve.... No, I don't feel regrets about it. The country elects him—we help him—do what the country wants. Nothing dishonorable about that (185).

Despite this rationalization, which indicates one dimension of the complexity involved in the tensions of loyalty and responsibility in the body politic, sophisticated readers understand that some actions cannot be permitted even if one invokes the doctrine of "substitute integrity," for such an ethic injudiciously applied can lead not only to the destruction of individuals, such as Senator Anderson, but also to the destruction of the body politic itself if the President becomes corrupt, mentally unbalanced, or unwise.

Through the character, then, of Senator Munson, the reader perceives and emotionally absorbs the vision of a declining America. Readers of *Advise and Consent* observe American workers who no longer take pride in their work and who are producing inferior products, an American military establishment lacking in the funds to compete with the ever-increasing Soviet military growth, and an American public beset by anxiety and fear induced by the threat of atomic warfare between America and Russia. Through the thoughts and actions of Senate Majority Leader Munson, readers also perceive several disturbing impressions of the nature of contemporary politics: politics is "the art of bargaining" and is the constant balancing of *quid pro quo* in order to achieve political goals that are not always in the best interest of the nation. Readers vividly perceive that political decisions and actions have unforeseen consequences in the body politic, as well as upon congressmen and senators whose political careers are vital to the political life and military strength of America. In addition, through the experience of Senator Munson readers perceive that the personal appeal of the President— the intimate exercise of presidential authority and power—can have a mesmerizing and corrupting effect upon even the most experienced Senator and that when presidential wishes and demands are of a dubious ethical quality, they possess the potential of seriously damaging the American body politic.

The second book of *Advise and Consent,* Seab Cooley's Book, develops the character of Senator Cooley and continues to dramatically integrate that "powerful" and "irascible" Senator into the action of the novel. Although Cooley emerges as a paternalistic racist in *A Shade of Difference*, the racist tendencies of his personality are not emphasized in *Advise* where Drury establishes his fundamental character. In *Advise* Drury emphasizes the seventy-five year old Senator's political experience, political intelligence, and political intuition, as well as his patriotism and dedication to his constituents in South Carolina, characteristics which are consistent with his character development in *A Shade of Difference* where he sincerely believes that his racist views are correct and that they should be reflected in both domestic and foreign policy. Not surprisingly, even in *Advise* Seab has detractors. Seab, his detractors say, "was out for what he could get for South Carolina, the South, and himself, in that order, and there was nothing he would not do to attain an objective once he had set it for himself" (154).

As we have already noted in the opening scenes of *Advise*, Seab Cooley is one of the power brokers in the Senate. Because Bob Munson, the Senate Majority Leader, knows that the powerful South Carolina Senator will oppose the Leffingwell nomination, he telephones the Senator in order to determine how fiercely Seab will oppose the nomination. Seab's strong personality immediately asserts itself, firmly establishing the basic tension between the Administration and the Senate. "I'm against it!" Seab tells the Majority Leader. "I don't like the man. I don't like him mentally, morally, physically, or Constitutionally." Shrewdly, Seab attributes a false motivation to his opposition, so that the Administration will miscalculate his ability to influence the Senate against Leffingwell. Thirteen years earlier, Senator Cooley angrily recalls, Bob Leffingwell called the Senator a liar in a committee meeting. After exploding his resentment into the phone, Seab promises to raise "hell" against the nomination and rudely assaults Bob Munson's ear by slamming the telephone into the receiver (19-21). Since both the Majority Leader and Seab are very sophisticated and effective members of the Senate, Seab's animosity is only temporary and has no lasting repercussions upon their personal relationship. Shortly after their lively conversation, both Senators share a cab to the capitol building and the South Carolina senator graciously pays the fare. When Senator Munson compares himself to a rock because of his firm commitment to the Leffingwell nomination, Seab responds with a metaphor foreshadowing the tragic events in *Advise*: "If you're a rock, Bob," the Senator retorts, "you've met a sledge hammer" (39). In *A Shade of Difference*, however, when Seab's opposition is primarily rooted in racial prejudice and political self-interest, the roles are reversed and it is Senator Cooley, rather than the Majority Leader, who will experience a traumatic political and personal defeat.

In "Seab Cooley's Book," after the narrator informs us that Seab's primary purpose is noble rather than ignoble, Drury presents a biographical narrative. The Senator possesses a genuine and sincere fear of Communist imperialism, and he perceives the Leffingwell nomination as an immediate danger to the welfare of the United States because of Leffingwell's sympathetic posture toward Communism. Although his friends and opponents are unaware, Seab views his opposition to Leffingwell as a patriotic duty and as "the final justification and culmination" of his fifty years of service in both the House and the Senate (149). As *Advise* evolves, readers observe how the shrewd Senator consistently strives to keep his options open as he explores tactics to oppose Leffingwell. This political posture enables Seab to respond flexibly to any opportunity for marshalling influence against the nomination. Even at the age of twenty-six, at the beginning of his political career, we are told that Seab already had possessed such political shrewdness.

As with other significant characters in his fiction, Drury presents for us in a lengthy biographical sketch information and events which help us to understand Seab's character, his political career, and his response to the opportunity to exercise power. The seeds of Seab's strength were sown in his childhood. His background was humble; his father was a storekeeper in Barnwell, South Carolina, a small, country town. When Seab's father died, Seab, who was the oldest of seven children, quit high school and assumed the responsibility of supporting the family. Despite such responsibility, Seab earned a high school degree by taking mail order courses. His intelligence and character were not unnoticed. Colonel Tom Cashton, a wealthy landowner and a political power in South Carolina, encouraged the young boy to attend the University of South Carolina and much more: he financed his college education and sponsored his political career. At the University, Seab continued to demonstrate unusual ability and strength of character. He was "good looking, sociable, likeable, and gregarious;" he was involved in sports and campus politics: football, chairman of the debating society, president of the junior class, and president of the student body (151-152). Through the Colonel's influence, Tom was appointed superintendent of a small, community school after he received his degree in education. Education, however, was only a momentary resting place for Seab who possessed political aspirations, aspirations which Colonel Cashton had anticipated. After Seab strengthened his credentials by attending Harvard Law School, political opportunity had ripened. He launched his political career with a speech at a Barnwell Fourth of July celebration at a time when the incumbent Congressman, conveniently, was ready to retire from political life. The only tragic event in Seab's early years was a traumatic romance with Colonel Cashton's daughter, a romance that was "a key to Seab's irascible personality," a personality which had won for him the unflattering epithets: "Seab the Irascible, Seab the Invincible, Seab the Holy Terror, the Scourge of the Senate" (160). However, there is a soft, as well as a hard side to Seab, and surprisingly, this soft side is revealed to Brig Anderson as soon as Seab realizes that Brig's life might be destroyed if the Utah Senator continues his opposition to Leffingwell's nomination for Secretary of State. Seab's sensitivity toward Anderson's difficulties parallels his growing awareness that he is getting old, that times are changing and that his image of being "intelligent, industrious, persistent, tenacious, violent, passionate, vindictive, and tricky" is no longer enough to awe and bluff his colleagues. Such Senators as Bob Munson, Orrin Knox, Stanley Danta, and Arly Richardson, Seab knows,

he had never been able to bluff, even though he had managed to beat them in open contest fairly often. It was only lately that he had begun to realize that perhaps he was no longer so strong as he once had been, that age was beginning to erode his position, that those who moved in awe of him just because he was Seab Cooley were dying off or were being beaten by younger men who came fresh to the Senate and learned early that while Seab was a man to be wary of, he was also seventy-five years old and neither immortal or infallible. Not yet had he really been toppled decisively from his throne, but he realized that there was a growing lack of respect for him among the younger members (150).

In *A Shade of Difference* Seab is toppled; but in *Advise and Consent* he still possesses enough power to contribute significantly to the defeat of the Leffingwell nomination.

In Book I of *Advise*, Seab, a Phi Betta Kappa, a master of parliamentary procedure and political rhetoric, demonstrates his political astuteness by offering to testify at the Senate Foreign Relations Committee hearings on the Leffingwell nomination. The Committee Chairman, Tom August, reacts as Seab anticipated; the Chairman appoints a subcommittee to examine and report upon the Leffingwell nomination, an action which will not only permit Seab to testify but which will also permit him to call and cross-examine witnesses in an open committee meeting. As a result, both Orrin Knox and Seab are able to challenge publicly Leffingwell's attitude toward Russia and thereby generate a lead (such as "Senator Seabright B. Cooley charged today that Robert A. Leffingwell will betray the United States in negotiations with Russia if he becomes Secretary of State") in newspapers that will be damaging to the Leffingwell nomination (190). However, Senator Cooley is able to do even much better.

After a committee member, Senator Richardson, receives a mysterious telegram from a Robert Gelman which alleges that Bob Leffingwell had Communist affiliations while he was a teacher at the University of Chicago, Gelman, who has a history of mental instability, is called to testify at the nomination hearings. At the hearings, Bob Leffingwell categorically denies Gelman's allegations, allegations that Leffingwell, Gelman, and an unknown third party—a pseudonym was used—were members of a Communist cell group that met on Thursday evenings. Shrewdly, Senator Cooley has staged events so that there can be two dramatic confrontations damaging to Leffingwell. The confrontations pivot upon Leffingwell's initial response to Gelman's telegram to Senator Richardson: his denial of ever knowing a man named "Robert Gelman." Gelman, upset by Leffingwell's denial, secretly makes contact with Senator Cooley and consents to appear as a witness upon the direction of the Senator. After Seab dramatically confronts Leffingwell with the Gelman allegations and Leffingwell reaffirms his denial, a second dramatic confrontation occurs when Gelman is then brought forward as a surprise witness. Although Leffingwell concedes that Gelman was at one time a student in one of his classes, the nominee denies the substance of Gelman's allegations—that Leffingwell, Gelman, and a "James Morton" were members of a Communist cell group. With this denial, it appears that the Leffingwell nomination will be recommended by the sub-committee. However, as a result of Scab's intelligence, memory, and experience, but especially because of his conscientious dedication to duty, the Senator significantly influences the momentum of the nomination by intensively studying the transcript of the committee hearings:

> First, by a conscious effort that he had found effective many times before, he deliberately drained his mind, as much as was humanly possible, of every preconception, every emotion, every prejudice, every thought that had filled it on the subject heretofore.
> Then he read through the transcript slowly and carefully from beginning to end, approaching it as though it were brand new and he a reader who knew nothing at all of what was involved, making a note or two from time to time on a large pad of lined Senate notepaper in his spidery old hand (273).

Then in a moment of illumination, his political intuition reveals the real name of James Morton, the unaccounted for member of the cell group. Rather than directly exposing the identity of James Morton, Seab directs Morton to call Senator Anderson, the sub-committee chairman, while also ordering Morton not to mention Seab's name or Seab's telephone call. The South Carolina Senator believes that the attack on Leffingwell will be much more effective if Anderson, not Seab Cooley, leads the political attack. There is no doubt that the shrewd Seab Cooley can sometimes be a calculating, vicious, cold-blooded character. There is also no doubt that Drury can create an intriguing, dramatic, political plot.

When Senator Van Ackerman vehemently supports the Leffingwell nomination and fanatically attacks those who oppose the nomination, Seab takes the measure of Van Ackerman and issues a verdict. Van Ackerman is dangerous to the Senate and the country; consequently, Seab advises the Majority Leader to destroy Van Ackerman before he causes major problems: "He means trouble, Bob; I've seen his kind come to the Senate before, and they always mean trouble, Bob. Destroy him, Bob, while you still can" (257-258). Since Van Ackerman is on the Majority Leader's side on the Leffingwell nomination, even though he agrees with Seab, Munson does not politically destroy Van Ackerman. As Seab suggests, five days later the Majority Leader is sorry he has not followed Seab's advice. When Van Ackerman attempts to blackmail Senator Anderson into supporting the Leffingwell nomination and Seab exerts a counter pressure by threatening to expose Anderson for withholding information about Leffingwell's Communist activity at the University of Chicago, Anderson commits suicide. Before Anderson commits suicide, however, Seab reveals a tender side of his personality; this tender side adds a sensitive dimension to his personality and makes Senator Cooley a more endearing character.

When Seab set his plan to defeat the Leffingwell nomination in motion, he "was much more interested in getting Bob Leffingwell and the President" than in Anderson's personal and political welfare (316). With his knowledge of Senator Anderson's character, Seab is certain that Anderson will bring forth Morton, thereby exposing Leffingwell's Communist activities and his lies to the sub-committee. In one respect, however, he miscalculates. Seab believes that Brig Anderson will communicate this information to his friends and colleagues, Bob Munson, Orrin Knox, and Lafe Smith, and that this information will then spread through the Senate, thereby relieving pressure from Anderson and shifting the public pressure to Leffingwell and the Administration. As events unfold and Seab suspects that Anderson may bend under presidential pressure, in a very effective scene, Seab guarantees his friendship and help to Anderson whatever the presidential pressure. To Seab, both the President and Leffingwell are "evil" men. Initially, however, his support to his "friend" is contingent upon his opposition to Leffingwell. Despite this qualification, the desperate Anderson is still grateful (413-415). As the pressure becomes greater upon Anderson and Seab realizes that the President can and will destroy Anderson if the Senator continues to oppose the nomination, in a credible reversal of character, Seab offers his unqualified support to Anderson. In a telephone call, a concerned and worried Seab informs the desperate Anderson that he will never reveal any information whatsoever about James Morton and that, consequently, no one will ever learn of James Morton. As for Van Ackerman—who is an "evil monster"— Seab counsels that Bob Munson and Seab will take care of him. In a noble manifestation of his character, Seab explains the motivation behind his change of heart to Anderson:

'Well, sir,' Seab said, 'I have decided that much as I despise Mr. Robert—A.— Leffingwell, and much as I would dearly love to get them both, the pleasure is not sufficient if it is really going to mean harm to you. No, sir, it isn't sufficient if that's what it means. I am quite an old man, Brigham,' he said, 'and I know by now when a fine young man comes to the Senate, and I suspect that much as it might satisfy my ego to get them, an old man's ego isn't worth a young man's career and happiness. I truly suspect it isn't. I don't know what they have to fight you with, but I don't like the sound of it. I don't like the sound of it at all. I think you could be most severely hurt. I think this would be a real tragedy for you, and for the country, and for the Senate. I think you are worth a hundred times any satisfaction I might get from beating Mr. Leffingwell. I gen-u-inely do' (443).

Seab's offer of help and friendship is total. He informs Anderson that he will be down in a little while and they will visit together over food. Such will not come to pass. After Brig commits suicide, Orrin Knox and Seab join together in defeating the Leffingwell nomination. Consequently, as readers turn to *A Shade of Difference*, they possess a highly developed sense of the character of Seab Cooley—a shrewd, conservative, patriotic Senator from the deep South who is in the twilight of his political power. *A Shade of Difference* adds another dimension to his character.

The third book of *Advise and Consent*, Brigham Anderson's Book, continues to present politicians in action and to develop the personality of Brig Anderson as a "real" rather than as an "ideal" political character. In this respect, Anderson is much like Bob Munson and Seab Cooley, politicians, who are neither "all good" nor "all evil." Though Anderson is neither "all good" nor "all evil," he is certainly decidedly different. Because of a World War II homosexual experience, Anderson's personal, domestic, and political happiness are inextricably intertwined. Consequently, when he is pressured by two strong, determined and powerful political personalities, he is painfully vulnerable. As the political plot moves inexorably toward its personal and political climax, both the President and Senator Cooley attempt to intimidate the central character in the novel. The President pressures Anderson, the Chairman of the Senate Foreign Relations sub-committee studying the Leffingwell nomination, to withdraw his fierce opposition to Leffingwell by threatening to leak evidence that Anderson is a homosexual. Simultaneously, Senator Cooley provides a counter-pressure: if Anderson does not inform his sub-committee that he has proof that Leffingwell had been a member of a Communist cell group when he taught at the University of Chicago, Cooley will destroy his political career by informing the press that Anderson had withheld crucial information involving national security from the Foreign Relations Committee. Such fear and anxiety about Communist infiltration of government and Russia's military threat to America were significant elements in the intellectual and emotional climate after World War II, an intellectual and emotional climate that significantly influenced the spirit of the age, a spirit which is crucial to the credibility and vitality of *Advise and Consent* as a novel.

To comprehend the dazzling popularity of *Advise and Consent* (1959), as well as the personality and political problems of Senator Anderson, one must understand the anxiety and apprehension rooted in the fear of Communist espionage, subversion, and atomic aggression which permeated America during the fifties and sixties as a result of Russian territorial expansion during and after World War II. Between 1939 and 1948, Russia's territorial and political expansion was almost without historical parallel: Russia either seized or absorbed Estonia, Latvia, Lithuania, Petsamo province, part of East Prussia, Ruthenia, Bukovina, and Bessarabia. In addition, Soviet satellites or puppet governments were established in Czechoslovakia, Hungary, Rumania, Bulgaria, Poland, Albania, and East Germany. The means of establishing these dependent Communist regimes which provided a territorial bulwark against the potential threat of Western aggression varied in particulars from country to country. Nevertheless, a general pattern of control followed the occupation of the Russian army during World War II and one historian has recorded this process as follows:

The existing or provisional government would first be denounced as fascist and reactionary and would be superseded by a coalition "popular front" cabinet in which Communists held key positions, such as minister of interior (in charge of the police) and minister of information (in charge of propaganda). Then the Communist ministers, backed by military aid, pressure, or threats from Russia, and led by a native who had been trained in Leninist tactics in Moscow, would get rid of their non-Communist fellow ministers and establish an authoritarian government. Next a constitution like that of the Soviet Union would be drawn up and ratified by an election theoretically democratic but actually controlled. Finally, the disciplined Communist party, even though a small minority, would take complete control and more or less rapidly liquidate all opposition parties and leaders. Thereafter, it was easy to control the schools, universities, newspapers, courts, and communications, to terrorize the churches, to suppress civil liberties, and to establish a thoroughgoing dictatorship, which would take orders from Moscow in both internal and external matters (Hayes, Baldwin, and Cole 791-792).[4]

Although Russia lacked the capability of attacking the American mainland in the years immediately following World War II, American troops stationed in Europe were constantly alert to repel a Russian surprise attack against America's European allies. In 1949, the hostility between totalitarian Communism and democratic Capitalism known as the "cold war" became more ominous when Russia exploded an atomic bomb, and America and Russia became engaged in an arms race whose goals were to invent, produce, and deliver atomic and nuclear warheads against "the enemy." In November, 1952, America exploded a prototype of a hydrogen bomb. The following year Russia responded by exploding the first hydrogen bomb. While America and Russia were simultaneously developing their atomic weapons and the rocket capability to deliver atomic destruction, the "cold war" became a hot war when the Soviet sponsored North Korean army invaded the Republic of South Korea in June, 1950. Without hesitation, President Truman committed American troops to repel the Communist aggression and requested that the United Nations provide moral support and aid in the defense of South Korea. After three years of bloody fighting between the United Nations and the combined North Korean and Communist Chinese armies, a truce was signed in July, 1953. Although South Korea's territorial integrity and freedom were preserved, twenty-five thousand Americans were killed in the conflict; American casualties were a third as many as were suffered in World War II. Needless to say, contemporary readers of *Advise and Consent* were painfully aware of the cost of repelling Communist aggression and of the future sacrifices that might be necessary to defend freedom, although no one could foresee at that time that over fifty-seven thousand Americans would be killed in the Vietnam conflict.

Not surprisingly, as Russian scientists became increasingly successful in competing with American scientists in the development of atomic weapons and delivery systems, Americans became increasingly anxious about Russian infiltration, subversion, and espionage. In 1947, President Truman ordered a loyalty check on all government employees, and in 1949 eleven American Communists were convicted of violating the *Smith Alien Legislation Act* which forbade the teaching of the desirability of overthrowing the United States government by force or violence, as well as the printing and circulating of written material that advocated the overthrow of the government. To strengthen the already existing legislation, Congress passed the *McCarran Internal Security Bill* (1950); consequently, Communists and Communist organizations were required to register with the Attorney-General; Communists were barred from obtaining passports; and, in the event of war, the federal government was empowered to hold Communists and other potential saboteurs in detention camps.

During the late forties and early fifties, charges of Communist infiltration and spying frequently dominated newspaper and magazine headlines. In 1948, Whittaker Chambers, a senior editor of *Time* magazine, reported to the House Committee on Un-American Activities that he was a former Communist spy and had once been a member of a Washington espionage ring. As a result of Chamber's testimony, Alger Hiss, who "seemed to represent the finest type of young intellectual drawn into government service during the New Deal era," was convicted of perjury and sentenced to prison despite his denial of transmitting secret state department documents to the Russians (Barck and Blake 549). Hiss was a Harvard Law School graduate who had served in the Agriculture and Justice Departments, as well as the Department of State. Hiss was also the temporary Secretary-General of the United Nations in 1945 before becoming the Director of the U.S. Office of Special Political Affairs prior to being named the president of the Carnegie Endowment for International Peace. Predictably, American anxiety and fear of Communist atomic aggression was compounded by the success of Russian espionage in England and America. In 1950, Dr. Karl Fuchs, a British atomic scientist, confessed that he had supplied vital data to Soviet agents and that American spies were also providing atomic information to the Soviet Union. Consequently, four Americans were tried and convicted of Soviet collaboration: Ethel and Julius Rosenberg were sentenced to death and Morton Sobell and David Greenglass were given long prison sentences. Three years later, the Atomic Energy Commission withdrew the security clearance of Dr. Robert Oppenheimer, the Director of the Los Alamos project that developed the first atomic bomb. After reviewing Dr. Oppenheimer's past associations with Communists in the thirties, associations that Oppenheimer had never concealed, and after noting that these associations were "far beyond the limits of prudence and tolerance," the Commission supported the judgment of a prior investigating committee. In addition, the fear of Communism also resulted in 6,926 "security separations" in government between May, 1953 and October, 1954 after President Eisenhower ordered an in-depth revision of government security (Barck and Blake 601, 602).

The anti-Communist spirit of the age was re-inforced and sustained by the political career of Senator Joseph McCarthy of Wisconsin. In February, 1950, McCarthy charged that there were "card carrying" Communists working in the State Department. Although the Senator charged at various times that there were (a) fifty-seven, (b) two hundred and five, and (c) eighty-one "security risks" in the State Department, when pressured to produce evidence he was unable to name one Communist working in the Department. As chairman of the Permanent Subcommittee of Investigations in 1953, Senator McCarthy launched over a hundred and fifty inquiries; and he charged that Communists had infiltrated the Voice of America, American overseas libraries, the CIA and an army post at Fort Monmouth, New Jersey. Senator McCarthy's inquiries were constantly in the headlines and the committee hearings concerning the army were televised. In December, 1954, because the Senator was unable to prove his numerous allegations of subversive activity, the Senate censured Senator McCarthy by a vote of sixty-seven to twenty-two. Undoubtedly, for many readers of *Advise and Consent*, characters and events depicted in the novel triggered images of characters and events that had captured their interest as a result of reading newspapers, listening to the radio, and viewing television. For instance, Robert Leffingwell, the President's nominee for Secretary of State, possessed the liberal orientation, record of public service, and intelligence similar to that found in Alger Hiss; and Leffingwell's Communist activities while teaching at the University of Chicago triggered mental associations with other college professors and public servants accused of subversive activities during the McCarthy era. The dilemma that engulfs Senator Anderson in *Advise and Consent* is an imaginative projection of a series of events that might have logically occurred as a result of the anti-Communist hysteria and witch hunting of the fifties. The Senate censure of Senator Ackerman, who politically exploits the nation's fear of Communism in his conflict with Senator Anderson, would recall to many Americans the Senate's censure of Senator McCarthy who politically exploited the anti-Communist feelings of the era and the threat of Russian totalitarian Communism to America and freedom throughout the world.

To an overwhelming majority of Americans during the fifties, then, the threat of imperialistic Communism was a constant and unalterable fact of life, and the anti-Russian, anti-Communist anxiety of *Advise and Consent* is an accurate reflection of their emotional experience. To transform American policy from a "hard" stand against Communism to a "softer" posture when such attitudes prevailed would be an extremely difficult political task. Because the President in *Advise and Consent* is a "strong" president who uses power quickly and decisively, he possesses the confidence to believe that he can change American foreign policy after he concludes that America needs better and more direct communication with Russia in order to avoid an atomic holocaust. Because the current Secretary of State has successfully taken a "hard" line with the Russians and thereby won their enmity, the President dismisses him so that he can apppoint a Secretary more likely to implement successfully a more flexible foreign policy. The President believes that his nominee, Ted Leffingwell ("well-tending-to-the-left") is sympathetic enough toward Russia to evoke their trust, yet still mentally tough and patriotic enough to stand firm in the presence of Russian threats and deceit. Senator Anderson is asked to chair the subcommittee hearings on the Leffingwell nomination. Despite the controversial nature of the nomination, Anderson chairs the sub-committee with competence until the committee drafts a report to the Foreign Relations Committee which states that the committee is deadlocked on the Leffingwell nomination.

At this juncture, the complex, political plot intensifies and becomes extremely compelling, a "pot boiler," when James Morton, the heretofore missing and mysterious third member of the Communist cell group that Leffingwell allegedly led when he was a teacher at the University of Chicago, telephones Senator Anderson and reports that these accusations are in fact true. Imprudently, without consulting his colleagues or the President, Senator Anderson immediately schedules a reconvening of the sub-committee and a reopening of the Leffingwell nomination hearings. Anderson believes, however, that the sub-committee meeting will not be necessary since he plans to inform the President privately of Leffingwell's perjury so that the President will withdraw the nomination. Because the President possesses a different political value system than the Senator, Senator Anderson's expectations are unrealistic.

Despite Leffingwell's youthful flirtation with Communism, unlike Anderson, the President believes that Leffingwell is a very responsible, loyal, and patriotic American. The President also believes that his new Secretary of State must combine mental toughness with guile in order to negotiate successfully with the Russians. Such a man, the President believes, will be able to negotiate peace with the Russians at a time when America's military power and confidence are deteriorating and America desperately needs to avoid a military confrontation. Consequently, when the President learns of Anderson's opposition, he has no intention of withdrawing the nomination; he views Anderson as an idealistic obstructionist. The President's reaction is to use every means at hand, even "evil" acts, to attain his "good" or desirable end. What, the cynical President asks, might be the price for purchasing Anderson's support as he probes for information that can be used to pressure Anderson to relax his opposition to Leffingwell (299).

Many critics have observed that plot can be viewed as character in action; in generic political fiction the primary action is political. As we have observed, Senator Anderson's tragedy occurs because he is pressured by two very powerful and politically astute characters who have differing views about what is absolutely necessary for the survival of America. The President believes that America needs to negotiate with Russia, but Senator Seab Cooley of South Carolina believes that negotiating is being soft on Communism and that Russia will interpret a more flexible policy as a sign of America's weakness and vulnerability. The South Carolina Senator fears for America's survival if Leffingwell becomes Secretary of State, yet there is more than just the patriotic in his opposition. As we have seen, cantankerous Senator Cooley still seethes because the nominee once implied publicly during a committee hearing that the much respected and powerful senior Senator was a liar. Thus in order to embarrass his foe and to save America from embarking on a potentially dangerous foreign policy, the aging, crafty Senator—not unlike the President—will adopt any means to achieve his end: the defeat of the Leffingwell nomination. As a result of his intelligence, long political experience and shrewd political instincts, the Senator intuitively concludes from Senate testimony that the mysterious third member of the alleged Leffingwell cell group at the University of Chicago was the current Assistant Secretary of Commerce for Economic Affairs. After a startled and shocked James Morton confirms the Senator's inference, Senator Cooley commands the Assistant Secretary to keep their telephone conversation a secret and then orders him to inform Senator Anderson that Leffingwell had indeed participated in a Communist cell group as Richard Gelman, the unstable sub-committee witness, had testified. As presidential pressure increases on Senator Anderson to support the Leffingwell nomination, Senator Cooley realizes that Senator Anderson may not be able to withstand the presidential pressure; consequently, Senator Cooley informs his young colleague that it was he who had advised Gelman-Morton to phone Anderson. If Senator Anderson does not "voluntarily" continue his "patriotic" opposition to Leffingwell, Senator Cooley suggests that he will "leak" the Morton information to the press and Anderson will be accused of cooperating with the President in the withholding of vital, damaging information about Leffingwell. Anderson's dilemma is acutely distressing. Whether he supports Leffingwell, remains neutral, or opposes the nomination, his public reputation and political career will be shattered. To understand additional causes of the Anderson tragedy, Drury presents an Anderson biographical portrait in "Brigham Anderson's Book."

In the Anderson biographical narrative, Drury explores the origins of Anderson's independent personality and probes the personality traits that prompt him to reconvene the foreign relations sub-committee without consulting his friends and advisors. As a pre-schooler, Brigham Anderson was an independent, self-reliant spirit. The predisposition to self-reliance and independence increased when he attended school, for his developing ego did not crave the approval of his peers. At play, Drury narrates, the school boy was "able to cope with the mercurial tides of liking and disliking, playing together and not playing together, being in a group or out of a group at a moment's notice, having his toys stolen, being in fights, bearing the brunt of mean remarks and at the same time making a few, without much jolt to his nervous or emotional system" (283). In high school and at Stanford he was very popular because he was an excellent student, a football player, and a politician. While serving as a pilot in World War II, Anderson confirmed to himself some facts of his own nature: he preferred responsibility to be a one-way street; he enjoyed working unselfishly for others, but he did not enjoy being accountable to them. Essentially, in the Air Force, Anderson reaffirmed to himself that he was a "loner." After the war, his successful pattern continued; he entered law school, became class president, graduated, and entered his father's law firm. Since Anderson was "one of those people...whose outward cordiality, responsiveness, and warmth persuade that they are giving much more of themselves than they actually are," astute observers were not surprised when his speeches at church suppers, social gatherings, service clubs, and professional groups evolved into a political career. His intelligence, education, war record, careful planning, and fortuitous political circumstances enabled him to become an immediate political success: at the age of thirty he was a member of the U.S. Senate (295).

In the Senate Anderson continued to impress his peers, and Senate leaders quickly perceived his potential to be a national political leader. This potential became even more obvious when Anderson demonstrated yet another essential quality of a successful politician. In his day to day senatorial duties Anderson demonstrated the ability to work effectively with his senatorial colleagues despite basic disagreements over their legislative and political goals. This diplomatic style is especially reflected in his friendship with Lafe Smith, a promiscuous senator his own age, and in his friendship with Illinois Senator Orrin Knox, whose affection for the Utah Senator is almost that of a father to a son. Although Anderson and Smith sometimes work at cross purposes to each other, there is never any personal strain at their differences. The same is also true of the Knox-Anderson relationship. In addition, when Anderson and Knox goals clash, neither tries to persuade the other to moderate their honest opinions; nevertheless, each maintains respect for the other, as well as their confidence that they will once again form an alliance when their political goals and values again converge. Although on the surface Anderson's life reflects a history of emotional stability, popularity, success, and responsibility, he occasionally experiences sharp moments of pervasive discontent. Except for a month in Hawaii during World War II, the Utah "lone wolf" Senator has never been completely happy. At the root of his sexual being, Anderson is different and different in a way that was socially and politically unacceptable: Anderson possessed latent homosexual tendencies.

Homosexual tendencies, undoubtedly, contribute to, or motivate Anderson's predisposition toward self-reliance and independence, for on the subconscious level he realizes that he is emotionally and socially vulnerable because he is "different." Latent homosexuality notwithstanding, Brig Anderson—the football star—had little difficulty satisfying his heterosexual instincts in high school and college. He was sexually responsive to attractive girls and his attentions were reciprocated. Although he enjoyed sex with many girls, he formed no significant romantic relationships before he entered the Army. At Stanford, the narrator informs the reader, one classmate suspected his homosexual tendencies, but Anderson did not want "what his fraternity brother wanted" (286). However, he did and does recognize within himself an unaccountable streak of moodiness, "a certain underlying feeling of incompleteness, of not having found something, he was not sure what, that he felt might make him happy" (286). During the war his heterosexual life flourished: he had hundreds of casual sexual encounters. Although Anderson had rejected almost all male propositions tendered to him in the Air Force, there was one exception. During a two month rest period in Hawaii, Anderson became intimately involved with another young service man whom he casually met at the beach. "For four weeks," Drury narrates, "he was happy, and he was unsparing enough with himself to realize that it was a perfectly genuine happiness" (288). Except for this one encounter that occurred ten years before the Leffingwell nomination, Senator Anderson's sexual experiences were heterosexual.

Because of Anderson's inability to become involved totally with a woman on an emotional and psychological level, his marriage seems inappropriate and out of character. From Anderson's perspective, his marriage after the war is not the result of a passionate, romantic commitment, but rather is the result of a mutual "liking" which occurs while he is ambitiously striving to become a United States Senator, a time when a wife and family would be a definate political asset. Senator Lafe Smith, Anderson's sexually promiscuous friend, offers a plausible explanation for the Anderson marriage. Marriage, Lafe suggests, is "a bargain between desire and custom, dream and reality, sex and society" (344). Though the Anderson marriage is not without difficult moments, the Senator is a conscientious and caring husband. Despite Brig's ability to heal domestic clashes by tenderness and physical love, Mabel Anderson eventually knows intuitively that Brig withholds something of himself from her and that at bottom she neither knows nor understands her husband. Nevertheless, despite Mabel's emotional insecurity, their marriage is a relatively happy one. Ironically, shortly before Senator

Cooley orders James Morton to make his catalystic phone call to Anderson, the Senator realizes that his five year old daughter provides him with moments of complete joy that are equal to the happiness which consumed him during his homosexual romance in Hawaii. Simultaneously, he admits to himself that Mabel is incapable of giving him the complete happiness that he desires. Consequently, when the Assistant Secretary of Commerce for Economic Affairs informs Anderson that Leffingwell has lied to the sub-committee, the time is now propitious for Mabel Anderson to provide the emotional support necessary to sustain the Senator's will to live when he is threatened with public disgrace and the ruin of his political career.

Once the "lone wolf" Senator unilaterally decides to reopen the Leffingwell hearings, events converge which make his suicide almost inevitable. When the sub-committee realizes that the wrath of the President and the "liberal" press will be directed at Anderson for the opening of the Leffingwell hearings, they give him a vote of confidence; in addition, his close friends plan to persuade their chairman to meet amicably with the President so that they may resolve their differences about the nomination. Senators Munson, Knox and Smith shrewdly conspire to work their will upon the Senator, but Anderson's newly acquired amenability is shattered when the President misjudges Anderson's ethical sensitivity and offers to "make a deal" prior to their scheduled meeting during a surprise phone call. The idealistic Senator is repulsed by the President's brazen *quid pro quo* political style and resents the presidential assumption that Anderson's opposition is based on self-interest: the placing of his personal and political profit before the welfare of America. Though anger, disgust, and hurt pervade Anderson, he consents to meet with the President in an attempt to resolve their conflict; but since he does not trust the President, he demands that Vice-President Hudson and Majority Leader Munson be participants in the meeting.

Unknown to Anderson but suspected by the Majority Leader, the President has already resolved to destroy Anderson politically if he continues his opposition. At the scheduled meeting, Anderson explains his reasons for reopening the Leffingwell hearings; and although the President suggests that Leffingwell's lie was not as serious as Anderson judges it to be, the President implies that he will withdraw the nomination without categorically stating that he will do so. Cunningly, the President asks Anderson to keep secret the President's change of plan so that the Leffingwell nomination can be gracefully withdrawn and a new nominee for Secretary of State can quickly be proposed for nomination. Because of party loyalty and because Anderson wants to believe the President of the United States is an honorable man, the idealistic Senator agrees not to reveal the evidence that Leffingwell is an "untrustworthy and dishonest man." Slowly, and then all too quickly, Anderson begins to discern in the next forty-eight hours that the deceitful

President has set in motion a black-mail scheme that will destroy his domestic happiness and his political career.

An anonymous phone call to Mabel Anderson is the first serious indication of impending catastrophe. Worried, Mabel is compelled to ask her husband what he did in Hawaii during the war that was "dirty." Confused and shattered by the unexpected accusation, Anderson's response is evasive. Pressed by Mabel for additional information, the normally calm and controlled husband can only respond by dazed confusion. During one of the more poignant scenes in *Advise and Consent*, Drury narrates Mabel's reaction to her husband's confusion:

But this change, so abrupt, so uncharacteristic, so utterly unexpected in one who had always seemed so strong and above any real need for her, so terrified her that she could hardly speak; and so instead of realizing that this was the moment to go to him, to accept and not to ask questions, to give him the strength he had never asked from her but desperately needed now, and that if she did they might weather whatever it was and he would be hers forever, she gave a sudden cry and ran from the room (408).

Stunned at his wife's departure, Anderson begins to understand that his homosexual affair is about to destroy his marriage, as well as his promising political career. Shortly thereafter, another emotional blow assaults Anderson's psyche when Mabel Anderson receives a telegram explicitly revealing her husband's homosexual activity. While Anderson is home awaiting and dreading the opportunity to explain the telegram to his wife, the surging events of his life force him to contemplate his years as a husband and father:

He realized now with a terrible clarity how terribly he must have failed her down the years, not as a husband, or a father or a provider, not sexually or in any other of the ways that mattered together but did not matter so much one by one, but simply because in none of these relationships that went into the total structure of a good marriage had he given enough of himself. Always, he could see now, there must have been some area where she felt herself barred and kept out, some minor kingdom of his being where she was forever alien. A heavy pity for them both touched his heart, for *he had never meant it to be that way, he had done his best, he had always tried to be kind, and apparently it hadn't been enough; and he knew now that it was inevitable, he couldn't have helped it, it had to be so, for it was his nature to walk his way alone, and with the greatest and most sincere will in the world he could not have overcome it no matter how he tried.* (431, Italics added.).

Although Anderson knows his wife loves him deeply and Mabel desires a harmonious and enduring marriage, such is not to be. In a very emotional and compelling scene in the novel, Mabel fails her husband. When Brig confesses his failure and begs her forgiveness, Mabel's suffering, soulful response is a disaster. Her sobbing "I don't know" is followed by the anguished, searching question which probes Anderson's sexuality of the past, present, and future: "How can I ever be sure again?" As Mabel perceives the devastating effect of her spontaneous response to her husband's need, she repeatedly attempts to repair her destruction by stating and restating "I didn't mean that, I didn't, I didn't, I didn't!" (433-434). As the domestic tragedy unfolds, the tightly constructed plot inexorably moves forward, and momentarily politics is submerged in the emotional chaos of the Anderson marriage.

The next devastating blow to the Anderson fortunes is a televised verbal attack by the opportunistic Senator Ackerman. After the "liberal" senator has identified and contacted the young man in the photograph that Justice Davis had given to the Majority Leader, Ackerman announces during a nationally televised COMFORT (Committee On Making Offers For A Russian Truce) rally that he will present information to the Senate that will prove that the Utah Senator who opposes the Leffingwell nomination is morally unqualified to hold public office. After this public threat, Anderson's homosexual friend telephones Anderson to beg forgiveness because he has signed an affidavit describing their Hawaiian affair. Generously and graciously, the Senator forgives him before reluctantly terminating their first contact since World War II. Then Anderson begins to contemplate suicide. Anderson's depression is not alleviated when the Director of the *Post* shows him a muck-raking column detailing Anderson's homosexual affair. The column, the Director of the *Post* explains, "isn't quite slander, it isn't quite libel, it's just enough to murder a man. He (the columnist) doesn't come right out with anything, he never does; he just skirts the edge of absolute evil, destroying people as he goes. I don't know why we continue to take his damned column, except that it's so entertaining and people want to read it." In this "cruel town," the *Post* director knows, one should not get on the wrong side of the "liberal" press. Although the *Post* will not print the column, the Director believes that at least one newspaper will print it and then the media will report the substance of the allegations in order to keep pace with the journalistic competition (439-440).

Following the departure of the *Post* Director, in another poignant scene, Anderson tenderly expresses his love for his daughter Pidge who returns his affection before her father leaves for his office for the last time. Ironically, because Senator Cooley believes that Senator Anderson possesses a bright future in the Senate and because the Carolina Senator has much affection and respect for his young colleague, the Senator telephones Anderson and informs him that he will not make good his threat to politically destroy Anderson over the Leffingwell nomination; the conservative Senator will not leak the Morton information to the press. After thanking Senator Cooley, who is troubled by Anderson's depressed state, Anderson makes a final telephone call to his loyal friend Lafe Smith before performing his final senatorial act: the writing of a report detailing both his homosexual affair and the attempted blackmail that links a Supreme Court Justice, the Senate Majority Leader, the President, and Senator Ackerman in a chain of dishonor. In an introspective narrative passage which illustrates Drury's ability to weave irony into plot and character, Drury reports the thoughts of Anderson as the Senator compares his sexual transgression with Leffingwell's Communist activities and thinks how their transgressions will be evaluated and presented in the biased media.

What...was the difference between them? Both were guilty of concealment, both were guilty of lying to the world, both had protected their reputations as best they could, and both had been discovered. The major difference then became that the nominee's was the popular cause, backed by all the combination of power and politics and press of Washington, while he was the unpopular, bitterly opposed by that combination; so that the nominee, if his luck held, might yet emerge unscathed, while he, driven to the wall by all the latent savagery of politics, must be the sacrifice. For he knew as surely as he knew Washington that if he had been a supporter of the nominee his past would never have been used against him; and by the same bitter token he knew that if it had been the nominee who had kept an inadvertent wartime rendezvous the fact would have been hushed up and covered over and hidden from the public, and under the protection of a bland united conspiracy of silence his nomination would have been triumphantly confirmed (445-446).

With final thoughts of God, family, and friend—and the fleeting memory of a joyful, happy time in Honolulu, Senator Anderson places a pistol to his head and, ultimately, as the captain of his own fate, takes his own life.

Much earlier in the novel Anderson had reflected upon the course of his life and had concluded that "both by religion and observation he had come to believe that luck or God or destiny or fate whatever men chose to call it had much to do with human endeavor and the tides of life" (282). This fatalistic streak, this note of fate or destiny which touches personal lives and political events, is thematic in Drury fiction. In some instances, Drury seems to suggest that man is a victim of circumstances; yet a more comprehensive view emerges to the effect that individuals and groups, as well as the body politic itself, have a significant role in the shaping of those circumstances that sometimes have tragic consequences. Heredity and environment, nature and nurture are causal factors, but one cannot overlook choice and personal responsibility when evaluating human activity. In the life of Anderson, though the biological pressures and the need for intimate human companionship during the war were extenuating circumstances which influenced his homosexual romance, there is nevertheless the recognition that man must accept the consequences of his actions even though the repercussions are tragic and the choice not totally free. On such a premise Drury constructs much of his political fiction. For Drury seems to suggest that just as man lacks complete control of the heart, man also lacks complete control over historical events, the body politic, and one's own political career. Though politicians and statesmen have only limited control over the present and the future, if man is to be responsible, and if the body politic is to remain healthy, individuals must accept their roles in the unseen consequences of their actions. Although Drury borders on the simplistic in the concluding novels of his political series in which he creates a world sharply divided into categories of good and evil, black and white, American and Communist, conservative and liberal, in *Advise and Consent* Drury demonstrates an understanding of extremely complex aspects of political reality and raises penetrating questions concerning the nature of evil in a divinely created universe. Consequently, in the climactic moments leading up to the death of Senator Anderson, Drury writes with an intellectual and emotional power that one identifies with enduring political fiction. In terms of structure, the death of Anderson is the high point in Drury fiction. Beyond this point, especially in other novels, plotting begins to become episodic and a vehicle for Drury's political message rather than an instrument to induce a "willing suspension of disbelief" and aesthetic pleasure. However, in *Advise and Consent*, Drury does continue the dynamic creation and development of political characters, including Orrin Knox who becomes the conservative political hero of the series.

Book IV of *Advise and Consent* is "Orrin Knox's Book," and Senator Knox will eventually become the most fully developed of Drury's characters. In *A Shade of Difference, Capable of Honor*, and *Preserve and Protect*, the presidentially ambitious Knox is a conservative Secretary of State; in *The Promise of Joy* he is elected and serves as president. (In *Come Nineveh, Come Tyre* presidential candidate Knox is assassinated, but his conservative personality continues to influence political events through his wife Beth, his son Hal, and his conservative friends and colleagues in the House and Senate.) In the early Drury fiction Knox demonstrates significant characteristics of what E.M. Forster terms a "round" character (103-109): Knox changes; he is modified by circumstances; and he sometime surprises in a convincing way. By the conclusion of *The Promise of Joy*, however, Orrin Knox becomes somewhat of a rather flat character: he functions more as a Drury mouthpiece, more as a purveyor of conservative ideology, than as a "round," multi-dimensional character. Nevertheless, Knox is a vivid and memorable character in each of the novels or anatomies. When we examine the Knox character, we should keep in mind that "flat" but memorable character depictions are quite common in the form of fiction that Frye describes as anatomy. Although the Knox character flattens out in *The Promise of Joy*, within the context of pure political fiction, that is, when we view Knox as a purely political character in a political novel or anatomy, he is clearly a politically "round" character whose thoughts and actions reflect complexity and provide insight into politics and politicians. In *Advise and Consent*, for example, Orrin Knox is already a multi-dimensional political character; he is a dedicated public servant who is consumed with presidential ambition. Brigham Anderson best summarizes his personality and character: Orrin "had an uncompromising honesty and a bluntly forthright way with the truth. Tart, tactless, impatient, fearless and unimpressed, the senior Senator from Illinois wasted little time on fools; but on those he liked who were not fools he conferred a friendship of absolute loyalty and a deep warmth of affection that appeared surprisingly from his shyly abrupt exterior" (292).

When Orrin Knox first appears in *Advise*, his good friend Brig wonders how the Senator will react to the Leffingwell nomination. "I think I'll oppose him," says Orrin Knox. "Yes, I know the man, and I don't like him" (29). Though Orrin speaks and sometimes acts impulsively, in the Leffingwell hearings he does not act decisively until after Senator Anderson's suicide. Senator Munson has indicated this rational, judicious aspect of his personality when he reports to the President the results of his lobbying attempt to win votes for the Leffingwell nomination. "Orrin is a fair-minded man," he reports, "but he did not commit himself to anything" (98). Earlier in the novel the reader has seen this responsible aspect of the essential Knox character. When grudge bearing Senator Cooley, a long time enemy of Leffingwell, solicits Orrin's support against Leffingwell's nomination for Secretary of State, Orrin forthrightly replies: "You can't decide a Cabinet nomination, particularly State, on the basis of a personal feud. At least, the Senate can't. Maybe you can, but the rest of us can't. There've got to be better grounds.... If you want anybody to go along with you, Seab, you're going to have to do better than that. We'll—they'll—want proof of things. Your word for it won't be good enough" (65). This, however, does not mean that Orrin Knox will rubber stamp the President's nomination, although he does believe that unless there is a serious question about the nominee's ability to preserve and protect the interests of the United States as Secretary of State, he has a responsibility to permit the President his choice of cabinet members. At the sub-committee nomination hearings, in an extended and heated exchange which reinforces the reader's impression of the "tart, tactless, impatient" and "fearless" Knox character, the Senator doggedly persists in his attempt to have Leffingwell articulate his principles concerning peace negotiations with Russia, since in a speech Leffingwell has said that "we must not bind ourselves arbitrarily to the outworn principles standing in the way of affirmative action for peace" (178). Even though Leffingwell's responses are unsatisfactory, a little "too soft" towards the Russians, Knox is still not unalterably opposed to the Leffingwell nomination. After Brig Anderson commits suicide as a result of being blackmailed by Senator Ackerman, who has been manipulated by the President, who was aided by the Senate Majority Leader, we see toughness and a streak of nastiness in the Knox character: he wishes the President dead; he thinks that he will never forgive his long time friend Senator Munson; he resolves to destroy the political career of Senator Ackerman; and he is determined to defeat Leffingwell's nomination for Secretary of State. However, political life is not quite so simple. Senator Knox continues his enmity against the President who will soon die of a heart attack; yet because of Knox's deep patriotism and sense of responsibility, he publicly supports the President in a reassuring and patriotic speech to the American people after the Russians have landed on the moon. Orrin Knox does not remain firm in his anger against Senator Munson; surprisingly, he forgives the Senate Majority Leader, but only after Knox has planned what he believes will be an effective attack against the Leffingwell nomination, and he perceives the Majority Leader's deep regret for his complicity in the destruction of Senator Anderson, whom the Senator loved as a son. Ackerman and Leffingwell, however, receive no mercy. Knox stages both the Senator's defeat of the Leffingwell nomination and the censorship of Senator Ackerman. The most effective or most convincing depiction of the Knox character occurs, however, when shortly after he has learned of Anderson's suicide, the President requests that Knox meet with him in the White House.

In the dramatic confrontation at the White House, Orrin experiences a series of emotions—sympathy, anger, self-righteousness, respect, admiration, surprise, distrust, cynicism—as the President searches for the key that will persuade Knox to vote for the Leffingwell confirmation. After sincerely congratulating Knox for "getting Fred Ackerman" and destroying COMFORT, the President attempts to persuade the testy Orrin to support his candidate. Since the Russians have probably landed on the moon and since they may possess the capability of launching an atomic attack from space, the President asks the Senator from Illinois to help him to unify the country by supporting Leffingwell, a man the President believes to be "an excellent and experienced public servant with a broad view of world problems' (549). In the current crisis Leffingwell, the President believes, is needed as a Secretary of State: he is tough enough to stand up to the Communists, yet he also possesses the sympathy and flexibility necessary to generate communication between Russia and America, a communication that is desperately needed because of the threat of atomic warfare. When Knox retorts sharply to the President's appeal to his patriotism, the President shrewdly shifts his appeal to Knox's presidential ambitions. If Senator Knox will advise and consent to the appointment of Robert Leffingwell as Secretary of State, the President promises to support Knox's presidential bid at the next national convention, thereby virtually assuring Knox the nomination.

Surprisingly, in view of the Knox reputation for "no deals," the Senator listens attentively to the proposition. Because of Knox's long standing ambition to become President and the shrewdness of the President, the scene is very vivid and convincing. Hours later an introspective Knox realizes that it was because of his almost obsessive ambition to become President that the "evil offer" had not immediately been rejected: "...that was why Orrin Knox had not acted like Orrin Knox, if truth were known; because there came a point, even with him, at which the imperatives of ambition gained triumph over the dictates of conscience, no matter how strong that conscience might be" (559-560). However, these thoughts are retrospective. It is only after the Senator and the President have shrewdly assessed Orrin's presidential possibilities both with and without the President's endorsement and only after Orrin has cynically asked the President to put the offer in writing that Knox has the presence of mind to reach this conclusion.

Once the President's "evil offer" has been made along with his assessment of the Knox qualities which would make him electable with the President's support (Knox "has three great qualifications. He is strong and he is honest and he is able to learn" [554]), the Senator has only a few hours to make his decision. As Drury depicts the emotional, political and ethical turmoil of Orrin Knox as he agonizes over his decision, Drury creates some of his most effective fiction. With the President's letter in hand, Knox returns to the Senate debate on the Leffingwell nomination where it is soon apparent that the Illinois Senator is wavering. To help him with his decision, he consults with his closest friends and advisors: Senators Dante, Smith, and Cooley, and Speaker of the House Abbott. Then he meets with his wife Beth and they drive to the Lincoln Memorial where he reflects upon his dilemma: if he does not support Leffingwell, he may never become President. Before making his decision, Knox reflects upon his dream:

And yet—and yet. Here within his reach lay all that he had dreamed of for thirty years, the chance to be President, the chance to run the country as *he* believed best, the chance to do the great things for America that he *knew*, he knew, he could do if he had the power. With all the vigor of his passionate heart he was convinced that he could serve the country in a way that would be to her great and ultimate good. He knew he could be a good President, quite possibly a great one; he had thought so often about what he would do, how he would handle it, the goals he would set and the ways he would achieve them, the clear direction he would chart and the strong leadership he would provide. Here it all lay, in the palm of his hand, needing only the bargain to be completed, the deal to be struck, for the hand to close tightly at last upon the prize it had reached for so long (572).

Then the Senator reflects upon the response of his wife and the responses of his friends. Not surprisingly, since Orrin's dilemma is a personal one with extremely serious and dramatic national and international implications, no one offers categorical advice. However, they do offer him insight into his own history and character. Before making his final decision, he reflects upon the voices that he has heard: "It is my observation that when a man deserts something he basically and fundamentally believes in, he loses something inside. Yes, sir, he loses something inside." And, "Whether you'd want to keep on living with Orrin Knox if you got it on a bargain of that kind, that, too, I don't know." And, "Orrin Knox has lived in a certain way and come to mean certain things to his country and his time. He has to decide now whether he wants to mean something else. It's as simple as that" (573). But it is not quite so simple on a personal and emotional level, for Orrin Knox wants to become President in order to continue to serve the country, for Orrin Knox wants "to save this blundering, helpless goodhearted nation that is fundamentally too decent to know how to deal with the ring of sharpies who encircle her, some with the face of enemies, and some with the face of friends" (573). Although Knox is torn by internal conflict, he perceives that he must be true to his first principles. He must vote with his conscience, not with his desire for power; consequently, the Senator returns the letter to the oval office and travels to the Senate to continue his opposition to the Leffingwell nomination.

The President's offer is consistent with the biographical information presented in Book IV of *Advise*, titled "Orrin Knox's Book." Through the mind of Orrin Knox, Drury presents for the reader Knox's life and his personality as he attends high school, the University of Illinois, Yale Law School, as he courts and marries Elizabeth Henry, and as he evolves in politics as a Representative in the Illinois House, as a Governor, and as a Senator with presidential ambitions while serving on the Foreign Relations Committee.

Though Orrin Knox makes the correct ethical choice in *Advise and Consent*, he is not a completely attractive or likeable person. His impulsiveness, as Knox himself knows, does sometimes cause him problems. Such was the case when his ambition, cynicism, and lack of trust caused him to leap to a regrettable conclusion concerning the character of Harley Hudson, the Vice-President, at the nominating convention seven years prior to the events that occur in *Advise and Consent*. At that convention, when the Governor of California and Senator Knox were deadlocked in their bid for the presidential nomination, Harley Hudson, the leader of the Michigan Delegation, had the power to determine the nominee. During a consulting session with Hudson, Knox quite firmly told Harley that he would make "no deals," whatever the circumstances. Despite Knox's unwillingness to offer some political commitments in exchange for his support, Harley expresses the hope that he will be able to support Knox's presidential bid and that "everything works out" (479). Since Orrin has a very low opinion of Harley Hudson's integrity, despite a note from Hudson stating that it is not true, when newspaper headlines declare that Hudson is backing the Governor of California in exchange for the vice-presidential slot on the party ticket, he fears and believes the worst. When Hudson is about to declare the Michigan votes during the peak of excitement at the convention, Orrin believes Hudson will declare for the Governor since Orrin believes "Harley was not strong enough to withstand that kind of offer, it wasn't human not to yield to a bribe of that magnitude." Consequently, when Orrin intercepts Harley on the way to the microphone, he insults him by stating that "I suppose you've decided to take it...I suppose you're like all the rest,...I thought I could count on your integrity, but I guess that wouldn't fix up too well, would it?" Too late, Orrin realizes that he has said "one of those things, nasty, horrible, not really meant but gone beyond retrieving, that break a heart, destroy a friendship, ruin a plan, or lose a nomination" (481). Moments later Governor Hudson casts forty-seven votes for the Governor of California, and Orrin loses the nomination. After the President dies in *Advise and Consent* and Harley Hudson becomes President, Orrin continues his low opinion of Harley, perceiving Harley as a bumbler who is beyond his depth as President. In short, Harley is a man who needs the advice of men wiser and smarter than the President if America is to survive the Communist threat. Believing that Harley needs the advice and moral and emotional support of Orrin, he is pleased when Harley summons him to the White House for a meeting. To his shock he learns, after he apologizes to Harley for doubting his integrity at the convention seven years past, at the time of Orrin's insult, Harley "was on" his "way up there to announce for you" (610). Although Orrin had gradually accepted his own responsibility for the loss of his nomination at the Chicago convention, this new information is still a stunning blow. It is more. It is another step in the maturing process of an intelligent, complex, sophisticated ambitious politician, a step which permits him to perceive his vanity, arrogance and self-righteousness and its consequences. President Hudson bears no grudge. He appoints Orrin Knox to be his Secretary of State and as the presidential party flies to Geneva to meet with the Russians, a still ambitious but wiser Orrin Knox ponders the evolution in his personality and character: "...he was no longer so restless, at least he was beginning to feel a reasonable equanimity, at least in the rushing events of the last three days, beginning with the shattering revelation of what he had done to himself at the convention and culminating in his appointment as Secretary of State, he had begun to take things as they came, without too much impatience and too much anguish and too much regret. And that, perhaps, was wealth enough of the Indies for him" (616).

Of the six plots in Drury's political series, the plot of *Advise and Consent* is the most tightly constructed. The external and internal conflicts are totally political, and professional politicians are both formally and informally engaged in a political conflict requiring the action of the Senate. All of the major characters are engaged in the same policy conflict-whether the strong posture of the United States should become more flexible in its negotiations with Russia—which builds to the political climax of the novel, the defeat of the Leffingwell nomination. In addition, all of the major characters are directly engaged in a political conflict with the President which causes intense emotional and sometimes traumatic political and personal conflict. When the President nominates Leffingwell to be Secretary of State, he pressures the reluctant Majority Leader to participate in dirty politics and seduces him to act dishonorably. As a result, Bob Munson is instrumental in the death of his good friend and colleague, Senator Anderson; he then re-evaluates his responsibilities and his performance as Majority Leader; he resigns as Majority Leader; and when he is re-elected Majority Leader, he announces his independence from the President and informs his colleagues that he will now function primarily as a spokesman for the Senators rather than as an advocate for the President. In a surprising change of character, Senator Cooley also reverses his thinking and his political tactics. After pressuring Senator Anderson to denounce Leffingwell publicly, Cooley informs Anderson that he may remain silent because Seab has concluded that Anderson's political career will be a greater good to the country than a guarantee of a Cooley personal and political victory over the President and Leffingwell. It is Anderson, however, who suffers most from his conflict with the President. Rather than reacting dishonorably by withdrawing his opposition to Leffingwell, he commits suicide. And Orrin Knox, the fourth major figure of the novel, decides that his presidential ambitions are less important than the defeat of the Leffingwell nomination, but only after being severely tempted by the shrewd, powerful, and unscrupulous President.

We have defined a political novel *"as a work of prose fiction which primarily focuses upon the exercise of political power within the body politic and where political ambition, political plans, and political acts permeate and unify the novel through plot and character;"* and we have suggested that *Advise and Consent* is a "pure" and serious political novel. In addition to the thoughts and actions of the main characters, politics is also weaved into the novel through descriptions, historical allusions, and symbols. From time to time, without destroying "the willing suspension of disbelief" of the reader, Drury describes capitol buildings and monuments which are symbolically inspirational to Americans, reminding them of their national and political heritage; he describes the daily activities of the Senators while the Senate is in session; he panoramically describes the diverse activities of Senate committees and committee members as they attempt to balance their personal and political interests with the welfare of the country; he describes social events—parties and luncheons—where politics is simultaneously discussed and practiced; and he creates subordinate characters, such as Dolly Harrison, Beth Knox, and Crystal Danta, whose thoughts and actions serve to promote and advance the political careers of the men that they love. To illustrate with one brief example, when Crystal Danta marries Hal Knox, Orrin and Beth's son, this signals the approval of politics as a profession "capable of honor" despite the sordidness of the Anderson scandal (538). Not surprisingly, in later Drury fiction Hal will become a congressman. In such ways does politics permeate the novel, and thus we can see that of its kind—a Washington based political novel which is "pure" and serious—*Advise and Consent* is a minor, if not a major classic, well deserving of the 1959 Pulitzer Prize.

Chapter IV
"Pure" Political Fiction as
Anatomy and Romance: *A Shade of Difference*

When we examine *A Shade of Difference* as a novel—an aesthetic whole with "real people" in a real world with a tightly constructed plot—*A Shade of Difference* is less successful than its predecessor, *Advise and Consent*. Continuity between *Advise and Consent* is sustained by the Washington setting and the continuing presence and development of characters presented in *Advise*: Vice-President Harley Hudson, who becomes President at the conclusion of *Advise and Consent*, and Senators Seab Cooley and Orrin Knox, who becomes Secretary of State. It is through the mind of Orrin Knox that Drury flashes back six months and reviews the final events of *Advise and Consent*: the President's fatal heart attack, the launching of a Soviet space satellite which the Russians believe establishes their superiority over America, the Russian demand for a summit conference, and President Hudson's departure for Moscow.

Because America, too, has landed on the moon, the military threat to the United States is not quite as threatening as when Harley Hudson acceded to the presidency. Even though America has succeeded in space, newspaper headlines in America and around the world reflect fear and anxiety as the United States delegation flies to Geneva: "WORLD ON BRINK OF DISASTER," "WILL U.S. CAPTIULATE," "WAR?," "WORLD AWAITS FATEFUL CONFERENCE AND HUMANITY MAY FACE EXTINC-TION." Such headlines are still very vivid to Orrin Knox as he reminisces in the United States on his new role as Secretary of State.

At Geneva, Orrin Knox recalls, President Hudson was much more than the Russians had anticipated; he returned arrogance with arrogance, boldness with boldness during the conference, and when the Russians made nine outrageous demands,—the abandonment and liquidation of NATO, the abandonment of all naval bases in Asia, Africa, South America and North America (except for bases in the United States), the termination of American missile and space exploration and the severe reduction of the American military, the appointment of cabinet members friendly to Russia, and an assurance that the media would take a friendly attitude toward the U.S.S.R.—the new President reacted with courage. Thus it is with pride in his President and his country that the Secretary of State re-lives the President's response to the Russian threat to "blow up the United States" and perhaps "destroy the globe." "Evil and despicable," Harley Hudson called the Russians; "I am in the presence of a maniac," he told Ambassador Tashikov, asserting that be what may, America would do nothing to placate the Russians (24). Then, abruptly, the President and his delegation boldly return to Washington. Although President Hudson's response increases world tension and anxiety, the Russian ultimatum proves to be without substance. The Soviet bluff is exposed as a result of the President's confident and orderly return to the United States. These events foreshadow and contrast with similar events in *Come Nineveh, Come Tyre*; in *Come Nineveh* "liberal" President Jason lacks intelligence and courage, he is unable to cope with the imperialistic Russian appetite, and the future of America is jeopardized in this concluding book of the series. Obviously then, this first confrontation in *A Shade of Difference* between President Hudson and the Russians has thematic overtones: if America does not react with courage, wisdom, and confidence to the Communist threat of a potential atomic holocaust, then America will eventually become a victim of the Communist imperialistic appetite. Harley Hudson, a "conservative," surrounded by conservatives, reacts positively to the Russian challenge. As we have indicated, in future Drury fiction such reaction will not automatically occur because America is becoming weakened by Communist infiltration. As a result, the American intellectual "elite" will eventually be unable to perceive the insidious nature of Communism and will unwittingly become an instrument of Communist propaganda and power. The propagandistic thrust of Drury's fiction becomes increasingly obvious as the political series evolves. The thematic thrust of *A Shade* compels us to view the second work in the political series as primarily anatomy. *A Shade* continues Drury's examination and dissection of politics and the spirit of the age in the sixties primarily for the didactic purpose of educating and shaping the political mind of the reader.

II

Homosexuality and a political "dirty trick" at the instigation of a "wheeler dealer" President, as well as the military threat of Russia, we have noted, are essential to the plot of *Advise and Consent*. Drury's second piece of political fiction introduces two new subjects for the education of the reader: the United Nations and racial prejudice. Like *Advise and Consent, A Shade of Difference* is elemental political fiction: the subject matter of the plot is primarily political, and the two most significant heroes of the novel are professional politicians serving their government; one serves in the Senate and the other serves in the House of Representatives. Both also serve their government by being delegates to the United Nations. The climactic moment of the novel is a political speech in the United Nations which is presented after the United Nations has defeated a resolution which contained a censure of the United States.

Although speeches, parliamentary procedures, and senatorial debates have substantial importance in *Advise and Consent*, such content, for most readers, does not impede the pace, movement, or impact of the novel. Much the same cannot be said of *A Shade of Difference*, which has four major parliamentary resolutions as the cornerstones of the plot. These resolutions and the processes surrounding these resolutions add a cerebral dimension to the anatomy, an intellectual challenge which is beyond the appetite of many potential readers. The first resolution occurs in the First Committee of the United Nations and contains a recommendation to the General Assembly "that the United Nations do all in its power to persuade the United Kingdom to grant immediate independence to the territory of Gorotoland" (66). This resolution, introduced by the Panamanian Ambassador to the United Nations, is vigorously and enthusiastically promoted by His Royal Highness Terence Wolowo Ajkaje by lobbying in the United Nations in a lobbying effort which is well received by the American "liberal" press, which tends to be sympathetic to "Terrible Terry" despite the African nation's woeful lack of social, political, and moral maturity. After His Royal Highness, "Terribly Terry," focuses world attention on racial problems in America by escorting a black girl to school in South Carolina in order to exploit the racial tensions generated by a court order requiring school integration and he, as a result, becomes a victim of mob violence, Felix Labaiya, the Panamanian Ambassador to the United Nations, introduces an amendment to the Gorotoland resolution. This amendment is extremely damaging to American prestige and influence since the resolution asserts that the United States may not be qualified to continue membership in the United Nations because of America's racial discrimination. The amendment also authorizes the Security Council to "make an immediate investigation of racial practices in America" (176).

In order to neutralize the anti-American sentiment that "Terrible Terry" has inflamed and exploited for the purpose of increasing his personal political power and promoting sympathy for abused blacks who desire Gorotoland independence, a joint resolution is introduced in Congress which expresses "the official apologies of the United States Government to the M'Bulu of Mbuele for 'danger and personal humiliation' suffered while escorting a colored child" to school. In addition, the joint resolution authorizes a ten million dollar grant to the African Prince for the "advancement and improvement of his people" and states that "the United States should 'move with increased rapidity to improve the conditions of its Negro population at all levels' " (250). Because of the joint resolution before Congress, the American delegation is able to persuade the United Nations to withhold action on the Gorotoland Resolution and Amendment until the Congress has reacted to the President's legislative request. After the joint resolution is passed by the Congress after a heated, prolonged debate and a filibuster, the Gorotoland Resolution again becomes the immediate business of the United Nations. Suspense is increased when the Amendment is reintroduced as a separate resolution in a parliamentary maneuver which would require that a simple majority vote, rather than a two-thirds vote, be required for the censure of the United States. Although a damaging blow to American prestige is to be expected after the United States chooses to vote with the United Kingdom and the minority on the Gorotoland Resolution, after much tension and a dramatic vote call, the resolution censoring the United States fails to win approval when France changes its anti-American vote after the votes have been tallied and a deadlock has been announced.

These resolutions in Congress, the Senate, and the United Nations are accompanied by formal speeches, motions, counter-motions, and votes which, for the most part, detract from the vitality of the anatomy. The parliamentary maneuvers and shifts of focus tend to weaken the illusion of reality and the "willing suspension of disbelief" which one normally associates with quality fiction. In addition, for readers who tend to be sympathetic to liberals or liberal causes, the recurring supporting themes in the novel have a disturbing, propagandistic thrust which becomes obtrusive. Such themes, focusing upon the deficiencies of "true liberalism" and the intellectual shallowness of "true liberals," involve several assumptions about liberals and their understanding of Communism which suggest that "liberals," in the context of Drury fiction, pose a threat to the security and well-being of America: "liberals" control the media—radio, television, and the press— and are easily manipulated by Communists and Communist sympathizers; "liberals" are grossly intolerant of perceptions of reality which conflict with "liberal" perceptions; "liberals" are unable to understand that some "liberal" positions may have their roots in a misunderstanding or misinterpretation of reality, especially realities pertaining to human nature, Communism, and politics; "liberals" have a naive trust of the good will of the Communists and refuse to acknowledge that subversion, political violence, and wars of liberation are the instruments for the implementation of the goals of imperialistic Communism; "liberals" have contributed to the lack of confidence and deteriorating moral character of America by exercising overwhelming influence on American education which neglects to instill traditional American values (discipline, Judeo-Christian morality, patriotism, and respect for intelligence and rationality) in the young. These themes will increase in shrillness and become more obtrusive in the concluding books of the political series; however, Drury very effectively integrates these same themes into the next book in the series, *Capable of Honor*, a very effective satire of the media.

Unfortunately, *A Shade of Difference* is also marred by too many characters in the novel for Drury's narrative skill to develop within the confines of his plots and subplots. Besides continuing the development of

Harley Hudson, Orrin Knox, Bob Munson, and Seab Cooley, four additional characters are introduced into the political series with accompanying biographical narratives: "Terrible Terry," Felix Labaiya, the Ambassador to the United Nations from Panama, Representative Cullee Hamilton, and Senator Hal Frye. Both Hamilton and Frye are delegates to the United Nations and both are political heroes who compete for the role of protagonist in the novel, thereby detracting from the impact of the novel by making impossible a primary hero in *A Shade of Difference.*

III

Hal Frye is a romantic political hero. He is an engaging, credible, Drury creation whose heroics in the United Nations require almost superhuman dedication to the United States and the cause of peace. The Senator would be a more engaging character, however, if he were not so obviously the bearer of Drury messages: the United Nations is a necessary, though an imperfect organization; America must continue as a member of the United Nations despite anti-American prejudice; the United Nations exploits American good will and generosity; however, it is one avenue for avoiding world conflict in a nuclear age; and, ultimately, men must love one another and work together despite differences of country and race. Through Frye, Drury presents international politics at the United Nations.

Through a biographical narrative, the sorrows of Frye's tragic life are presented in the climactic fourth and final book of the anatomy-romance. Perhaps because of loneliness and the belief that something essential was missing in his life, the no longer young Frye married a girl who was unable to provide him with domestic harmony and sexual satisfaction. Gradually, Hal became aware that his wife Kay possessed a warped religious sensitivity — her conception of the divinity was an unsympathetic and extremely demanding God of wrath. An additional dimension of anguish occurs in the Frye household because of an accident during Kay's pregnancy. As a result, a physically beautiful but brain damaged son causes an irreparable breach in the Frye affections, a breach which expands when Kay's religious guilt and fear become a part of the young boy's personality. Though the Senator tried to be sympathetic to his wife's religious views, Drury narrates, he no longer found it possible to be so after his small boy, Jimmy, pathetically asked his father a question pertaining to his physical and mental development: "Daddy," he said, "Why is God mad at me?" (499).

Problems in the Frye household were not to diminish. Jimmy's brain damage continued to worsen and following the best medical advice available, the once dynamic child, who had regressed to a vegetable state, was institutionalized. Finally, Kay Frye, after many years of attempting to cope with her personal and domestic happiness, resolved her personal and domestic conflict by taking her own life. The Senator's response to his wife's suicide was a renewed dedication to his work, a renewed commitment to a life of service in the United States Senate and the United Nations. His distinguished career, however, is threatened by leukemia. Much more than most men, Hal Frye is prepared to cope with this, his final misfortune. As a child, Hal was reared in a household where sincere religious conviction and hard work were a way of life. These, along with prayer, "instilled in him an acceptance of God's will" and a desire to serve his fellow men, qualities which help him to attain noble stature in his chosen profession—politics (485).

The "idealistic, wide-eyed, romantic damned fool," as the Secretary of State describes the Senator, insists on continuing as Chief Delegate to the United Nations although the best medical advice has convinced him that he has only a few, short, painful weeks to live (516). As the Chief Delegate, the Senator courageously works to blunt the charges of racism against America, accusations more difficult to counter because the United States supports the United Kingdom in its opposition to the Resolution recommending immediate independence for black Gorotoland. Following the passage of the Gorotoland Resolution granting independence to a nation which still permits human sacrifice, cannibalism and slavery, and in the midst of circumstances which would permit even the most heroic of men moments of despair, the dying Senator views the challenge as "some final justification of his life" and as, perhaps, the explanation of the cross that "the Lord had placed upon him for some reason he could not understand." The excruciating painful leukemia, he perceived, enabled him "to clear his mind and life so that he could make one last appeal to mankind" (559).

To the surprise and delight of the United States Delegation, Senator Frye's diplomatic skill and rhetorical efforts bring positive results; the motion to censure the United States for its racial practices is narrowly defeated in a dramatic vote. Bitter-sweet, however, is the time of triumph. Before the session is adjourned, Senator Frye addresses the United Nations for the last time. With an exuberant spirit but with a rapidly deteriorating body, the Senator from West Virginia delivers an appeal for peace and brotherhood. "Let us love one another" is his final plea to the world as he reminds his friends and fellow delegates that men are no longer able to flee from one another, that no one can save man unless man saves himself. "Though we fly to the moon and far beyond," he warns, "we shall take with us what is in our hearts, and if it be not pure, we shall slaughter one another wherever we meet" (584).

For everyone in the world to love one another is perhaps a utopian dream, but while Frye speaks, for a moment in Drury fiction, the dream seems a reality. Later, at the United Nations ball after the session had adjourned, Caucasians and Orientals dance with one another, and color blindness prevails as representatives of diverse and sometimes contradictory ideologies talk, drink, and share a spirit of good will in an atmosphere where "no shade of difference" exists. The United Nations, the United Nations ball and Hal Frye are symbols of the best in the human spirit. At the conclusion of *A Shade*, the Secretary General suggests a corollary to the Senator's exhortation to love. Though such love and harmony may not be easily or readily achieved and may be, even permanently unattainable, nevertheless he reminds the United States Delegate from Iowa "we must always try" to make them become a reality (600). The courage of Hal Frye, his utopian vision, and his optimistic message of love to the United Nations merges the propagandistic and didactic with the romantic. The character of Hal Frye is credible, but Hal Frye as protagonist is an idealistic hero whose dream is bigger than life.

IV

The second political hero of *A Shade of Difference* is not a Caucasian. Cullee Hamilton, a Congressman from California who becomes a United Nations Delegate at the conclusion of the novel, is a black whose "shade of difference" traumatically affects his personal life as well as his political career. Like Senator Frye, Cullee Hamilton is a bearer of Drury messages: (1) although there is much racial exploitation and prejudice in America's past as well as in the present, even impoverished blacks can succeed if blacks have respect for themselves, respect for hard work, and ambition to rise above their present circumstances. (The Hamilton family produced not only a Congressman, but also successful members of the medical and teaching professions); (2) there are many kind and decent whites who are deeply disturbed by the racial injustice which exists in America who are willing to accept blacks as individuals and who are willing to help blacks improve the plight of the Negro in the United States; (3) blacks, even though they are still being exploited and discriminated against, are doing better in the present (fifties, early sixties) than they have done in the past; and (4) though racial injustices and the effects of racial injustices can never be totally eliminated, America is working to eliminate racial injustice; (5) though integration is desirable and necessary, integration in itself will not solve the Negroes' problem, unless Negroes, as the Hamilton family illustrates, are prepared to take advantage of opportunity; (6) black leaders who tend toward moderation will run the risk of being ostracized by blacks, as is Cullee Hamilton, who is accused by his wife of being "an uncle Tom, a white man's nigger, a stooge, a patsy, a traitor to his people" (270); and finally, (7) Drury wants his readers to understand that more good can be accomplished by working constructively within the political framework of the body politic than by choosing to withdraw from the body politic and working to destroy it by violence and subversion. Despite Drury's sympathetic presentation of a successful black politician, Drury oversimplifies the problems of black America and presents an unflattering impression of

American blacks, as well as the blacks in Gorotoland. Since the Kerner Report suggested that there was much unintended racism in America, perhaps some of the popularity of *A Shade* might have been influenced by unconscious racism in the minds of some white readers.

Like Hal Frye, Cullee's life is a very troubled one. Both in South Carolina, where he was born, and in the North, where he attended school, Cullee has learned the significance of "a shade of difference." The future Congressman's life was never easy and life became even more difficult when his father, a hard drinking field hand, was killed in a tractor accident; and his mother, a housemaid, was faced with the demanding task of rearing five children in a segregated environment. As an adult, Cullee is never able to forget the pain of racial bigotry and discrimination. He remembers that

Something as simple as going to the bathroom became a major issue when you were in town with your mother. There were only one or two widely separated places where you could go, and very early you learned that on shopping days you mustn't drink too much water in the morning because you wouldn't be able to urinate, unless you used back alleys, which your mother's pride wouldn't permit you to do, until you got home again. And you sat on certain places in buses and streetcars, and you entered only certain doors that were marked for you, and you attempted to walk down the street in an inconspicuous manner, and you learned not to listen to what the white man was saying, unless of course you were supposed to hear, in which case you learned to laugh just a little too loudly and just a little too heartily to reassure him that yassuh boss, he was indeed the Lord of Creation and you his admiring vassal, constantly surprised anew by his wisdom and his all knowing superiority and his ineffable and incomparable wit (325).

Through the perseverance, hard work, and wisdom of his mother, the Hamilton family not only survives, but also becomes successful. After outstanding academic success in high school, Cullee decided to venture North to Columbia University. New York and Columbia were not what the young track star had anticipated. Before not too long, "he began to be aware that for all their outward comaraderie there was a subtle shade of difference, invisible but unmistakable, tenuous as fog but hurtful as acid, that separated him from his newly found friends" (327). To Howard University he transferred in his sophomore year, where he met his future wife, Sue-Dan, and LeGage Shelby, who will become the founder of a militant, black organization, an off-shoot of the much more moderate NAACP, titled DEFY (Defender of Equality for You) and who will also become Hamilton's best friend until Shelby's radical solutions to radical problems become unacceptable to the Congressman who has chosen a more moderate, conservative approach to achieve the same results.

Before their bitter differences evolve, however, Cullee's life has been one of public attention. When the young track star establishes an Olympic record, he is featured in *Life* magazine. Later, after graduation from law school in California, the talented young lawyer is once again the focus of the media when a torrent of racial abuse erupts after he and Sue-Dan purchase a home in an all white section of San Fernando Valley. The papers report his successful meeting with his white neighbors who are persuaded that the intelligent, sophisticated Hamiltons are not a threat to the neighborhood and their property values, but are, instead, a potential asset to the community. Not a man to miss an opportunity, in the glow of favorable newspaper reports, the black man from South Carolina, sensing that the moment is ripe for his entry into politics, becomes a candidate for Congress. His political intuitions are sound: the all white congressional district elects the intelligent, talented black to Congress. Fortunately, the Hamilton election occurs at an opportune time. Because Cullee is black and the Administration wants to strengthen its image with emerging African and Asian nations, the lawyer from California is given a coveted committee appointment: membership on the Foreign Relations Committee.

As a black member of the Foreign Relations Committee, Cullee is responsive to the Administration's request that he accompany "Terrible Terry" to South Carolina and attend a dinner in the M'Bulu's honor. At "Harmony," the Southern home of Ted Jason, the liberal Governor of California, the Congressman is challenged by the ruler of Gorotoland to actively participate in the integration of the local elementary school. The choice reflects a strength of Drury fiction, an awareness of the complexity of racial problems and the diverse pressures that occur in politics: if the Congressman chooses to accompany the M'Bulu as he escorts an eight year old girl to school, he will be dramatically visible in the struggle for racial justice; however, the Congressman's ego-satisfying participation would perhaps be offensive to the all-white-constituency which elected him in California; and, as a reaction to his meddling in the racial struggle in South Carolina, his constituents might exercise their right to send a different candidate to Congress at the next election. On the other hand, if Cullee Hamilton chooses to function as a public relations representative for the administration and refrains from participating in the confrontation between whites and blacks at the school, the Congressman will continue to be in an establishment position where he can exercise influence for the good of black Americans in the House and perhaps, eventually, in the Senate; but in such an instance, because of his failure to participate in the confrontation, he will lose respect, prestige, and influence among militant, black Americans. Rather than risk the destruction of his political career and the possibility of helping black Americans by remaining within the overwhelmingly white political power structure, Congressman Hamilton rejects "Terrible Terry's" request that he immerse himself directly and immediately in school integration. Predictably, "Terrible Terry's" presence at the school provokes an angry crowd reaction and the black prince of Gorotoland is pelted with fruit and eggs, causing both national and international repercussions.

The international reaction to the media coverage of the pelting is strongly anti-American and damaging to America's influence and prestige in the United Nations. To bolster the American image and power in the world body, and to defuse the potential public relations damage that "Terrible Terry" could inflict on the United States, President Hudson and Secretary of State Knox request that Congressman Hamilton introduce the joint resolution in the House expressing an apology to the M'Bulu and authorizing a ten million dollar grant to Gorotoland. Cullee Hamilton's alliance with the Administration and the "white establishment" severely destroy his health and happiness: his wife leaves him to sleep with "Terrible Terry;" his best friend, LeGage Shelby, rejects him—he too will eventually be Sue-Dan's lover—because he will not actively support the militant black movement; and he is savagely beaten by agents of the radical black movement for being an active member of the white establishment.

Although these misfortunes bring the Congressman to the brink of despair—he wishes "to crawl in a hole and not get out"—he is persuaded by the courage of Senator Frye to leave his bed and to appear at the United Nations to participate in the debate of the resolution to censure America because of its racial discrimination (524). Still bearing the physical marks of his beating by the black extremists, Congressman Hamilton, as a United Nations Delegate, illustrates with his presence and words the evidence that blacks can become a part of the American power structure and that though injustices still remain, blacks can succeed and actively participate in the resolution of racial problems. Like most members of the United Nations, Cullee Hamilton is much influenced by Senator Frye's courage, dedication, and commitment to the practice of love. As *A Shade of Difference* nears conclusion, the central image of love also becomes embodied in the character of the Congressman. The much maligned and rejected Hamilton attains a degree of peace and harmony through his suffering which generates a re-learning of the nature of love and permits him to contemplate that some day he will find a woman deserving of his love and that together they will be able to share this gift with the world. The kind of love that he, and the world needs, Cullee understands, does not

...come from outside. It came from inside. It was something you had to work out yourself, from your own being—then maybe if you really achieved it inside, somebody who had also achieved it inside would come along, and you could have it together and it would really be something—then you could give it to the world, too. But only after you had achieved it inside. Only then (596).

Like Hal Frye, Cullee Hamilton too is a romantic hero who is credible, but yet not totally convincing. In the creation of Cullee Hamilton, Drury focuses upon an example of black success which was very exceptional at that time in American history. Though many black people achieved success in the fifties and early sixties, such political success stories were exceptional indeed. For a black growing up in South Carolina, the prevailing attitude among white Southerners was that of Seab Cooley, the powerful Senator from South Carolina.

V

Seab's conception of honor is at the root of two conflicts in *A Shade of Difference*: Seab conflicts with both Cullee Hamilton and "Terrible Terry," who in turn conflict with each other not about the goals of blacks, but rather about the time frames and methods whereby those goals will be achieved. Seab possesses a racist attitude toward these two blacks; however, he respects Congressman Hamilton. On the other hand, he has no respect for "Terrible Terry," His Royal Highness of Gorotoland. When "Terrible Terry" travels to South Carolina to attend a Jason dinner in his honor, the foreign diplomat raises the wrath of Seab Cooley by becoming involved in South Carolina's school integration. Although segregated schools were outlawed in the United States in 1954 by the Supreme Court's Brown v. Board of Education decision, the South was slow in integrating its schools. Consequently, American readers of the sixties could easily visualize "Terrible Terry's" actions in *Shade* as well as the reactions of Southern whites. In order to speed integration, "Terrible Terry" escorts a six year old black girl to an all-white school through a crowd of angry whites. These are "Christian souls," who shout "Go on home, you God-damned niggers," "We don't want no niggers messing with our kids," and who carry banners: "THIS IS A WHITE SCHOOL: NO NIGERS APPLY" (sic) and "KEEP YOUR BLACK BASTIDS IN YOUR OWN BACK YARD" (sic) (132). After Terry gently kisses the girl and presents her to the superintendent at the school door, the crowd assaults him with eggs, tomatoes, bricks, sticks, and rocks. As Terry has anticipated, his presence has helped to precipitate racist violence, and the media response assures an embarrassing focus on the racial injustice prevalent in America. Although the President quickly extends an apology to Terry and expresses the hope that South Carolina can comply with the Brown v. Board of Education Supreme Court decision, anti-American riots erupt in Tokyo, Moscow, Jakarta, Cairo, Stanleyville, Mombasa, Lagos, Accra, Casablanca, Rome, Paris, London, Caracas, Havana, Port au Prince, Rio, and Panama City. In addition, the incident in Charleston has immediate repercussions in the United Nations where as Krisna Khaleel, the Indian representative explains to the Secretary of State, "the Asian-African states are concerned by everything that touches upon the question of color. It is one of the major things that divide the world, of course. Sometimes it makes for a shade of difference in the way various states approach various matters" (143). To complicate American embarrassment and to increase America's loss of prestige throughout the United Nations and the world, Seab Cooley furiously denounces "Terrible Terry" in the Senate. As *Shade* nears conclusion, Senator Cooley makes clear that he views Terry as an outside agitator who has been manipulated by foreign powers in order to embarrass the United States. The Senator also believes that Terry is a pawn of Governor Jason who uses Terry to project a pro-black image and thereby to win support for his attack against the Hamilton Bill, a bill that will help blacks in America and Gorotoland and which is the administration's response to the damage to America's prestige in the United Nations. Surprisingly, despite the racial eruption in South Carolina, Senator Cooley does not mount a personal attack against Cullee Hamilton, the black who sponsored the bill. Cullee, like Seab, is a native of South Carolina, and though he too is an enemy of "Terrible Terry," Hamilton perceives segregation from a vastly different perspective than Seab Cooley.

A Shade of Difference was written between November, 1960 and February, 1962, a time of racial turmoil in the United States, a turmoil which erupted with a bus boycott in Montgomery, Alabama in February, 1956, and extended into the seventies. Statistics and historical facts are inadequate to communicate the racial hatred that permeated—perhaps to a lesser extent, still permeates—America, a racial hatred that was frequently presented graphically on the evening news and which was a significant part of the information and emotional base of all—white and black—educated Americans, whether they lived in either the North or the South. In February, 1956, during the Montgomery bus boycott which was led by Dr. Martin Luther King, thousands of racist handbills were circulated at a white citizens' rally. They suggest the racial animosity of that time and place, a time and place which touches the historical orientation of a fictional character such as the seventy-five year old South Carolina Senator:

When in the course of human events it becomes necessary to abolish the Negro race, proper methods should be used. Among these are guns, bow and arrows, sling shots and knives. We hold these truths to be self evident that all whites are created equal with certain rights, among these are life, liberty and the pursuit of dead niggers. In every stage of the bus boycott we have been oppressed and degraded because of black, slimy, juicy, unbearably stinking niggers. The conduct should not be dwelt upon because behind them they have an ancestral background of Pygmies, Head hunter, snot suckers.... If we don't stop helping these African flesheaters, we will soon wake up and find Reverend King in the white house (Oates 91-92).[1]

Ten years later, four years after the publication of *A Shade of Difference*, Martin Luther King led demonstrations in Chicago which were designed to focus upon and to ameliorate racial injustice in the North. After a violent confrontation King said that "I've never seen anything like it.... I've been in many demonstrations all across the South, but I can say that I have never seen—even in Mississippi and Alabama—mobs as hostile and hate-filled as I've seen in Chicago." King made this observation after leading a demonstration through a neighborhood of second generation Poles, Italians, Lithuanians, and Germans where Confederate flags and Nazi insignias were prominently displayed and where there were racist shouts and comments: "Nigger go home!" "We hate niggers!" "We want Martin Luther Coon!" "Wallace for President!" "Kill the Niggers!" and Hate! Hate! Hate!" After violence erupted and order was restored, an old woman said: "God, I hate niggers and nigger lovers." An old man: "I worked all my life for a house out here, and no nigger is going to get it!" (Oates 412,413).

Nevertheless, some racial progress occurred. In September, 1962, James Meredith, an Air Force veteran, successfully integrated the University of Mississippi even though there was violent opposition. When Meredith first attempted to register, he was turned away from the administration building by the governor and state troopers "while armies of white students waved Confederate flags and chanted 'Glory, glory, segregation' to the tune of 'The Battle Hymn of the Republic' " (Oates 206). When Meredith received a federal escort, he was able to register and attend classes.

In *A Shade* readers are informed that Cullee Hamilton applied for admission to the University of South Carolina, but rather than force a dramatic confrontation as his wife and his best friend, militant LeGage Shelby, desired, he decided to attend law school in California instead. In the context of the times, in the fiction of Drury, Hamilton exercised prudence. After graduation from law school, Hamilton successfully integrates an all-white neighborhood despite initial white opposition. It is against a background of racial injustice, animosity, and conflict in America, that Drury creates a Southern Senator who has sympathy—but certainly not enough—for blacks and one who has worked diligently to pass legislation which has helped blacks to improve the quality of their lives in South Carolina. On a personal level, Senator Cooley likes and respects Cullee Hamilton; nevertheless, he is unintentionally patronizing, racist, and ignorant of the complexities of black difficulties. Although the Senator disrespectfully refers to "Terrible Terry" consistently as a "kinky-haired Kinkajou," he does not direct racial slurs against Hamilton. He considers Hamilton to be "smart;" he wishes him "well;" however, the Senator does possess a racist view of Hamilton's intelligence. "For an educated colored man," Seab tells Orrin Knox, "he does very well," but in Seab's estimation he does not possess enough intelligence to conceive of the Hamilton Resolution without the help of the Administration: Seab "was not about to admit that a colored man could have been clever enough to think of anything like that, even an intelligent colored man like Cullee" (114, 281). With similar sincerity, Seab believes that the natives of Gorotoland are not ready for freedom because human sacrifices and cannibalism might be still found there. In addition, there are "signs of Russian and Chinese Communist infiltration" (86-87). If Congress and the President were to concede to Terry's pressure in either the United States or in the United Nations, Seab believes that America's prestige and influence in the world would erode. Such actions would be tantamount to upsetting world order and to denying the innate superiority of the white man: "If every little black man who cared to raise a hollar could grab the attention of the nations and make great states bow and scrape before them, where was it all to end? Certainly not in any conclusion that he as a white man, or even as a self-respecting citizen of what he liked to think was still a self-respecting nation, could contemplate with casual calm" (282). Now, Cooley believes, because of the world threat of Communism and the eroding will of the American people, is the time to take a stand. Communism is becoming successful because of "a lack of guts on the part of the free world. The cowardice of the West was the Communists' secret weapon." Consequently, Seab believes that since the Gorotoland and the Hamilton resolutions combined both the issue of race and Communism, "he has no other alternative than to register his determined opposition" (282). Seab's position is not without some merit; Cullee Hamilton also perceives Communist imperialism as a threat and Hamilton is aware that black organizations, such as DEFY and the Black Muslims, are helping the Communists to weaken America. In an argument with his best friend, LeGage Shelby, Shelby expresses his disenchantment with Cullee's alignment with the white power structure and his impatience with a gradual approach for gaining black equality and freedom:

'All my life,' LeGage said with a strange tone of lonely anger Cullee had never heard in his voice before, 'I've been trying to play it your way, the way so many of us have tried to do in the past. I've been trying to get along with them on their terms. Even when I've led DEFY out picketing someplace, it's been to accomplish something in a way they could understand, so they would do something about it. 'Well'—he drew a deep breath—'well, maybe now I'm not going to do it like that, anymore. Maybe I'm going to do it the way we think is right, for things we want, and let them sweat, for a change. Maybe I've just decided I've got to be true to what I think is best for us, not what they think.' He paused somberly. 'That's about it, Cullee. And maybe I think it's time for you to stop playing their way, and help us' (226).

In response, Cullee accuses his friend of being "a stooge for Terry and the Commies" as he tears America apart. "That's what Russia wants, for us to fall to pieces fighting over race," said Cullee (227). This linkage of Communism with the Civil Rights Movement—though not named directly as such within *A Shade of Difference*—reflects the thinking of some influential Americans during the fifties and sixties. In June, 1963, President Kennedy told Dr. Martin Luther King that two of his friends, Stanley Levison and Jack O'Dell, who were on his staff were Communists and that FBI Director Hoover believed that Levison was "a conscious agent of the Soviet conspiracy" (Oates 247). Even though an FBI security investigation found no evidence of Communist influence upon King, Hoover disbelieved the report. When William Sullivan, in charge of the Domestic Intelligence Division of the FBI, was pressured by Hoover concerning King's alleged Communist affiliations, Sullivan stated that because of a demagogic King speech, he now thought that King stood "head and shoulders" over all other Negro leaders put together when it comes to influencing great masses of Negroes. "We must mark him now, if we have not done so before, as the most dangerous Negro of the future in the nation from the standpoint of Communism, the Negro, and national security (Oates 264-265). By 1966, after King had led opposition against the Vietnam War (a war which King believed was partially motivated by "our paranoid anti-Communism" and the result of "racist decision making") with the same philosophy of peaceful dissent that had characterized his leadership of the Civil Rights Movement, his philosophy of love and civil disobedience were frequently challenged by black militants (Oates 431, 468). Stokley Carmichael, for instance, denounced the Vietnam War "as a white racist war" and called the black American soldiers in Vietnam "white men's mercenaries." President Lyndon Johnson was a "hunky," a "buffoon," and Carmichael saw integration as "a white subterfuge for the maintenance of white supremacy." In a SNCC document (Student Non-Violent Coordinating Committee) this black civil rights organization, then led by Carmichael, stated that "if we are to proceed toward true liberation, we must form our own institutions, credit unions, co-ops, political parties, write our own histories," and "construct an American reality defined by Afro-Americans." To black audiences Carmichael stated that "if we don't get justice we're going to tear the country apart" and he urged blacks to "fight for liberation by any means necessary" (Oates 419-420). In the summer of 1968, when riots occurred in over a hundred cities, the difference between the nonviolent rhetoric of Martin Luther King and the violent rhetoric of younger black leaders was irreconcilable: Carmichael urged Negroes "to kill the honkies;" H. Rap Brown who had replaced Carmichael as chairman of SNCC "exhorted the Negroes to 'get out your guns' and 'burn the town down,'" and the Chicago Chapter of SNCC stated that "we must fill ourselves with hate for all white things. We have to hate and disrupt and destroy and blackmail and lie and steal and become blood brothers like the Mau-Mau" (Oates 447). Such sentiments contrast sharply with the words, philosophy, and actions of King, who consistently affirmed his love for America despite its racial injustice and who, in 1958, chose to go to jail to protest racial injustice and police brutality rather than pay ten dollars and court costs. In Montgomery, Alabama he addressed the judge, but he had the nation in mind when he said:

I also make this decision because of my love for America and the sublime principles of liberty and equality upon which she is founded. I have come to see that America is in danger of losing her soul and can so easily drift into tragic Anarchy and crippling Fascism. Something must happen to awake the dozing conscience of America before it is too late. The time has come when perhaps only the willing and non-violent acts of suffering by the innocent can arouse this nation to wipe out the scourge of brutality and violence inflicted upon Negroes who seek only to walk with dignity before God and Man (Oates 136).

Although *A Shade of Difference* predates a significant amount of the racial violence in America during the sixties, through the character of LeGage Shelby Drury anticipates the clash between King's philosophy of non-violence and the Black Muslim's philosophy of violence after black militants perceived that non-violent protests and demonstrations were ineffective in achieving black goals. The impatience of LeGage and the racist personality of Seab Cooley make inevitable a clash between blacks and the white power structure, a clash which did—and does—reflect the danger of America, in King's words, "losing her soul" and drifting into "tragic Anarchy" and "crippling Fascism." As we have seen, Cullee Hamilton, despite his painful experiences with racism, remains a moderate, choosing to work non-violently within the white power structure of the body politic in order to improve the plight of blacks in America and throughout the world, and because he chooses to work within the body politic to affect change, he has a dramatic confrontation with Senator Cooley before Senator Cooley filibusters against the Hamilton Resolution in the Senate.

In addition to the conflict between blacks and blacks, Drury creates and adds another level of tension in the novel by creating a conflict between whites and whites. The President, Secretary of State, and the Senate Minority Leader believe that the Hamilton Resolution is necessary for the welfare of America and that justice dictates the need. Secretary Knox and Majority Leader Munson, though firmly committed to change, are troubled by their conflict with Seab, an old friend and a respected colleague whose political power is eroding in both South Carolina and the Senate. They fear for his health. Consequently, Bob Munson attempts to persuade Senator Cooley to make only a formal and token opposition to the Hamilton Resolution. As a result of mounting only a formal opposition, he would not lose significant support from his racist constituents, and at the same time the Senator would be able to conserve his health as well as his waning power in the Senate. Secretary Knox, too, takes action to support the man who was his ally in the battle against the Leffingwell nomination. Knox asks Cullee Hamilton to compromise on the wording of his resolution so that the South Carolina Senator might save face. Shrewdly, however, he suggests to Hamilton that the Senator is open to change and that Seab wishes to meet with him and to make a compromise. Hamilton agrees providing that the Senator will personally ask for the change. With good intentions, but deceitfully, Bob Munson and Orrin Knox purposely communicate misleading messages. Bob Munson advises Seab that Hamilton is willing to compromise and desires a meeting with Seab to work out a compromise on the Hamilton Resolution. Not surprisingly, because of their experiences and cultural orientations, when Cullee and Seab meet to discuss changes in the Hamilton Resolution in a climactic scene, race—"a shade of difference"—is a barrier to communication. A very much surprised Seab gradually begins to understand that the Hamilton Resolution will pass because the black Hamilton has amassed the voting support to pass it; nevertheless, because of his perverted sense of honor, the aging Senator cannot bring himself to avoid what will be, for him, a fatal conflict in the Senate; he cannot resist his personal history; he cannot "ask a colored man" or beg from a "colored boy" even when his political and physical life depend upon it. The Southern Senator cannot understand Cullee's lack of gratitude for all that he has done for the blacks, and Cullee cannot make the Senator understand that the Senator is patronizing to blacks, that changes should be made because white Senators should "like us." As Bob Munson and Orrin Knox anticipate, though they hope for the best, that is, that by some miracle Cullee and Seab would reach a compromise, neither Seab nor Cullee is capable of compromise. Before the conversation is concluded, Seab offers further evidence of his racial prejudice: "I sometimes think you're beyond help," he tells Cullee, and then he firmly expresses his position: "It (the Hamilton Resolution) may defeat me, it may be the death of me, but I'll fight it through my way, because that's how I am" (427-432). Since his fellow Southern Senators perceive that times are changing, that despite Cooley's opposition the Hamilton Resolution will pass, they do not support the Senator when he unleashes racist rhetoric during a filibuster in a futile attempt to defeat the Administration bill. Except for Senator Van Ackerman who taunts and goads the tired but determined Seab, Senators, as well as spectators in the gallery, are distressed by the strain that the Senator places upon himself. After the seventy-six year old Senator filibusters for over eight hours and suffers from exhaustion, the Hamilton Resolution is passed. Spurning the solicitous concern of his senatorial friends and colleagues, Seab takes a Washington walk and remembers his past. Before expiring on the grass before the Capitol Building, he asks the Lord if He has been satisfied with "Your servant Seabright" and the answer he receives is "Yes" (477). The death of Seabright Cooley, as with the deaths of the President and Senator Anderson in *Advise and Consent* and Hal Frye at the conclusion of *A Shade of Difference*, is a significant juncture in the multi-plotted maze of Drury fiction.

Chapter V
"Pure" Political Fiction as
Anatomy and Satire: *Capable of Honor*

When we examine *Capable of Honor* from the perspective of Frye's "Four Forms of Fiction," we find that this third book of the political series is primarily anatomy. In *Capable* Drury continues his examination of politics against the background of the spirit of the age, and he expands upon a theme he introduced in *Advise and Consent*: the role of the press in politics or, to put it another way, the exercise of power by the media in the body politic. Somewhat ironically, Drury attacks the abuses of advocacy journalism through the medium of advocacy fiction, and his attack against liberals in the media is within the traditional framework of political fiction. "The main purpose" of the political novelist, according to Speare, "is partly propaganda, public reform, or the exposition of the lives of personages who maintain government or the forces which constitute government" (ix).

Although the central journalistic character in *Capable of Honor* does not become a candidate or an elected public official, he does actively participate in the presidential nominating process and in the determination of the foreign policy plank of the party platform. Through the character of "Wonderful Walter" the role of the press is critically examined and satirized. "Wonderful Walter" is a comic character—vain, affectatious, and hypocritical—who appeals to our sense of the ridiculous provided that our egos are not emotionally and intellectually intimately identified with the liberal segment of the media. The dedication of *Capable of Honor* is ironical: although the novel is "dedicated to all the many sincere and objective newspapermen and women, in Washington and elsewhere, who are not a part of Walter's world," the overwhelming impact of the novel is the impression that most journalists are imperceptive, biased, intellectually dishonest, and hypocritical. *Capable of Honor* was a best seller for forty-one weeks in 1966 and 1967. During those weeks American soldiers were fighting and dying in Vietnam, and the media was reporting daily this war against Communist expansion which originated in the fifties.

While Drury was composing *Advise and Consent* (1957-1959), America was already supporting South Vietnam's efforts as it struggled against Communist insurgents who were assassinating government officials and infiltrating men and weapons down the Ho Chi Minh Trail into South Vietnam, and the first American soldiers were killed in combat. While Drury was composing *A Shade of Difference* (1960-1962), the Communist insurgency continued: Hanoi formed the National Liberation Front (Vietcong); America sent 12,000 military advisors. Between the time that Drury completed *A Shade of Difference* in 1962 and began to compose *Capable of Honor* in December, 1964, America's involvement in Vietnam had intensified and domestic opposition to America's Vietnam commitment became a public issue. Although Washington learned in 1963 that President Diem's generals were plotting a *coup d'etat*, his government was overturned and President Diem was murdered. After two unprovoked attacks against American destroyers in August, 1964, Congress passed the Gulf of Tonkin Resolution which authorized the President "to repel any armed attack against the forces of the United States" and "to take all necessary steps, including the use of armed force, to assist any member or protocol state of the Southeast Asia collective Defense Treaty requesting assistance in defense of freedom." The Tonkin Gulf Resolution provided the legal basis for America's full scale military commitment to Vietnam; however, the facts concerning the attacks against American destroyers were seriously disputed.

Because of conflicting accounts of the "unprovoked attacks" in the Bay of Tonkin, a serious credibility gap was created between the military, the government, the President, the press, and the public, a gap that would become both wider and unbreachable during the Vietnam conflict (Karnow 374-376, 344, 360-363). Even before Senator Morse challenged the Bay of Tonkin facts, (only two Senators, Morse and Grundy, voted against the Bay of Tonkin Resolution) a Vietnam credibility gap existed. In February, 1964, James Reston of *The New York Times* had warned of government duplicity: "The time has come," he wrote, "to call a spade a bloody shovel. This country is in an undeclared and unexplained war in Vietnam. Our masters have a lot of long and fancy names for it, like escalation and retaliation, but it is a war just the same" (Karnow 414). And while Drury was writing *Capable of Honor* (1964-1965), the war became even more bloody, confusing, and frustrating. American troops increased their attacks against the Vietcong; the Vietcong increased their attacks against the Americans and the South Vietnamese. Casualties mounted and President Johnson responded with a stick and a carrot: North Vietnam was bombed; American troops were increased to 400,000; and a peace offer was extended. All was to no avail. During the months that *Capable of Honor* was on the best seller list (October, 1966-July, 1967), more and more Americans were becoming painfully aware that the concept of honor was sometimes more complex than it first appeared and that the price tag for honor was distressingly high. As millions of readers were enjoying *Capable of Honor*, members of the media were more and more frequently beginning to question the wisdom of an American ground war in Asia. In *Capable of Honor*, when President Hudson addresses the American public, he directly connects or links the Gorotoland war with Korea, Vietnam, and Santo Domingo; in addition, a CBS Special Program juxtaposes the two: GOROTOLAND: ANOTHER VIETNAM? Just as the press attacked Presidents Johnson and Nixon because of American involvement in Vietnam, President Hudson and Orrin Knox are attacked because of American involvement in Gorotoland.

II

As the plot of *Capable of Honor* begins, Harley Hudson has been President for six months. Despite his promise to Congress and the American people that he would not become a candidate for the party's presidential nomination, there is much speculation that he will go back on his word and become a candidate although he has solemnly promised the American people not to do so. As President, Harley Hudson adopts a foreign policy "of patient and unafraid firmness" which does not meet with the approval of the media. A Communist-backed rebellion in Gorotoland—a fictional parallel to the Vietnam War—causes a crisis for his Administration. After insurgent forces murder American missionaries and destroy the property of American Standard Oil, the President dispatches American troops to the newly independent African nation which is legitimately governed by "Terrible Terry." This American intervention enables Drury to employ the dominating, recurring focusing technique which he has woven into the plot of *Capable*: the foreshadowing of an event, the event itself, and the national and international reactions to the event. In this instance, there are ominous signs that a Communist backed army will commit violence against American citizens and American property as a part of a plan to overthrow the legitimate government of Gorotoland. Despite the President's warning to the rebels that they should not harm Americans or American property, doctors and nurses are massacred at All Faith's Hospital and the property of an American oil company is destroyed. The President immediately dispatches American troops to Gorotoland, and then he report directly to the American people via television the reasons for his actions in a formal speech.

Drury has the President speak directly to the American people and the reader who hear, see, or read the serious speech in its entirety. Responses to the President's speech then follow: an interpretive and expository column by an antagonistic journalist, a United Nations debate in the Security Council which includes exchanges between the Soviet Ambassador and the Ambassador from the United Kingdom; reporters then comment upon this verbal conflict. More follows: the American Delegation makes a response to the Russian reaction in the United Nations, the Russians then reply, the Americans again respond. Then there is a United Nations vote which condemns the United States intervention, which again generates newspaper headlines, which thus reflect the UN resolution and the United States' veto of that resolution. After this, the reader is presented with reactions to these events which occur around the nation and throughout the world. Finally, there appears the commentary of syndicated columnists reacting to these events and the President's response to this journalism. The President is especially sensitive to "Wonderful Walter" Dobius's commentary.

That the pace of *Capable of Honor* diminishes as a result of this technique, (foreshadowing, action, reports, commentaries, interpretations) a technique which critically examines the journalistic process and requires an intelligent and interested reader, is to be expected. This critical examination of the media constitutes a significant theme in Drury's novels: although the press is *Capable of Honor*, the press acts dishonorably by pretending to be objective and disinterested when in fact the news is selectively presented and slanted to depict positively those who are favored by the press and to depict negatively those that the press holds in low esteem. Throughout the anatomy "Wonderful Walter" Dobius symbolizes and epitomizes the intellectual and emotional corruption of the press as he spearheads opposition to the President's policies, the President's bid for reelection, and the political ambitions of Orrin Knox, the Secretary of State.

In *Capable of Honor* the media response to American intervention in Gorotoland is extremely hostile, and resolutions in the House and Senate which endorse the President's policy are hotly contested. The position of the Administration becomes even more threatened when Felix Labaiya, backed by Soviet and Chinese Communists, leads a "Government of the Panamanian People's Liberation Movement" in a revolution which hopes to evict the American presence from the Canal and to reclaim the Canal for the Panamanian people. President Hudson's reaction is predictable: American troops are dispatched to the Canal Zone in order to protect American personnel and property.[1] Again, as in American intervention in Gorotoland, the President receives the wrath of the press: "few Presidents have received his condemnation," especially for acts in defense of American or national security. Ironically, because of the inflammatory attacks of the press, instead of withdrawing from the political arena, the President feels compelled to defend his policies and to provide the American people with a clear-cut choice. Despite his solemn pledge in *Advise and Consent* not to become a candidate for the presidency, Harley Hudson does so in *Capable of Honor*.

This presidential decision is a devastating blow to his Secretary of State who passionately aspires to become president. Though Secretary Knox is disappointed, he firmly supports the President in his policy and in his bid for re-election, despite the President's decision to have an open convention for the purpose of choosing his vice-presidential running mate. At the convention the popularity of Ted Jason, a liberal Governor from California who challenges the President's foreign policy decisions on Gorotoland and Panama, is swelled by media support which laments the grim fact that American soldiers are fighting and dying in two separate wars, both far from American soil.

As the plot evolves, Ted Jason's vice-presidential ambitions evolve into presidential ones; consequently, he joins forces with radical groups who violently oppose the Hudson-Knox foreign policy. "Coordinated demonstrations" persuade the convention to refrain from endorsing the Administration policy on Gorotoland and Panama in the party platform. Conservatives at the convention become appalled at the violence generated by the Jason supporters, violence which Jason implicitly condones since the media unfairly blames Orrin Knox's supporters for the eruptions. By a narrow margin of 658-635, President Hudson receives the nomination of his party. In his speech to the convention he strikes the keynote theme of the novel: honor. Honor, the President believes, is not so much what a man does, but how he does it. Ted Jason is humiliated when the President labels him—without mentioning his name—as a man who possesses neither conscience nor honor and then selects conservative Orrin Knox for his running mate, even though "Wonderful Walter" and the press have made a concentrated effort to discredit the Secretary of State as a viable vice-presidential candidate.

III

At the center of *Capable of Honor*, the core of its vitality as fiction— his thoughts and actions significantly affect the lives of Harley Hudson, Orrin Knox, and Ted Jason and significantly contribute to the shaping of the spirit of the age in *Capable*—is the character of "Wonderful Walter" who is presented as the preeminent journalist of the twentieth century. In the real, non-fictional world, the preeminent American journalist of the twentieth century when *Capable of Honor* was written was Walter Lippman (1889-1974), the author of twenty-six books, ten thousand articles, friend and advisor to presidents and confidante of international figures such as Nehru, DeGaulle, and Khruschev. To many Americans, Walter Lippman's finest hour was his opposition to the Vietnam War. As early as 1963, Ronald Steel reports in *Walter Lippman and the Twentieth Century*, Lippman questioned our involvement in Vietnam by writing that "the price of a military victory in Vietnam is higher than American interests can justify" (541). Years later, such a belief was deemed unpatriotic by many Americans, including President Lyndon Johnson who had once looked kindly upon Lippman. After giving Lippman his "famous treatment" in the spring of 1964, "telephone calls for advice, birthday gifts, private lunches at the White House, invitations to state dinners," Johnson put his arm around Lippman before a large gathering of press, labor, and business leaders, the Security council, and government officials and declared that "This man here is the greatest journalist in the world, and he's a friend of mine" (547-548). Johnson's mood changed, however, after Lippman consistently disagreed with the President about Vietnam in his weekly columns. Lippman's barrage against

Johnson and his Administration sometimes included striking samples of vituperation, such as "self-righteous use of military power," "foolish and ignorant men," and "messianic megalomania" (577). President Johnson, Lippman wrote in 1967, was "a primitive frontiersman who wants to be the biggest, the best, the first, a worshiper of what William James called the bitch-goddess success" (577). On another occasion Lippman wrote: "The root of his (Johnson's) troubles has been his pride, a stubborn refusal to recognize the country's limitations.... Such pride goeth before destruction and an haughty spirit before a fall." The preeminent journalist of the twentieth century also wrote that "There is growing belief that Johnson's America is no longer the historic America, that it is a bastard empire which relies on superior force to achieve its purposes, and is no longer an example of the wisdom and humanity of a free society...it is a feeling that the American promise has been betrayed and abandoned" (577). Not surprisingly, Johnson retaliated by lashing out at Lippman publicly and by labeling him a "political commentator of yesteryear" (578). The Johnson-Lippman conflict was so open and so bitter that their conflict became an additional news story reported by the press. In May, 1967, Robert Herlock of *The Washington Post* wrote that if Johnson and Lippman "had lived in the days of Thomas More and Henry VIII, he (Lippman) would have lost his head completely" (578).

Although Lippman bitterly opposed President Johnson's conduct of the war, he had perceived Goldwater, Johnson's opponent in 1964, as a less attractive alternative even though Lippman had once thought "it would be a good idea for the Republicans to run an archconservative and get it out of their system." Lippman also had strong negative feelings about the conservative candidate's ability to be a successful president. Lippman

accused Goldwater of being a "radical reactionary," the mouthpiece of the "newly rich on the make." With a foreign policy that promised "victory" by bomb-rattling and a domestic program that would deny federal aid to the indigent, Goldwater was truly a unique candidate. "We all know of demagogues and agitators who arouse the poor against the rich," Lippman wrote during the campaign. "But in Barry Goldwater we have a demagogue who dreams of arousing the rich against the poor" (554).

Walter Lippman's emotional commitment against the Vietnam War was not in character with the conspicuous public image of detachment that he had projected during his distinguished career as a Philosopher-Journalist. This image of detachment existed despite the fact that on one occasion, when he was the guest of honor at a dinner given by the Academy of Political Science, he was hailed by his peers in the words of *Time* as "their Moses, their prophet of Liberalism." Lippman's ideal of a detached, disinterested, unemotional observer was expressed in a column during Wilkie's campaign against Roosevelt. Lippman wrote:

Columnists who undertake to interpret events should not regard themselves as public personages with a constituency to which they are responsible.... It seems to me that once the columnist thinks of himself as a public somebody over and above the intrinsic value and integrity of what is published under his name, he ceases to think as clearly and disinterestedly as his readers have a right to expect him to think. Like a politician, he acquires a public character, which he comes to admire and to worry about preserving and improving; his personal life, his self-esteem, his allegiances, his interests and ambitions become indistinguishable from his judgment of events.

In thirty years of journalism I think I have learned to know the pitfalls of the profession and, leaving aside the gross forms of corruption, such as profiting by inside knowledge and currying favor with those who have favor to give, and following the fashions, the most insidious of all the temptations is to think of oneself as engaged in a public career on the stage of the world rather than as an observant writer of newspaper articles about some of the things that are happening in the world. (388)

Although Lippman publicly projected an image of disinterest and detachment, he was frequently consulted as an advisor by presidents; his newspaper columns benefited from inside information, and he frequently used his columns as a vehicle to express publicly his advice to presidents. An indication of his influence occurred during the Cuban missile crisis. After Lippman suggested in his column a plan to resolve the Cuban missile crisis, John Scali, a journalist who was acting as an intermediary between the Soviets and the State Department, was compelled to tell the Russians: "Everything Mr. Lippman writes does not come from the White House" (535). Since Lippman attended Kennedy parties, was solicited for advice, participated in deliberative councils, and even had successfully suggested changes in President Kennedy's inaugural address, the Russian inference was not an unreasonable one. The Kennedy White House viewed the philosopher-statesman "as one of their prime assets" (525). President Kennedy was extremely skilled in manipulating the press in his favor, and like Johnson before Lippman's break with him over the Vietnam War, Kennedy enjoyed an excellent relationship with the most influential American journalist of the century. On one occasion when Kennedy was queried about inviting Lippman to a minor ceremony, President Kennedy rejected the idea. "No," he said, "We're doing so well with him, let's not spoil it" (538).

In April, 1964, before his conflict with Johnson, Lippman reiterated the need for detachment for the responsible journalist; this time, however, he emphasized the ideal relationship between journalists and great men. While being interviewed on television Lippman said:

There are certain rules of hygiene in the relationship between newspaper correspondents and high officials—people in authority—which are very important and which one has to observe. Newspapermen cannot be the cronies of great men. Once a man, even if you have known him more or less as a crony for years, becomes something like a governor—much less a President—it's all over. You can't call him by his first name anymore. I've known several Presidents whom I knew by their first names long before they were President, and I would never think of calling them by them when they got into the White House. I think it is advantageous for the President to be able to talk to somebody who won't exploit him, or betray him, or (to whom he can) talk his mind, and it's certainly an advantage to the correspondent to know what's really going on so he won't make a fool of himself. But there always has to be a certain distance between high public officials and newspapermen. I wouldn't say a wall or a fence, but an air space that's very necessary (548).

Just as Walter Lippman was a friend, adviser, and confidant of presidents and international dignitaries, who professed disinterest and detachment, so also is "Wonderful Walter" the "solemnly portentous" "statesman-philosopher" of the press in *Capable of Honor*. In addition, both Walters were highly influential authors and columnists. Walter Lippman's "Today and Tomorrow" syndicated column was published in two-hundred newspapers. "Wonderful Walter's" syndicated column, which is graced with his "solemnly portentous" and "pompous countenance" at the head of his column, titled "The Way It Is" is published in 436 papers, including the Walla Walla Union *Bulletin*. Within the context of *Capable*, Drury informs the reader that "Wonderful Walter" is considered a better writer than Walter Lippman. The "peasants who read newspapers agreed that 'Wonderful Walter' indeed did know 'The Way It Is' " and "that of all those writing in Washington, the Bakers, the Drummonds, the Krocks, the Lippmans, the Pearsons, the Restons, and the rest, Wonderful Walter was indeed the greatest of them all" (8). Through the first name of "Walter" and the tag words of his column, "The Way It Is," Drury also associated "Wonderful Walter" with Walter Cronkite, the CBS anchorman considered by many to be "the nation's most reliable journalistic commentator" who concluded his evening news with the words "and that's the way it is" on this day (Monday) and date (June 7) and who, according to one politician, "by a mere inflection of his deep baritone voice or by a lifting of his well-known bushy eyebrows...might well change the vote of thousands of people (Karnow 547-548). "The greatest of them all," Drury satirically suggests, leaves much to be desired. As we have already indicated, by presenting the thoughts, comments and actions of journalists, Drury presents and demonstrates the methods used by some members of the media to slant the news. Drury obviously satirizes the arrogance that he perceives in contemporary journalists through the person of "Wonderful Walter" Dobius, the most revered of all syndicated columnists, who is a greatly respected "philosopher-statesman" as well as a journalist. Drury's characterization of "Wonderful Walter"—the "Wonderful Walter" being a biting, ironic epithet—is a caricature which focuses upon Dobius' egotism and arrogance, which lead him to advocate authoritatively and dogmatically "liberal" positions while simultaneously promoting and projecting an image of objectivity and disinterestedness to the public. Ironically, "Wonderful Walter" sincerely believes that his liberal ideals and his foreign and domestic policy statements are in the best interests of the country. However, because Drury presents additional information to the reader, the reader is compelled to perceive that his "liberal" position is wrong and potentially disastrous to America.

Because of "Wonderful Walter's" monumental ego and the admiration of the majority of his peers and the public, "Wonderful Walter" is psychologically unable to understand problems from any perspective other than his own. This personality flaw is common knowledge to Washington insiders. Beth Knox, the Secretary of State's wife, tells her husband what he already knows, that "Wonderful Walter" has "a terrific messianic complex" (12); Patsy Labaiya, the sister of Governor Jason of California, flatters and manipulates Walter in order to gain his support for her brother's presidential bid. Patsy "knew as well as anyone how delicate you had to be with Walter, his ego was so monumental and his dignity so insecure, and altogether he was such a pompous little a———————" (14). When Drury permits us to enter the mind of Walter while Walter is contemplating his achievements, Walter's thoughts, as well as his actions, confirm to the reader Beth's and Patsy's perception of Walter's oversized ego. After a vicious argument with his wife, Walter's nerves are calmed by thoughts of his influence and achievements. These self-aggrandizing thoughts "restore him once again to what he was—what he was and would be for the rest of his life, and no one could take that away from him, no one—America's leading philosopher-statesman, in whose presence the great and the little of the world bowed down" (454). Again, after Walter has joined with Frankly Unctuous as a reporter and commentator of the nominating convention, he reflects upon who he is and what he has become: "It was good to be just himself again, Wonderful Walter, for whose wisdom the nations waited and the world bowed down" (518). Walter's vanity and arrogance are so great that they permit him to be hypocritical without suffering the pangs of conscience one would normally expect from a professional journalist.

Nevertheless, as a professional journalist, Walter espouses a desire to be "objective" and "fair" in reporting political campaigns. Walter also prides himself on his "spirit of fierce independence." Early in *Capable* the philosopher-statesman assesses his responsibility to be "objective and fair" and expresses a determination to be impartial in the soon to occur nominating convention where "liberals" and "conservatives" will battle over foreign policy and the selection of candidates for President and Vice-President: "I do have some obligation to be objective and fair," Walter tells Patsy Labaiya when she pressures him to support her brother's presidential bid. "These aren't just words that one takes lightly or evades, you know," Walter pontificates. "In an honorable profession, these are the stoutest guideposts. For twenty-five years I have tried to abide by them and I shall do so now" (16).

Despite such convictions, Walter is unable to do so because of his deeply rooted antagonism toward Secretary of State Knox who vigorously supports the presidential decision to dispatch American troops to Gorotoland to repel the Communist attempt to take over the country. Walter's personal animosity toward Orrin Knox is very deep. He once told the director of the *Post*— who has agreed to cooperate in Walter's endeavor—that he "was going to get Orrin Knox if it's the last thing I do" (22). Because Walter believes Orrin Knox is "misguided" and his presidential ambitions constitute a danger to the country, Walter believes that "any misrepresentation in the column is justified, any smear is reasonable, any cruelty excusable" (45). As the action evolves in *Capable*, Walter becomes a self-proclaimed advocacy journalist, despite the lip-service that has been given to objectivity earlier in the anatomy. In a climactic scene with Anne Carew, his former wife, he reveals his journalistic practices through the formation of rhetorical questions: "I ask you, is it wrong for me to use my column and my position to fight for the policies I believe in, and against those I honestly think are destroying the last chance of ever arriving at a workable arrangement with the Communists?" (452) In order to promote peace negotiations as a means of ending the Gorotoland war, Walter pressures the Governor of California to become a peace candidate. When Governor Jason is not selected on the party ticket, Walter suggests that a third party be formed.

Walter's political activities are not restricted to newspaper columns. He also makes behind the scenes telephone calls and attends meetings designed to pressure potential candidates whose views can be influenced and directed to reflect Walter's. When Walter arrives at the United Nations building while an anti-war, anti-American riot is in progress, the philosopher-statesman speaks encouraging words to the rioters, rather than categorically rejecting the violence as one would normally expect of a responsible public figure. When his encouragement of the anti-war rioters is categorized as "close to treason" by Senator Smith of Iowa, the "philosopher-statesman" reaffirms his support of the rioting anti-war demonstrators: "I was happy to endorse their protest against the irresponsible, inexcusable act of a war-mad administration. I would do it again. I *will* do it again, in my column and in everything else I say" (136).

Walter's commitment to the anti-war faction of the party takes a surprising turn at the nominating convention. After Walter has created a political climate extremely advantageous to a Jason presidential bid by making a speech which polarizes choices between "hawk" and "dove," Governor Jason finds himself in the unenviable position of having either to endorse Walter's pro-peace speech or of being labeled a war-monger. At the convention, after Jason has become a leader of the anti-war faction of the party, Walter—despite his earlier declaration of being fair and impartial in election campaigns—acts as an emissary to Jason from three anti-war groups (DEFY, KEEP, and COMFORT) that have extremist tendencies. At Walter's meeting with Jason, an agreement is reached whereby the anti-war groups will take over the Jason demonstrations promoting his bid for nomination as Vice-President. These demonstrations become increasingly demagogic and violent, thereby threatening to subvert the democratic process. During the convention Walter's pro-Jason column helps to promote this climate of violence, a climate that will culminate in the beating of Crystal Knox, which causes the still-born birth of Orrin Knox's grandson. Prior to the assault upon Knox's daughter-in-law, Walter has written: "It is time to abandon concepts of 'fairness' and 'honor' which have up to now hampered and hindered the Governor of California and his supporters. It is time to be as ruthless and tough as Orrin Knox and his master at the White House. It is time to act" (369).

Although Walter possesses the right to his personal political philosophy, he also possesses a responsibility to alert the public to his biases. Not only does "Wonderful Walter" become actively involved in promoting and consciously manipulating candidates so that they will implement "Wonderful Walter's" political and social philosophy, he also conscientiously promotes a disinterested, detached image to the public as he does so, thereby concealing his biases and his political activities from his readers. Because syndicated columnist Helen-Anne Carew, Walter's ex-wife, believes that he has betrayed the ethical ideals of journalism, she verbally blasts him for publicly affecting impartiality, slanting the news, and reporting it inaccurately. After violence erupts at the convention, Helen-Anne, who, ironically, has also become personally involved in the campaign by tentatively agreeing to become Orrin Knox's press secretary if he is nominated, pounces upon Walter in the press room while he is typing his column. In a comic scene "Wonderful Walter" loses his temper when his ex-wife sarcastically refers to him as "that great statesman and philosopher," calls him a "demagogue" who tells boobs what to think, yanks his paper from the typewriter, and labels him a "monster" who "lies and knows that he lies," who possesses "an ego grown so great, so convinced of its own infallibility, so fawned upon and made so much of by the world that you have just about lost touch with reality." During Helen-Anne Carew's hysterical tirade, Walter attempts to remain calm and controlled by remembering "that he was Walter Dubius whom all the world admired and to whom nobody said and did such things." Before the ex-wife concludes her tirade, she slams her handbag on Walter's typewriter, hysterically summarizes the unethical activities of the "liberal" press, and declares the results of its biased reporting of the political campaigns.

Listen! she said. Listen to me, Walter! You have almost killed Crystal Knox. You have actually killed two other people. You and your friends have created a climate in this country in which it will be a miracle if the President himself isn't assassinated before this is over. You and your friends have destroyed every pretense of objectivity, fairness, decency, nonpartisianship, honor, that the press was ever supposed to have. The lot of you have spewed out a steady stream of deliberate misinformation, twisted, slanted, dishonest reporting, photography and analysis from the day the crisis began in Gorotoland right on through Panama to this very hour (450).

When Helen has finished her highly emotional verbal assault, Walter trembles violently and can barely see the typing paper before him as he tries again to compose his column.

Henry Fielding in his Preface to *Joseph Andrews* writes that "the only source of the true Ridiculous is affectation" and that the roots of affectation are to be found in vanity and hypocrisy. Vanity, Fielding believed, "puts us on affecting false characters, in order to purchase applause," and hypocrisy "sets us on an endeavor to avoid censure by concealing our vices under the appearance of their opposite virtues" (Fielding 7-12). In the dramatic conflict between Helen-Anne and Walter in the press room, the philosopher-statesman's vanity and hypocrisy are comically unmasked before stunned reporters, reporters who talk about, but do not report the confrontation in the news stories or gossip columns though the confrontation possesses interesting and dynamic conflicts with David and Goliath overtones: superior male versus inferior female; dominant husband versus submissive ex-wife; world renowned philosopher-statesman versus gossip columnist; calm, detached, rational male versus emotional female; the "intelligent liberal" versus the "dull conservative." However these conflicts are viewed, Helen-Anne Carew wins the sympathy of the reader. "Conservative" David slays "liberal" Goliath. Amused and entertained by Drury's comic scene and the caricature of a pompous columnist, the reader sympathizes with and applauds the victor. Although, as we have already indicated, *Capable of Honor* is "dedicated to all the many sincere and objective newspaper men and women, in Washington and elsewhere, who are not a part of Walter's World," the overwhelming impact of the anatomy is the impression that most journalists are unlike Helen-Anne Carew; they are more in the mold of "Wonderful Walter"—imperceptive, biased, intellectually dishonest, and hypocritical. In *Capable of Honor*, the slanting of the news is the norm of journalistic behavior.

IV

"Wonderful Walter" is just the most visible part of a pattern which demonstrates the political power of the press in the body politic. Journalistic bias and slanting are also habitual in the Manhattan office of *The Greatest Publication That Absolutely Ever Was*. The executive chairman of the most influential American newspaper knows that his paper consistently takes a partisan posture but the paper never overtly expresses this bias except during the two weeks prior to the presidential elections. Nevertheless, through the mind of the executive chairman we learn that his newspaper frequently pours "hot coals upon the heads of those below of whom it disapproved" while disguising "these attacks as fair, objective news stories which permitted it to cling tenaciously to its non-partisan mantle" (173-174). At times the executive chairman believes that *The Greatest Publication* "was taking standards too harshly intolerant, printing stories too obviously slanted, publishing headlines that clearly placed it on just one side of the great issues that gnawed at the vitals of the world" (174-175). When the executive ponders his biased stories, photographs and headlines, he wonders: " 'Aren't there more people friendly to America who might have been interviewed?' Or, 'Isn't war hell for non-rebel soldiers, too, when they get captured by the rebels?' " (175). Such sophisticated slanting is not unnoticed by the President who is constantly under attack by the media.

The President whose Gorotoland policy is bitterly opposed by *The Greatest Publication* details the slanting techniques of the media in a direct address to the American people, an address which permits Drury to link the biased reporting of the war in Gorotoland to what Drury believes to be the biased reporting of the Vietnam War by the liberal, anti-war press:[2]

What are the techniques, the President asked, which are used by these people— this small but influential group whose power is out of all proportion to their numbers?...   There is the headline or bulletin so phrased that it instantly gives the American citizen the impression that his own country is in the wrong, no matter what the truth is.

There are the shocked disclosures of how disorganized and corrupt and irresponsible the loyal government is—and the admiring reports of how shrewd, well-organized and invincible the enemy government is.

There are the diligent—one might say, the eager—reports of the American losses and mistakes, somehow never quite matched or balanced by reports of enemy losses and mistakes....

And there is, finally, the indirect and vicious attack (upon government officials) which concentrates upon their financial practices, or their personal lives, or their private morals, but never honestly comes into the open to tell you that the real argument is with their *political philosophy*....

This is what has become, in this partism century, of once inviolate integrity of a once inviolate profession (227-228 Italics added.).

Since "Wonderful Walter" is presented as the most influential journalist in America, he symbolizes both the conscious and the unconscious prejudices which permeate the "liberal" media. Nevertheless, Drury also directly satirizes the less well-known journalists who compose the bulk of the press by labeling them as "sheep" because of their tendency to agree with the philosophy and the policies of "Wonderful Walter" without subjecting them to their own critical analysis. In a devastating comic scene-at an "Aid-the-People's-Republic-of-Free-Gorotoland-party" given by Mrs. Roger Castleberry, the "liberal" sister of the "liberal" Governor Jason—Drury depicts the press as ignorant, fawning admirers of Prince Obi, the pro-Communist leader of the Gorotoland rebellion. In the person of journalists from *The New Yorker, The New Republic, Newsweek,* the *Nation, Reporter,* and the *In-Group Quarterly,* Drury caricatures their *naivete.* At the party readers hear the Vice-President of the Most Right Thinking Book Publishers, Inc. report that they are going to publish an autobiography of Prince Obi titled *New Star Over Africa: My Struggle for Justice* and that The Most Darling Right Thinking Hollywood Producer will bid five hundred thousand dollars plus 30% of the gross for a movie about "the greatest leader in Africa" (77). When Prince Obi exchanges insults with a Ghana Princess in their native language while they maintain smiling faces and pleasant voices, the "liberal" journalists from *The New Yorker, The New Republic, The Reporter,* and the *In-Group Quarterly* gush with praise at what they believe to be an ideal example of black harmony, not understanding that the actual words of the conversation are mutually and grossly insulting:

"I see," Obifumatta said in the same polite tone. "Whore of the earth," he added pleasantly in Twe, "you are doing well in the white man's world."
"Anus of the universe," the Princess responded cordially in the same language, "swallow your own excrement."
"They like each other." Selena cried ecstatically to the billowing room."They speak the same language: These two are making such progress in world relations, right here in my humble flat. Oh, it's wonderful" (78).

Again, the reader's confidence in the media as perceptive, unbiased observers and reporters of the war in Gorotoland and of the presidential campaign is severely challenged at the nominating convention. At the convention Drury creates two devastating scenes involving interviews which are presented to the public in a severely distorted fashion. After the "lady from CBS" asks loaded and irritating questions of members of the Knox family and rudely tells Mrs. Knox that she does not enjoy talking to her, the "lady from CBS" informs a colleague that "I've just given the Knox women a fit, and I am going to have fun with them in my broadcast." In the broadcast, the "lady from CBS" presents a distorted report unfavorable to the Knox women and detrimental to Orrin Knox's bid for the vice-presidency. The report is slanted both by emphasis and by omission. Although Crystal Knox responded to a request for a comment by stating that "I think there has been a deliberate attempt to smear my father-in-law, to attack him, to blame him for something for which neither he nor his people are responsible; to place the whole proceedings on violence, demagoguery, and fear. I think this is foreign to our way of doing things in this country. I think Governor Jason will live to regret it," the reporter omits this forthright and newsworthy response from her report (422-423).

In her interview with Ceil Jason, the "lady from *Newsweek*" reveals similar unprofessional behavior. After the reporter expresses her preference for Governor Jason, Ceil's husband, and receives little encouragement, she reflects that Mrs. Jason is a "tough bitch" and wonders "if she doesn't know we're on her side." Although Mrs. Jason calls the lady from *Newsweek* completely despicable when the reporter asks if she agreed that Orrin Knox is a murderer "as your husband's people said" and is "responsible for the violence at the convention," the reporter nevertheless files a pro-Jason story, neglecting the larger story that the Governor's wife is upset at the actions of her husband's supporters because she does not intend "to help Orrin Knox with anything" (423-425). As deplorable as these breaches of journalistic ethics are, they pale in comparison with the reporting of violence during the nominating convention. Because "Wonderful Walter," Frankly Unctuous the Anchor Man, and the overwhelming majority of the press begin with conscious and unconscious biases, they do not intensively investigate the roots of the violence that occurs and they misrepresent or misinterpret the convention violence based on the unstated assumption that conservative factions are responsible for violence. Drury the narrator permits the readers to see the events and to learn the autobiographical background of the major participants, thereby permitting the readers to observe the blatant discrepancies between the actual events, the perception of the events, and the reporting of those events by the media.

When the President watches the convention demonstrators on television, he perceives demonstrators who are "solidly packed, virtually expressionless, barely moving, hardly speaking, silent, hostile, and...menacing" carrying banners which are "all of war, and of the fear of war, and of the hatreds of vicious minds let loose, as though their masters had pried open some giant manhole cover and out of it they had crawled from the sewers of the race" (375). Frankly Unctuous has a different perception of the same event. The anchor man perceives the demonstrators as "more serious than some faces you saw on your screen yesterday." They have "sprung spontaneously" from three Democratic groups that are gradually coalescing behind Governor Jason, he reports to the television audience as he explains that the demonstrators are charging the convention with the "great responsibility" of choosing, "in effect, between two policies: one which many believe can lead only to a deeper involvement and greater war-and one which can ultimately lead to a restored and revitalized American prestige in a peacefully united world" (376). The purr of positive words associated with the Jason policy—"restored," "revitalized," "peacefully," and "united world"—reveal the sympathies of the "objective" reporter as he makes a dichotomy—peace and war, liberal and conservative—that both expresses and helps to shape a polarization in America at a time when there is a need for emphasis upon points of agreement rather than upon difference if the potential for violence is to be avoided. When a Knox demonstrator is viciously beaten, Frankly Unctuous rationalizes the attack with muted language that slants his report so that his readers will not react negatively to the Jason demonstrators and thereby damage Jason's chances for a vice-presidential nomination:

It is believed that the incident occurred when the youthful Knox demonstrator made some joking comment to the Jason group standing in the lobby of the Palace. The remark was apparently misinterpreted, but our reporter who was standing close by, tells us he is convinced there was no real malice in the spontaneous and probably quite unthinking reaction of the Jason backers. They were apparently just carried away for a moment by the feeling here, which is beginning to run...a little high here as you can see (377).

This muted response contrasts sharply with Frankly Unctuous' later report of a convention riot involving several hundred persons which results in thirty injuries. In his televised report, Frankly Unctuous expresses the presumption that the now "angry spirit of violence" was initiated by Knox supporters who were "angered by this morning's earlier episode in which a backer of the Secretary of State was *roughed up a bit* at the Palace hotel" (383-384 Italics added.) Although Frankly Unctuous has earlier disavowed knowing who causes the immediate violence being reported, he concludes by pointing out that Governor Jason has demanded a "fair-play" convention, thereby implying that there can be little blame for the violence upon the liberal faction, and that Jason's opponent and associates should "heed the call," thereby leading the audience to believe that the Knox supporters had started the riot. Shortly thereafter, again without evidence, newspaper headlines proclaim that "KNOX FORCES START UGLY RIOT IN UNION SQUARE" and "IGNORE JASON CALL FOR FAIR PLAY." With both an hyperbole and a demonstration of the irresponsible use of unidentified sources, Drury continues to depict for the reader the techniques of journalistic abuse in the media: "On five-hundred newscasts across the country five hundred newscasters began their reports: 'A bloody riot which observers believe was started by supporters of Secretary of State Orrin Knox today turned San Francisco's Union Square into a shambles' " (384). The readers know differently since Hal Knox, the Secretary of State's son who is present at the riot, reports to his father: "I was there, I know our people didn't start it. I saw it begin" (389).

A second convention riot occurs when Williman Everett Hollister II strikes a Knox supporter because he thinks "the smart-ass college" kid is laughing at him. Hollister is described in terms some have associated with stereotyped anti-war demonstrators of the sixties: he had "bounced along from boarding school, wound up at the University of California, discovered in himself little aptitude for study but great aptitude for protest; organized riots, planned campaigns, uttered fiery slogans, screamed dirty words, toppled chancellors, harried legislators, protested everything, graduated at twenty-one with nothing to do but hang around the grown up world and keep on protesting." When he and Booker T. Sanders—who at the age of twenty had already "drank, took dope, raped, robbed, and murdered"—are critically wounded in the riot, they are idealized as martyrs by the "liberal" Jason faction (400-401). The reader knows differently and so does Senator Munson, who addresses the convention. As the President did in his televised speech to the American public, Senator Munson bluntly unveils the bias of the media which has instantaneously assumed and asserted that Knox followers "initiated" the riots: "Not one single solitary witness of any credibility whatsoever has come forward to claim, with proof, that it was Knox-inspired, Knox-authorized, or Knox-started. The so called 'Knox-riot,' " Munson announces to the convention and to a live television audience, "is the pure and simple creation of a handful of commentators and a group of powerful journalists, all of them deeply hostile to the Secretary of State and deeply committed to the candidacy of the Governor of California. It is they who have charged the Secretary of State with fostering violence—in order to cover up the violence of the other side" (420). When Frankly Unctuous and "Wonderful Walter" respond to Senator Munson's allegations, they continue to reflect their "liberal" biases. Unctuous responds with "a humorous, candid smile and a mock pretense of wiping his forehead" as he explains to the audience that the Senate Majority Leader is a Knox supporter, that the convention "is influenced if not completely controlled," by the Hudson-Knox faction, and that no one has proven that the Knox supporters did not start the riot. However, he further explains, their reporter "on the spot" had "the impression" that they did. Walter Dobius, in his commentary, projects "a spiteful distaste he made no attempt to conceal" and emotionally asserts that attacks upon the press and the "personal smearing of them or of the press" cannot change the fact that "They were *murdered*" (420). Because the reader is permitted an overview of the events by the narrator, when the President and Senator Munson attack the press, the readers know that these "conservative" attacks upon media abuses are fully justified. It would require an extremely knowledgeable and highly sophisticated reader not to transfer

either consciously or unconsciously the knowledge of press abuses and
slanting techniques presented in Drury fiction to the reporting of "real"
events in the "real world" of the Vietnam War and the ideological conflicts
between "liberals" and "conservatives," "hawks" and "doves." This is so
because Drury plants such associations in the reader's mind early in *Capable*
when newspapermen perform a skit at the annual Washington Gridiron
Dinner where the "liberal" press is lampooned in song by "conservative"
reporters:

> "Oh—
> You—
> Can—
>
> "Slant the news,
> Twist our views,
> Warp the facts,
> Give us the ax—
>
> "But—
> If—
> You—
>
> "Stand tall in Georgetown,
> Stand tall in Georgetown,
> *Stand tall in Georgetown,*
>
> "You're
> ALL
> RIGHT!

Drury the narrator then emphasizes the reflection of the real political and
media world in his fiction by allusions to Bobby Kennedy, Adlai Stevenson,
Richard Nixon, and Barry Goldwater: " 'Got to stand tall in Georgetown!
Somebody will grin, skillfully boasting Bobby, villifying Dick, sanctifying
Adlai, black-guarding Barry. 'Better watch out or you won't stand tall in
Georgetown!' Someone else will chuckle to a friend who has inadvertently
been fair to the other side' " (29).

To make certain that readers are aware of slanting techniques in televised
news, after indicating to the reader that some "pro-liberal" headlines are
larger and more prominent than "pro-conservative" headlines and that some
positive news stories involving the "conservative" cause are placed on the
bottom of the first page or perhaps even on pages three and four, Drury
as a narrator ironically compares television news reporting with that of
newspapers: "The evening televised programs were *equally balanced and
informative,* filled with *disapproving dissertation* on the *motives* of the

President and the Secretary of State, heavy with analysis of *the awful things* being done by Washington to world peace and an innocent and dreadfully wronged UN" (200 Italics added.). Then Drury focuses upon body language and voice projection as instruments of slanting:

> With a lifted eyebrow here, a *skeptical* smile there, a chuckle, a frown, a *knowing* tone of voice, a *bland* omission, a *gracefully* damaging turn of phrase, all the lesser Walters went at it with a will. Somberly they sketched the world in collapse as the result of vetoes, *smoothly* they shifted the blame from America's enemies to America's President, suavely they telescoped the Administration's arguments and gave extra time to the opposition's. Then with a *portentous* sadness they bade the viewers good night, having spent a brisk thirty minutes blackguarding their country, encouraging its enemies, and doing all they could to undermine its citizens' confidence (200 Italics added.).

Later in *Capable*, when Frankly Unctuous and Walter Dobius are reporting the convention, Drury presents us with television commentators who slant the news in exactly the way that he suggests; consequently, alert readers are able to compare their reporting, their voice tones, and their body language and see for themselves that Unctuous and Dobius serve as excellent models of biased television reporters.

In addition to vividly portraying body language and voice projection as effective tools of slanting, Drury also shows how television commentators can slant the news by omission. When Cullee Hamilton, a black conservative Congressman from California addresses the convention in support of the conservative Knox-Hudson Administration, instead of presenting Hamilton's speech live to the American public and thereby directly providing evidence that some blacks are intelligent, successful, and conservative, Unctuous and Dobius casually decide to omit live coverage of the speech. The narrator underscores their omission. "...the convention faded away, and it was guaranteed by two intelligent, earnest, sage, and thoughtful faces agreeing with each other diligently for the next fifteen minutes, that on one network, at least, the sentiments of one of the few Negro leaders, not backing Governor Jason, would be very smoothly, logically, and skillfully withheld from the country" (435).

V

So far we have looked at some parallels in the world of Drury fiction and "the real world" as we have examined Drury's critical examination of the media as it slants the news. As Drury satirizes the "liberal" media, "Wonderful Walter" Dobius is at the center of *Capable* as a symbolic figure. The name Dobius itself suggests simultaneously a paradox of ego and lack of credibility: "Do Be Us" who are "dubious." "Wonderful Walter" is also at the center of the novel as a significant character in the action. In *Capable*

Walter significantly influences the course of events that will shape the political ambitions of President Hudson, Secretary of State Knox, and Governor Ted Jason, the major political characters in the anatomy-novel. As we have indicated, what Walter Dobius thinks, what he writes, and what he does has a significant impact upon presidential policies and the exercise of political power. Let us now turn to the third book in Drury's political series and explore the impact of "Wonderful Walter" and the spirit of the age upon their political careers and personalities.

Although Harley Hudson gives little indication that he will be a competent President during his tenure as Vice-President in *Advise and Consent*, after the death of his predecessor he surprises both his friends and his critics by becoming a "strong" President in the area of foreign affairs: he rebuffs the Russians at a Geneva confrontation and when Communist instigated rebellions occur in Gorotoland and Panama, without hesitation he dispatches American troops to defend the freedom in these countries. His firmness in confronting the threat of imperialistic Communism in Gorotoland and Panama requires much political courage, for the "liberal" press views this defense of freedom as American acts of aggression, and the media's constant criticism of his policies erode his popularity and threaten his political future.

President Hudson, though perceived by the "liberal" media as inept and impulsive, possesses a shrewd understanding of the political climate as the climate evolves and shapes the spirit of the age. President Hudson identifies the "century's major theme" while he observes that America is sinking "rapidly and perhaps irrevocably into a welter of chaos, uncertainty, and violence;" there is, he perceives, "insensate rebellion against everything, for no reason, no purpose, no logic, no nothing. Out of the great creeds of liberation, uplift, and reform had come finally—nihilism, heartless...mindless...useless" (430). Closely associated and identified with this nihilistic spirit is senseless violence, and such violence once begun, the President believes, becomes uncontrollable. Violence in this context is viewed with supernatural significance: "He didn't believe in letting the devils out of the box. He believed in sitting on the lid, for history had shown on too many occasions lately what happened when you let it open. You couldn't tuck the Thing that came out neatly back inside, once it had broken loose to ravage the world" (430). Dobius, the philosopher-journalist, by not rejecting violence as a political instrument and by supporting the leaders of COMFORT, DEFY, and KEEP, both actively and passively contributes to the violent and nihilistic temper of the times and makes Harley Hudson's political life much more difficult.

President Hudson, besides being a vehicle for presenting Drury's version of the spirit of the sixties, also permits readers to witness the insidious effect of power upon an essentially good and patriotic American. Because of the nihilism and violence which characterizes "liberal" opposition to his foreign policy, President Hudson slips into political *hubrism*. Even moral, well-meaning and perceptive Presidents, Drury indicates in the personality portrait of Harley Hudson, are not immune to the corrupting effects of power when a nation is on the brink of anarchy. However, because of his success at the Geneva Conference where the President "saved" America from atomic war and Russian imperialism and because—despite bitter opposition from Walter Dobius and the media—he believes that his foreign policy in Gorotoland and Panama is essential to the spiritual and physical health of America, President Hudson concludes that he is the "best" of all potential presidential candidates and that, therefore, despite his solemn promise to the American people, he must become a candidate for President. Nevertheless, the President recognizes "that it is probably the height of egotism—or insanity—or something—to equate his own personal fortunes with the preservation of the United States. And yet, this, too, is something Presidents have to believe, if only to rationalize what they do through the imperatives of ambition" (309).

We continue to see the rationalization of this process as it occurs in Hudson's mind, a process which enables us to appreciate Drury's perception of the human personality as it evolves through history in the political arena, a process which has very few, if any, ethical absolutes:

There comes a point in this office, he realizes now, where it is literally impossible for the occupant to distinguish any longer between his own interests and the interests of the United States. The White House in time, even for the most determinedly idealistic, gradually obliterates the line between self and service. Presidents after a while—and sometimes a much shorter while than in this case—reach a point where they simply cannot regard themselves objectively any more...

So—pledges are broken. Decisions are reversed. Yesterday's absolute becomes today's maybe and tomorrow's negative. History bends Presidents to its will as it bends other men (309-310).

At the conclusion of *Capable of Honor*, after the President has rebuffed the liberal attempt to strip him of his power and influence by denying him the party's presidential nomination, the President reflects upon recent political events as he returns to Washington on Air Force One. Little does it matter that he has broken his word to the American people and that he is a "grasper of power" since he believes "that he could see a road that led at last, through whatever dark forest, toward some ultimate benefit for the United States. If a man saw somewhere ahead some shining upland where the puzzled, unhappy, beloved republic might rest at last, if history had given him a chance to lead her to it, then he had a right to hold it as the Lord gave him strength to do" (529). After experience in the presidential office Harley Hudson is beginning to believe that "most," and perhaps "all things were justified by this." Ted Jason, the "liberal" candidate, shares a similar political philosophy, and this philosophy will cause his destruction in the fifth novel of this political series, *Come Nineveh, Come Tyre*. The significant difference between the *hubrism* of Harley Hudson and the *hubrism* of "Wonderful Walter" and Ted Jason is that the President possesses wisdom and prudence. President Harley Hudson is a conservative.

Ted Jason, the liberal Governor from California, symbolizes one type of "liberal," significantly different from both Walter Dobius and Senator Fred Van Ackerman, who also become prominent anti-war leaders in Drury's fiction. Ted Jason's family is enormously wealthy: he is intelligent, sophisticated, and handsome. He has attended the finest schools. At root, when he first appears in Drury's fiction, he is an honorable man. Ted Jason enters politics to serve the people of California and his presidential ambitions are noble ones. Although he is undecided about the wisdom of President Hudson's decision to commit American troops to Gorotoland, he begins with honest and sincere misgivings after studying the national and international implications of American involvement in a civil war that is a Communist backed "war of liberation." When Ted Jason decides to challenge President Hudson at the national convention by becoming a candidate for the presidency after he has agreed to compete with the Secretary of State, Orrin Knox, for the vice-presidential office on the party ticket, his change of mind is dictated by thoughts which are very similar to those that we have observed in the mind of the President. During the convention Ted Jason expresses his rationale for his presidential ambitions in a conversation with his campaign manager, Bob Leffingwell: "No man tries for these offices at the top unless he has some conviction that he personally feels that he has a mission to try to put into effect. There has to be—there is in all of us—some inner conviction that *we know best* and that we have simply got to try to do it" (427). As we have observed, President Hudson possesses the same *hubristic* strain; however, Drury's conservative president possesses a sounder grasp of reality, a more penetrating understanding of imperialistic Communism, a more penetrating grasp of the potentialities of human nature, and a keener understanding of the limitations of power than his "liberal" opponent. Unlike Ted Jason, Harley understands that sometimes a man can be powerless to change the course of events, even though he may act with intelligence and courage. Because "liberal" Ted Jason believes that he can shape or control the flow of history and that he can, whenever he chooses, exercise control over his advisors and supporters in his anti-war candidacy, he will bring America to the brink of destruction in *Come Nineveh, Come Tyre*.

As an ambitious politician of the sixties, Ted Jason is extremely sensitive to the power of the media as a communicator and shaper of his image. Although the Jason family is too sophisticated to attempt directly to undermine the integrity of the press, they are sophisticated enough to manipulate America's fourth estate. Not surprisingly, then, Ted Jason and his sister Ceil possess multiple motivations when early in *Capable of Honor* they decide to confer the prestigious Good and Faithful Servant Award on Walter Dobius at the annual Jason award dinner. The Jason's believe that as a result of such flattery "Wonderful Walter" who is already kindly disposed toward Ted Jason, will subtly be pressured to continue supporting the liberal Governor—whatever the Governor's political ambition or whatever the issue. Ironically, both manipulators—Jason and Dobius—will themselves become manipulated and intimidated by radical elements in the anti-war movement. "Wonderful Walter's" acceptance speech at the Jason dinner exploits anti-war sentiments and creates a political ground swell for Jason as an anti-war candidate. The manipulator is manipulated. Jason is pressured to declare himself a vice-presidential candidate while he is still uncertain whether American troops should be involved in Gorotoland.

Indecision, too, is Jason's posture when the press queries him concerning the correct policy after his brother-in-law, Felix Labaiya, has initiated a "Panamanian People's Liberation Movement" to eject American troops from the Canal and to claim Panamanian Canal ownership. Immediately after the Good and Faithful Servant Award dinner, President Hudson invites Governor Jason to the White House in order to have Jason participate in a decision involving American intervention. Sensing the political implications of being associated with a South American intervention, Ted Jason equivocates. The potential presidential candidate searches for middle ground. When the President suggests immediate and direct intervention, Jason responds, "I'm not against you, certainly. Neither am I whole-heartedly for you. There must be middle ground, there always is, in democratic experience" (268). Rather than directly criticize the President's decision to intervene in Panama, Jason shrewdly equivocates with the press. "Sometimes," he tells reporters, "there is a patriotic duty to disagree. Conscience must decide the issue" (269). Despite his equivocation, Jason remains the darling of the press and equivocation becomes the characteristic posture of Jason. While this posture ultimately leads to his presidential nomination and election in *Preserve and Protect* and *Come Nineveh, Come Tyre*, his equivocation at the national convention in *Capable of Honor* causes his wife and Ted Leffingwell, his campaign manager, to leave him.

The decisive factor which propels Ted Jason to become a candidate for the vice-president's office is President Hudson's decision to run for President. Such also is the wily President's intention. With an uncharacteristic streak of nastiness, the President calls "Wonderful Walter" to inform him that the emotional, vigorous, and unfair journalistic attacks upon him and his foreign policy have made it imperative that he test his popularity and the popularity of his foreign policy with the American voters. Consequently, the President informs Walter that not only will he run for re-election but he also is inviting a contest between the Secretary of State and the Governor of California as a forum for an open discussion of foreign policy within the party. Shortly thereafter, a very antagonized Walter informs the equivocating Ted Jason that the energies of many "powerful people" are being directed at his candidacy and that he is a fool if he believes that he will be able to refuse the nomination. Although Governor Jason angrily tells Walter that he will make his own decision about his candidacy and that he is "not taking any more pressure," Walter knows better; the syndicated columnist immediately informs the leaders of COMFORT, DEFY, and KEEP that Ted Jason will be "their" candidate. Later, at the convention, these radical organizations will become instruments of political violence in the Jason campaign for nomination and although Walter will fear for his life and property, he will not repudiate them.

At the convention Walter Dobius acts as a "go-between" to Jason for COMFORT, DEFY and KEEP as they offer "to take over the demonstrations," to furnish "all the supplies, all the financing, all the people" (361). Although the Governor accepts their support, he equivocates in his acceptance. Jason instructs his campaign manager to meet with the "unholy" three organizations and coordinate plans, explaining that this is "politics" and he needs their help; however, his commitment to them is unspecific. "You can tell them," the liberal candidate advises Walter Dobius, the ostensibly impartial television commentator who is actively partisan," that any assistance they deem me worthy to receive I will accept" (362). This arrangement permits Jason to disassociate himself from the violence and political intimidation which will permeate the convention. Because of bias, all convention violence is perceived by the news media as being instigated by Secretary Knox's supporters. Newspapers proclaim "Knox Forces Start Ugly Riot in Union Square" when in fact Jason supporters were the instigators. Soon, through the media, this violence is termed a "Knox Riot," thereby seriously tarnishing the Secretary of State's image with voters. When a disturbed Orrin Knox asks Governor Jason to join with him in repudiating the convention violence, Knox is rebuffed. Since Jason does not know for certain who instigated the violence and since the violence is helping to weaken the Knox reputation as a man of integrity, the "liberal" Governor refuses to commit himself against political violence. After two anti-war demonstrators are killed in a riot and a disciplined, anonymous group chants "Withdraw, Murderer" and "Watch-it" when Knox advocates attempt to make convention speeches, Robert Leffingwell, Jason's press secretary, again asks the Governor to repudiate violence, but to no avail. Instead of repudiating violence, Jason declares: "If the wild-eyed Negroes, the half-assed liberals, and the crazy conservative kooks want to link hands and dance around the May pole, that's their problem, not mine. I think it's great to have their support, if it helps me with this nomination" (426). Later, after Jason has declared himself a presidential, rather than a vice-presidential candidate, he explains to black Congressman Cullee Hamilton, that the ends justify the means. More specifically, one can rationalize anything in politics "In terms of power and in terms of what can be accomplished by what has been done" (462). Even after Crystal Knox, the pregnant daughter-in-law of the Secretary of State, is severely beaten at the convention, Governor Jason equivocates concerning political violence. If the attack "was made by individuals carrying my banners and supporting my causes," he announces at a press conference convened to announce his presidential bid, "I condemn them" (444). Little will the Governor lose in this equivocal repudiation of convention violence, since the press will focus upon his challenge to the Hudson-Knox ticket rather than upon the violence and intimidation which has created a climate conducive to a Jason presidential nomination.

If the major antagonist of *Capable of Honor* is "Wonderful Walter" as a symbol of a biased, "liberal press," the emerging hero of the anatomy and Drury's political fiction is Orrin Knox. For Orrin Knox, "Wonderful Walter," makes the price of honor very steep and painful: on a personal level, Orrin is the designated enemy of "Wonderful Walter," who at an unguarded moment reveals he is "out to get Knox." On a political level they are also in opposite camps which permit no room for compromise: Walter and his liberal companions view Orrin Knox as the architect of American intervention in Gorotoland and Panama, an intervention that they believe is immoral, illegal and unwise. Consequently, Walter feels fully justified in practicing against Orrin Knox the highly sophisticated art of biased reporting that he learned as a young reporter: "the knack of the prejudicial word, the smoothly hostile phrases, the sarcastic jape that substitutes for decency, the bland omission of friendly facts, the deliberate suppression of honors and achievements, the heavy dependency upon unidentified 'informed sources' who believed, or stated, or predicted, or thought unfavorable and unkind things about chosen targets of editorial disapproval" (46).

As we have already indicated, when riots occur at the convention and Crystal Knox is assaulted, Helen-Anne Carew identifies Walter and the press as creators of a climate of violence that significantly contributes to the anguish of the Knox family as Orrin Knox attempts to win the vice-presidential nomination. The violence is central to Drury's political fiction. The "Thing," as Drury designates the evil of violence, is the "monster...that stalked the unhappy twentieth century" (459). Violence it is that drives Orrin Knox to withdraw from his campaign for the vice-presidency and to retire to private life after the media has irresponsibly blamed him for the Communist inspired riots, hecklers have charged "murderer!" at him at the televised convention, and anti-war protesters and Jason supporters have savagely beaten his daughter-in-law. Within the power of the press, Drury seems to be saying, lies the ability to create a climate of violence and to determine candidates for national office, and in doing so, shape the foreign policy of the nation.

Because of the political astuteness and shrewdness of President Hudson (in his political moves he is beginning to resemble his shrewd predecessor), the press is defeated in its attempt to dominate the political process. The President realizes that his Secretary of State is disheartened and that Knox harbors a desire to withdraw from his campaign for the vice-presidency against Governor Jason. With excellent acting, President Hudson reverses the situation before Orrin can announce his retirement from politics: the President solemnly informs the Secretary of State that he is disheartened by the malicious press coverage of the wars in Gorotoland and Panama, as well as their biased and irresponsible reporting of the violence at the convention; the President announces that he is in a state of despair over the current political situation—he is being challenged by Governor Jason, of his own party, for the presidential nomination because the press, much of the nation, and almost fifty percent of the delegates at the national convention repudiate his foreign policy since they believe that it is blatantly imperialistic and immoral. Consequently, President Hudson craftily declares his withdrawal from his bid for the presidential nomination. Not surprisingly, the dedicated, responsible Secretary of State forgets his own problems and his own decision to withdraw as he immediately and patriotically implores the President to continue to campaign. Quickly, as a result of his argument, Orrin realizes that it would be out of character for him, as well as for the President, to withdraw from the battle with the violence that threatens to destroy America and the American political system. Therefore, he courageously acts within his character and accepts the vice-presidential nomination. Orrin Knox, like president Hudson, despite Wonderful Walter's media attacks and the press's allegations, is a man of honor. Wonderful Walter is not.

As in *Advise and Consent* and *A Shade of Difference*, the primary plot in *Capable of Honor*, as well as the sub-plots, is political. The plots pivot upon presidential politics and the formation and implementation of foreign policy: the decision to commit and to continue to commit American ground forces to Gorotoland and Panama in defense of freedom. The major characters are totally political; they are constantly engaged in or preoccupied with exercises of power within the body politic, even the allegedly professionally detached journalist, "Wonderful Walter" Dubius. *Capable of Honor*, then is "pure" and serious political fiction. In its examination, analysis, and depiction of the role of the media in politics, *Capable* is a political anatomy that dissects media abuse, an abuse which transcends ideology. Like *Advise and Consent*, *Capable of Honor* is a classic of its kind.

Chapter VI
Orrin Knox: Conservative Political Hero

E.M. Forster in the *Aspects of Fiction* presents useful terminology for the discussion of political characters in Drury fiction (103-109). Characters, Forster suggests, are either "flat" or "round." Extremely flat characters are one dimensional; "they are constructed around a single idea or quality." In Drury, all of the significant characters are dominated by one quality or temperament: Drury's characters are easily identifiable as either "liberals" or "conservatives." Once authors create characters in fiction who have an additional "factor," Forster suggests, "we get the beginning of the curve towards round." Even though flat characters are one dimensional, many—such as are found in Dickens' novels—are vivid and memorable characters who evoke feelings of depth and take on a life of their own even though they are not significantly changed by circumstances. Dickens, Forster further explains, uses types and caricatures, "yet achieves effects that are not mechanical and a vision of humanity that is not shallow" (109).

On first acquaintance, Orrin Knox, the protagonist in Drury's anatomy, might be perceived as a flat or one dimensional character. A closer examination reveals, however, that Orrin Knox is more than a one dimensional creation. If he is not completely "round" or multi-dimensional, he is at least a two dimensional or semi-round character. Orrin Knox is dynamic rather than static; unlike completely flat characters, Orrin Knox changes or is modified by circumstances.

In addition to being dynamic or changing as contrasted with being static or flat, Forster believes that "the test of a round character is whether it is capable of surprising in a convincing way" (118). If as Forster suggests, birth, food, sleep, love, and death are the main facts of human life (75), in political fiction there is an obvious sixth: politics. Politics, in Drury's fiction, is the informing, organizing, and vital principle of plot and character. It is Drury's comprehensive knowledge of politics, the political process, and political personalities that generates the energy or power in this fiction. And it is convincing and surprising change in the personality of Orrin Knox as his political personality evolves in *Advise and Consent, A Shade of Difference, Capable of Honor, Preserve and Protect,* and *A Promise of Joy* that provides a curve or some roundness to his character. The motivating force in the Knox personality, the roots of his personality, are his conservative beliefs or principles. It is these principles which constitute a tightly linked and hierarchical system of thought that make Orrin Knox an intellectually complex character, even though many readers may disagree with his conclusions about political realities and philosophical truths.[1]

In *The Republican Right Since 1945* David Reinhard cogently demonstrates that there is "no tidy way" to define The Republican Right since there are constant shifts within the conservative spectrum and shifts of ideological identity are sometimes very complex and subtle (viii). Nevertheless, all conservative members who constitute the Right Wing of the Republican Party embrace one belief which significantly influences their political consciousness: "fierce anticommunism" (vii). Though Orrin Knox is a proud conservative who evolves and grows in Drury fiction, he never becomes a member of the Radical or the Far Right. Although Knox is fiercely anticommunist, it would be a serious mistake—and a disservice to Drury fiction—to identify Knox with ultra-conservatives such as those who joined the John Birch Society or the Minutemen. Members of these groups were political extremists: John Welch, the founder of the John Birch Society, wrote and taught that Dwight Eisenhower was "a dedicated and conscious agent of the Communist conspiracy" (Reinhard 174 and Rusher 61); the Minutemen, 2,400 patriots divided into twenty-three guerilla units, prepared to fight a guerilla war on American soil in "the final battle against communism" (Reinhard 174). Rather than associating Knox's anticommunist beliefs with such extremist groups, it is more accurate to associate his views with those groups closer to the center of the conservative spectrum. For example, the principles expressed by The Young Americans for Freedom in the Sharon Statement of 1960 seem more appropriate to Knox's temperament:

> That we will be free only so long as the national sovereignity of the United is secure; that history shows periods of freedom are rare, and can exist only when free citizens concertedly defend their rights against all enemies;
>
> That the forces of international Communism are, at present, the greatest single threat to these liberties;
>
> That American foreign policy must be judged by this criterion: does it serve the just interests of the United States? (Rusher 91)

Such views about freedom, the defense of freedom, and Communism constitute only one segment of Knox's belief or value system.[1] In addition, some beliefs enunciated by Russell Kirk in *The Conservative Mind* provide insight into Knox's intellectual vision, an intellectual vision that is constantly tested in the hard world of the practicing politician and statesman. When Knox is confronted with difficult and sometimes traumatic problems in an imperfect world not of his own making, he is guided by the following beliefs:

A divine intent rules society as well as conscience, forging an eternal chain of right and duty...

Political problems, at bottom, are religious and moral problems.

Affection for the proliferating variety and mystery of the traditional life, as distinguished from the narrowing uniformity and egalitarianism and utilitarian aims of most radical systems.

Conviction that organized society requires order and classes.

Persuasion that property and freedom are inseparably connected.

Faith in prescription and distrust of "sophisters and calculators."

Recognition that change and reform are not identical (7-8).

There can be no doubt that Orrin Knox reflects a responsible conservative vision and that the Knox character sometimes flattens out and functions narrowly as a Drury mouthpiece, a function which is comfortably associated with anatomy. In spite of sometimes functioning as a mouthpiece, Orrin Knox is a vivid, memorable, political character whose thoughts and actions illustrate truisms about the practice of politics and the nature of man: "Politics is the art of the possible." "Politics is the art of compromise." and "Power corrupts, and absolute power corrupts absolutely."

II

Thus far we have examined Orrin Knox as a senator in *Advise and Consent* who becomes Secretary of State after his victorious opposition to the Leffingwell nomination. In *Advise* Orrin Knox is a major character who is faced with a moral and a political conflict: should he soften his opposition to Leffingwell in exchange for an opportunity to become president and to implement his political philosophy. After a painful struggle of conscience, the "tart, tactless," impulsive, and sometimes blunt senator retains his integrity. On the basis of his ability and character, President Hudson appoints Knox his Secretary of State. As Secretary of State in *A Shade of Difference*, Orrin Knox continues his significant role in Drury fiction: he is central to the first scene, and the first scene generates the plot and the central theme of *A Shade of Difference*.

When Orrin Knox enters the United Nations Lounge, he is introduced to "Terrible Terry" (His Royal Highness of Gorotoland), who is seeking independence for Gorotoland from English rule. Without embarrassment, black "Terrible Terry" requests a formal White House dinner and informs the Secretary of State of his plans to attend a Jason Foundation luncheon in Charleston, South Carolina, although his visit may stir the fires of racial unrest in the racially troubled city. Because of anti-American feeling in the emerging third world countries, the Secretary of State is confronted with severe diplomatic challenges when Terry attends the luncheon and initiates an embarrassing racial confrontation. Knox's duties are additionally complicated when Terry announces to the press that he has been invited to the White House for dinner, although no such invitation has been offered. Although Secretary Knox advises the President to accommodate "Terrible Terry," despite his rudeness and despite the affront such an accommodation would be to the British, the President chooses not to bend to Terry's pressure. As a result, four parliamentary resolutions will be generated in *A Shade of Difference* and the Secretary of State will be deeply involved with each of them. The first resolution is favored by the "liberal" press in America and by the Communist and third world nations, but is opposed by the United Kingdom and the United States; it is a recommendation to the United Nations General Assembly "that the United Nations do all in its power to persuade the United Kingdom to grant immediate independence to the territory of Gorotoland." An amendment to this resolution which states that the United Kingdom may not be qualified to continue membership in the United Nations because of its racial discrimination is the second parliamentary resolution and is extremely damaging to American power and prestige. The third parliamentary resolution is a congressional joint resolution initiated by Orrin Knox as "damage control" in response to strong United Nations support for "Terrible Terry" as a result of his politicizing the racial unrest in America in order to strengthen anti-American feeling in that world body. The joint resolution, which is introduced in the House by a black Congressman, expresses "the official apologies of the United States Government to the M'Bula of Mbuele for 'danger and personal humiliation' suffered while escorting a colored child" to school. In addition, the joint resolution authorizes a ten million dollar grant to the African prince for the 'advancement and improvement' of his people and states that "the United States should 'move with increased rapidity to improve the conditions of its Negro population at all levels.' " After this joint resolution is passed, the action shifts to the United Nations where an amendment is added to the original United Nations resolution—the fourth parliamentary resolution—whereby the United States may be censured by a simple majority vote rather than by a two thirds vote of that body.

Although Orrin Knox possesses a subordinate role in *A Shade of Difference*, he continues to be both an evolving and convincing character as he meets the challenge of being Secretary of State. When the Secretary realizes that "Terrible Terry" will cause a loss of power and prestige if he is not invited to the White House, he counsels the President to have a small buffet for the black prince, but to no avail. Knox's initiative for compromise indicates a change in his political style, and the President berates him for suggesting that he give in to "black-mail." The President laments a "lack of starch" in the Secretary's soul. In this instance, the Secretary is more astute than the President. Knox realizes the importance of image and public relations in the United Nations, with the American press, and

with the voters. The Secretary attempts to educate the President in defense
of his advice:

'God knows I'd like to tell the little worm to go to hell,' Orrin said, 'but, you see,
he isn't a little worm in the eyes of his fellow Africans, the press, and the New
York cocktail circuit. Or if he is, they're doing an awfully good job of keeping it
quiet. He floats around this place on a wave of favorable publicity that hasn't been
matched since Castro spoke to the newspaper editors. He's the world symbol of freedom
and liberty at the moment. It doesn't make any difference that he's really the exact
opposite. It's the public image that counts, and I must say the public image is crowned
with laurel and ten feet high (82).'

Such advice is in keeping with Drury's creation of an Orrin Knox who
is capable of growth. It is an Orrin Knox who possesses a keen intelligence
and an ability to perceive duties and relationships from the perspective of
shifting governmental roles. As Secretary of State, he no longer possesses
the power he once wielded in the Senate. As he begins a lobbying effort
on the hill, he reflects upon the change that has occurred in his relationships
because he is no longer a Senator; he is now Secretary of State. In the past

His ties to the Congress were so strong that they were an instinctive, implicit part
of his being; yet here he was in a position where he must deal with it, not as one
of its most powerful and commanding insiders, but as an emissary from the Executive
Branch, forced to rely upon argument and persuasion to secure the support he once
could secure just by being Orrin Knox, with all that meant in power, influence,
and personal authority. Now he was an office, not a man; the Secretary of State.
It separated him from the sources of his power, put up a barrier, silken but distinct,
between his colleagues and himself, forced him to rely upon subtler persuasions and
gentler arguments (231-232).

Even though the power and the style of Orrin Knox has shifted, his positive
vision of America and his vigilant defense of America is maintained. In
this context, the conservative Orrin Knox consistently maintains a them-
us attitude. In *A Shade of Difference* he continues to lament the erosion
of confidence and will in America and the threat that this poses to his country.
The intelligent American college graduates educated after World War II,
he believes, have been taught

to accept the idea of their country as not-quite-best, [and they] labored with a suave
and practiced skill to gloss over the anguish of unnecessary decline. Experienced
in the glib rationalization of failure, the smooth acceptance of defeat, they found
cogent arguments and reasonable explanations for each new default of will on the
part of their government and could always be found hovering at the elbows of those
officials, like himself, who still held firm to some vision of America more fitting
and more worthy than that. There they smoothly offered their on-the-other-hands
and their let's-look-at-it-from-their-point-of-views and their but-of-course-you-must-

realize-the-people-won't-support-its. Meanwhile the Communist tide rolled on, explained and rationalized, possibly, but not stopped (277-278).

As the title *A Shade of Difference* indicates, racial conflict and its national and international political implications are at the core of the novel. Consequently, as Orrin Knox attempts to solve national and international problems, we see him in personal contact with people who are racially different from himself, and this permits Drury to present another aspect of the Knox political personality and character. Good will, sincerity, intelligence, responsibility, patriotism, shrewdness, affection and deep, personal concern are all manifest in Knox's relationship with Cullee Hamilton, a black Congressman from California. Through several brief but convincing scenes, Drury very effectively develops the relationship between the black Congressman and the white Secretary of State. In order to stop the erosion of American prestige in the United Nations, the Secretary of State places the Congressman in an awkward position. He asks him to help the white power structure by introducing the joint resolution in the House which offers an apology to "'Terrible Terry" and financial aid to Gorotoland along with the stated goal of improving the quality of life among blacks in America. Though the resolution is beneficial to the blacks in America and Gorotoland, Congressman Hamilton's help would make him appear as a moderate in a polarized racial conflict and make him appear to some as a "stooge" of Orrin Knox and the white establishment. Because of his association with the white establishment, Cullee will lose his wife and his best friend; and because of their influence, the Congressman feels compelled to ask: "Can I trust you...you're white," as he confronts Knox with the fact that blacks will see his help as a self-interested bid by a black politician in order to court the white votes necessary if he is ever to become a Senator. Orrin Knox responds directly, but he places the decision upon the shoulders of the black Congressman: "...do you know what they're going to say about me? That I'm just trying to get black votes for President, aren't they? So what do we do about it, you and I, sit around crying because they call us names and don't understand us, or go ahead and do what we know is right? You tell me. You tell me. We start equal with our own people, Cullee, so you tell me what you'd like us to do, I'll follow your advice, and that's a promise" (233-234). Although Hamilton agrees to introduce the resolution, pressures become so intense that Knox, "in a direct and unadorned approach" presents him with an opportunity to withdraw graciously. To counter Hamilton's fears that he may be being used by the white Secretary, Knox shrewdly articulates the Congressman's unverbalized accusation: "I have ambitions too, you know....Maybe I'm just using you for all your're worth. Maybe my only motive is to line up the colored vote to help us in the nomination. You'd be a powerful asset if I had you on my side. Of course you know that. Better think about it carefully.... I may be a bad and evil white man, out to use you all I can" (296). Again, the somewhat hesitant Congressman is persuaded by Knox's blunt but sophisticated appeal. To firm up the commitment, Knox offers a final note of concern and trust in his characteristically direct style: "Promise me one thing,...if you begin to doubt later on—if you feel you can't trust me, or the pressure gets too great from your own people or mine—don't hesitate, I'd rather have you out of it altogether than dragging along reluctantly. Then I couldn't trust you, and right now I do implicitly" (297).

Although momentarily reassuring, this telephone conversation does not completely relieve Hamilton's apprehension about the motivation and commitment of Orrin Knox. Consequently, after the Hamilton Resolution has passed the House and is being debated in the Senate, the Secretary is faced with an enormous task when he asks Hamilton to modify the wording of the resolution in order to enable Senator Cooley—the South Carolina Senator who has a racist reputation among blacks—to lose with dignity and maintain a public record which may help him if he wishes to run for reelection. Hamilton reacts bitterly to the suggested rewording of a sentence in the last paragraph, accusing Knox of doing what his extremist friends had warned him Knox would do, use him for his presidential ambitions: "You're afraid the resolution will offend too many people in the South, and that will hurt your chances for the nomination, and that's why you want me to water it down. That's what they told me and I said it wasn't so. I said I believed in Orrin Knox. My God! What a laugh!" (423) A maturing Orrin Knox suppresses his anger and patiently presses his case, explaining his motivation and political philosophy to the angry Congressman: "Sentiment. I guess. Loyalty to an old friend. A foolish belief that things are best accomplished in this mixed-up land of ours when they are accomplished with the broadest general agreement and the least individual hurt. Some feeling that you might be able to understand; apparently mistaken" (425-426). Slowly, Hamilton does begin to understand; the Congressman suggests yet another alternative wording, providing that Senator Cooley will come to him and personally request the change. Again, Orrin Knox has demonstrated his considerable powers of persuasion in the most difficult of circumstances.

As it happens, Seab Cooley is unbending; he does not consent to those changes necessary for his personal and political welfare. Instead, he filibusters in the Senate, becomes overtired, and dies of a heart attack. When Orrin laments the death of his long time friend and frequent political ally in the Senate in a conversation with the President, Orrin wonders aloud whether he has been a good Secretary of State, whether he has given good counsel, or whether he has become a "trimmer." The President assures him that he is pleased with his work and that he has maintained his principles, he has not become a "trimmer." The President, and the reader, have observed Orrin Knox evolve and grow in the challenging position of Secretary of State. He will continue to grow in *Capable of Honor*. He will also suffer.

III

We have examined the development of Orrin Knox in *Advise and Consent* and in *A Shade of Difference*, and we have briefly observed his role in *Capable of Honor* as a politician whose political career is dramatically affected by a biased and antagonistic press. Now let us more closely examine Orrin in the context of *Capable of Honor*. Although there is no book titled "Orrin Knox's Book" or "The Secretary's Book," the last book of *Capable* could comfortably be titled a Knox book because Orrin Knox is designated a "man of honor" by President Hudson when the President nominates Orrin to be his vice-presidential running mate at the nominating convention. The President "will accept no other"—but only after Orrin has suffered severe personal and political trauma. In *Advise and Consent* Drury creates an Orrin Knox who possesses an almost obsessive ambition to become president, an Orrin Knox whose ego declares that he would be a dynamic and effective leader of America. In *A Shade of Difference*, as we have seen, Orrin continues his life-time patriotic service to his country, not as a Senator, but as Secretary of State. During his tenure as Secretary of State, Orrin prepares himself for the moment when he can once again declare himself a presidential candidate. This political tension, Knox awaiting the optimal moment to declare himself as a presidential candidate, is sustained in *Capable of Honor* and provides the momentum for one of the climactic scenes in *Capable*.

As we have already observed, Walter Dobius and the press are the antagonists in *Capable*, and "Wonderful Walter" is a vehement opponent of Knox because of his successful attempt to defeat the Leffingwell nomination in *Advise and Consent* and because of his conduct of foreign policy during "Terrible Terry's" visit in *A Shade of Difference*. Because of "Wonderful Walter's" low opinion of Knox, Walter believes that any action—even printed lies and slander—that will impede Knox's presidential ambitions is ethical or morally justified for the greater good of the country. Despite their deeply rooted mutual antipathy, "Wonderful Walter" invites Orrin to a luncheon for the ostensible purpose of learning Orrin's views so that Walter can make an "objective" decision to support either Orrin's or Ted Jason's presidential bid. During the ensuing meeting, which includes—unbeknownst to Orrin and Beth, who do not expect other guests—Ted and Ceil Jason, Bob Leffingwell, and Helen-Anne Carew, Walter and Orrin bluntly, frankly and emotionally exchange views which are in harmony with the personalities that Drury has created in his fiction. Orrin is blunt, forthright, and aggressive, as one would expect him to be when faced with someone who attacks his foreign policy as "blood thirsty insanity" and who expresses the hope that he be "driven forever from public life." But *Capable* also reveals an evolving Orrin Knox who matures within the context of family, political ambitions, disappointment, and tragedy.

Central to Orrin Knox's presidential ambitions is the foreign policy decision to commit American troops to Gorotoland. However, even before the American intervention in Gorotoland—an intervention that will become the most significant public and political factor, as opposed to personal ambition and the fascination of power, in persuading Harley Hudson to become a presidential candidate—Orrin Knox is evaluating his opportunity to become president in an attempt to determine the optimal moment to declare his candidacy for president. As *Capable* begins, Orrin is politically frustrated. Harley Hudson has promised the American people that he will not seek another term as president, yet he has wavered in making a Shermanesque statement (If nominated I will not run, if elected I will not serve) concerning his availability. Consequently, since Orrin is Harley's Secretary of State, he is in an awkward position to declare as a candidate because this would promote divisiveness within the Administration and negatively affect the implementation of foreign policy. On the other hand, Ted Jason, the liberal opponent within the Hudson-Knox political party and a potential anti-war candidate, has no such obstacles in declaring a candidacy and thereby obtaining a political advantage by becoming an early candidate. Predictably, early in *Capable* Orrin and the President discuss their reciprocal political dilemma, and a loyal, patriotic Orrin Knox frankly discusses his political ambition with the President. During their discussion the President challenges him by asking: do you think you are capable of being a good President? This, after Orrin has jokingly observed that since Harley has doubts about whether he will be a candidate, he will resolve those doubts in his favor by becoming a candidate since "Power corrupts— and absolute power is absolutely delightful" (61). Moments later the President soberly observes that his power is far from absolute because his knowledge is limited and the job of being President is too large for any one individual. As in the real political world, Presidents in political fiction do not possess total power or control over people and events:

Who can possibly have all the facts in a world as complex as this? Our society believes that the President has, because for the sake of its own sanity it has to believe it. But I don't know—no mortal man can know, of his own knowledge—all facts on which a President acts. The thing is too big. I can't tell you—of my own knowledge— that if I push that button, so many ICBM's will blast off for Russia or China or Indonesia. All I know is that somebody below has told me so—and somebody in turn has told him—and he in turn has gotten it from somebody else. I act in the faith that I have been given a true account. The country follows me because it believes I know. But I don't know. What single individual could? (62)

Despite the President's depiction of the perils of office, Orrin maintains his confidence, "I think I am big enough," Orrin slowly responds, and then later, the Secretary of State adds: "Do you doubt it?" The President's response is as honest as Orrin Knox's would be in the same situation: "I don't doubt your courage, Orrin," he said finally. "The public record is full of that for the past twenty years. It goes deeper than courage. It goes to—acceptance, I think you might call it—of what this job is, and what it does to you, and what it can do to the country and to all of humankind. You can talk about it. But can you do it?" (63) Orrin's political intuitions tell him that the President really wants to stay in office-that the President believes that the current President is the best man for the job and owes a duty to the country to seek another term—so Orrin advises him: "Stay." Since Orrin is an ambitious politician who also believes that Orrin Knox as President would be good for the country, and probably a better President than Harley Hudson, and since one can never foretell with certainty political events and the enduring success of political careers, Orrin will declare also as a candidate. This political decision is made prior to his discussion with the President; as best he can, Orrin Knox will control his own future.

Although Orrin makes this personal and political decision early in *Capable*, he does not mount a public campaign as a candidate, he does not "hit the political trail" as Beth so aptly puts it. Instead, he is preoccupied with his duties as Secretary of State: he requests and encourages support for the administration's Gorotoland policy in the form of Senate and Congressional resolutions and he masterminds the defense of the Gorotoland policy in the United Nations while he waits for the President to declare his candidacy. Because of political realities, as well as for the welfare of the country, he would not be a candidate once—or if—the President decides to run. And the President makes such a decision, because, as he tells Orrin Knox in a memorable and vivid scene, the country is divided and he feels compelled—for the good of the country—to defend the record. In this meeting, the largeness of the Knox character—the generosity, the complexity—is demonstrated; correlatively, the growth indigenous to this demonstration of character is intensely painful. Readers have closely observed Knox's obsession for service in the form of the presidential office through *Advise and Consent* and *A Shade of Difference* and now, to Orrin Knox, that dream is shattered in the twilight—if not the evening—of his political career.

This emotional Hudson-Knox scene is especially effective because we sympathize with both the President and the Secretary of State: we wish that *both* of their ambitions could be realized, but we know, as they know, that their ambitions are contradictory and thus are mutually exclusive. The hurt is more because they are friends; they share experience, service, affection, respect, and admiration. In anticipating their meeting, the President recalls the multi-faceted career and complex character of Orrin, his friend. Orrin, he knows, is "idealistic, practical, sentimental, tough, iron-firm on issues, sometimes too soft on people, predictable one minute, unpredictable the next; the great ambition, the great ability to accept ambition's denial—a many-sided man, not entirely understood by his President, who is now about to seek understanding from him." The President trusts that the meeting will go well, for "Orrin is always, in the long run, a logical man.... Surely Orrin the loyal and forgiving servant will be the loyal and forgiving servant again" (284-285).

When they meet in the presidential office, the President immediately informs Orrin that the conversation will not be easy for the President—because Harley is going against his promise not to run for president, and he hopes—asks—Orrin "to help with it" (303). During this emotional scene, Orrin maintains control over his emotions, but his control is precarious as Harley informs him that he will run for the presidency and asks Orrin, for the good of the country, to compete for the vice-presidential nomination, so that there can be an open debate between Orrin and Ted Jason as an emotional safety-valve for the country. As the conversation nears to a close, the President suggests that there still may be time, during another presidential campaign, for Orrin to succeed in his presidential ambitions. True to his character, Orrin accepts the President's suggestion that he run for the vice-presidency even though the President will not support his Secretary of State's bid for the nomination. Only when the President says "Orrin, my friend: thank you and good luck," does Orrin lose the tight grip on his emotions. "Thank you," Orrin responds, and turns away hastily to conceal his emotion from the President (306).

Later, after dinner, the emotional impact takes hold after he and Beth watch the President's speech.

It was only now when Beth snapped off the set to leave a sudden terrifying silence in the room that the event and its full implications came rushing upon him in such a fierce attack that he thought for a moment his being might not be able to stand it. Everything up to the moment had gone so well and so fast that he really had not had time to think about it very deeply. Now nothing stood between him and that abyss from which men's hopes, once toppled, rarely re-emerge (306-307).

Despite Beth's consolation, love, and support, Orrin is extremely despondent. Orrin believes that "my somedays are running out," and that since he is in his late fifties and since this is "the third time around the track," he will never bloom again as a presidential candidate (307). He has doubts also about his ability to defeat Ted Jason in their competition for the vice-presidency because Walter Dobius and the press "have created such a mood in the country that a candidate upholding the Administration's policy cannot win," especially since the anti-war candidate, Ted Jason, is "riding the popular wave" (308). Wistfully, a very emotionally torn Orrin Knox lets

go of his hope when he tells Beth "it would have been nice—to be President."
Poignantly, the scene ends as Beth continues to console her husband of
wounded ambitions: " 'Oh, my dear,' she said softly, taking his hand again
in hers and turning her head to the fire so that he would not see the tears
in her eyes,   'one can't tell of these things. If it's meant to be, it still
will be. If it doesn't happen, then we'll just have to conclude that we were
the only ones who meant it to be—not someone else...' " (308-309). This
powerful, emotional scene is both surprising and convincing. We had felt—
on the basis of the Knox character and his conversation with the President—
that the highly disciplined and emotionally tough Orrin had passed the
point of deep, emotional suffering. This is what sympathetic readers had
hoped; but such was not to be. In retrospect, Orrin's passionate, emotional
response is very understandable. We thought, on the basis of the Knox
personality developed over *Advise and Consent* and *A Shade of Difference*,
that Orrin possessed a stronger, tougher personality. Instead, Drury shows
us rather than tells us that Orrin suffers deep disappointments on the personal
and professional level the same as you and I, the same as every man or
woman would.

Such experiences, traumatic as they may be, contribute to the maturity
of the Secretary of State. His intense disappointment at not being a viable
presidential candidate pales in comparison with the heartbreak which is
destined to follow. Since Orrin as Secretary of State has the responsibility
of explaining, implementing, and defending foreign policy, he is an obvious
target for the anti-Gorotoland segment of his political party who actively
and emotionally oppose American intervention in Gorotoland. At the
convention, the media misrepresents the Hudson-Knox foreign policy and
actions in their militant opposition to Orrin's candidacy for the vice-
presidency. When violence occurs at the convention, the violence is
erroneously identified as a "Knox Riot" in newspaper headlines and is
reported as such on television. When two Jason supporters are killed in
the convention violence, the blame is placed directly upon the shoulders
of Orrin Knox, and pro-Jason anti-Gorotoland supporters chant "murderer,"
"Withdraw Murderer" on the convention floor. The most devastating blow
to Orrin's psyche occurs not directly as an assault against Orrin Knox, but
rather as an assault against his daughter-in-law Crystal who suffers a
miscarriage after being beaten by a pro-Jason mob at the convention. Unable
to cope with this trauma, the hatred and violence directed at him through
a surrogate, his daughter-in-law, Orrin is hospitalized and given Seconal.
Despair permeates the soul of Orrin Knox when he awakens.

Unfairly, Orrin accepts blame for Crystal's miscarriage, perceiving this
as a "deserving punishment from the Lord" for his inability to cope with
his political ambitions in a world of violence. In the hospital Orrin Knox
broods upon the spirit of the age:

Now he was contending against something alien, the monster of violence that stalked the unhappy twentieth century: an evil grown great, come to visible life, rampant and voracious in a land that perhaps had been lucky too long in escaping it, and now must be made to pay the price by the jealous Furies.

How could he fight that? He could condemn it, as he had—he could order his people to refrain from it, as he had—but it came nonetheless. Good intentions and decent behavior were not enough when the citizenry were not unanimous in their rejection of it. The Thing only needed a few friends to open the gate and let it in, unless everyone stood firm it entered. And where it entered, the world tore open and society collapsed.

It has entered in Union Square, it has entered in blankly hostile faces at the Cow Palace—it has entered, at the start, in savage columns and hysterical editorials and slanted headlines and one-sided photographs—it has entered in suavely supercilious and blandly ruthless rearrangements of the facts in commentaries and roundups and special programs and news reports (459).

Although Orrin was able to withstand the personal attacks against himself, he lacks the emotional stamina to withstand the suffering inflicted upon his family. Consequently, because of his own misplaced sense of guilt for what has happened, he voluntarily decides to abandon his political ambition. He decides to withdraw his candidacy for the vice-presidency.

This resolve is not sustained, however, because of the persuasive powers of the wily Harley Hudson who informs Orrin that he—the President— is withdrawing from public life because of the violence and the President's inability to cope with the nation's problems. Not surprisingly, Orrin Knox becomes revitalized as he responds to the President's decision, and the Secretary of State articulates the reasons why the President should not withdraw from the political arena. As we noted earlier, illumination strikes Orrin during his attempt to persuade the President: Orrin should remain in the political arena for the same reasons that the President should.

In "The Roots of Honor" John Ruskin identifies five great intellectual professions relating to daily necessities of life. Ruskin writes about these professions and their responsibilities. In connection with the daily necessities of life, the soldier, the physician, the pastor, the lawyer and the merchant have specific responsibilities that must be met if civilization is to continue. The soldier must "defend" the nation, the physician must keep "it in health," the pastor must "teach it," the lawyer must "enforce justice" on it, and the merchant must "provide" for it. When the occasion demands, Ruskin points out, four professions may be required to make the ultimate sacrifice, to die for their profession:

The Soldier, rather than leave his post in battle.
The Physician, rather than leave his post in plague.
The Pastor, rather than teach falsehood.

The Lawyer, rather than countenance Injustice.

For the merchant, physical death is not professionally required, but in time of dire economic necessity, the loss of profit and the loss of wealth is (39-40).

The political profession in the context of statesmanship and government is also a great, intellectual profession—or is capable of being so in a man of intelligence and honor. And just as the soldier, the pastor, the physician, and the lawyer have the duty, in most extreme instances, to offer their lives in the exercise of their duty, so also, in extreme instances, does the politician who is elected to office and who identifies himself as a statesman. In *Capable of Honor* bomb-threats are levelled at the Knox family, Crystal Knox is assaulted and suffers a miscarriage, and Orrin Knox is confronted with the question, why campaign for Vice-President in the presence of such volatile hatred? Honor and duty is the response. In order for democracy to work, the most capable people within a society must participate in the electoral process, and when such people have the ability to serve their country successfully in high office, there is an additional imperative to duty, despite the personal risk and sacrifice such a candidacy would entail, even if the nomination may be lost. Only in this way will citizens be presented with viable choices; otherwise the political process becomes, or will become, weakened and perhaps corrupted. Within this context—a sense of duty despite risk and personal sacrifice—Orrin Knox continues to be a candidate for Vice-President even though he knows that the President may reject his Secretary of State as a political liability sometime in the not too distant future. Nevertheless, the President expediently albeit honorably nominates Orrin for Vice-President, and in doing so he labels him as a man of honor. "I do know a man of honor" the President announces to the convention:

He has served his country and his party without stain or blemish for twenty years.

He has occupied high position in his state, in the Senate, in the Cabinet.

He has fought hard and valiantly and with great courage all his life for what he believes in.

He has made enemies, but they have been enemies honestly made, in battles honestly fought.

He has not been devious.

He has not been cynical.

He has not been cruel.

He has not been weak.

He is as convinced as I am that only with unflinching firmness and the willingness to accept, and act immediately upon our international obligations, can this nation, and the free world that depends upon her, survive.

He is direct, forthright, courageous—and honorable.

Like him or dislike him, take him or leave him, there he stands—a man, in all senses.

A man, the President concluded quietly, I believe the country needs—I believe the world needs.

I know I need him.

I nominate for the office of Vice-President of the United States, he said, so quietly and calmly that they hardly realized he was doing it until it was over, a great and *honorable* American, Orrin Knox of the State of Illinois (508-509).

In his acceptance speech, Orrin Knox also speaks of honor. To the Secretary of State, honor and conscience are not the things—the decisions themselves—these are destined or fated. Honor is rather, he tells his audience, "only the way you do things. The things themselves are what history has placed upon us. Conscience and honor are only the style in which we meet them. They do not permit us to escape from them, or to pretend that they are not there. Conscience does not decide the issue: the issue has long been decided. It is only how we meet it that matters. It is only from courage and integrity, our fortitude and grace, that honor springs and conscience is upheld" (516-517). Knox has learned through his painful political experiences that hard choices must be made for the good of, indeed for the survival of, the country and that sometimes great personal sacrifices must be made because of the noble ideal of honor. To choose not to follow the dictates of professional and patriotic conscience, for Orrin Knox, would be to choose to live dishonestly, and such a choice would disintegrate and shatter his personality, shaping for him a life devoid of joy and peace of mind. In a sobering discussion at the conclusion of *Capable of Honor*, Orrin and the President discuss the threat of political assassination. Both realize that they are vulnerable, as the President recalls Calvin Coolidge's remark: "Any well-dressed man who wants to give his own life can kill the President." Orrin's response blends a realistic, sobering, and anti-romantic note to the conclusion of *Capable of Honor*.

What I regret about it is not the danger to you or to me—or to Ted, say, if somebody on our side gets unbalanced enough to go after him—but the fact that all Americans can get in such a state of mind about each other at all. That we could have the really terrifying things that have occurred at this convention. That out of this seemingly decent land could come such monstrous subversions of decency. The rational people—leave aside the kooks and the oddballs, the *rational* people— who begin with reasoned argument can end with the sort of ghastly sincerity that could produce death for their opponents.... You expect it in other countries, but somehow it always surprises you here, even though the record certainly has its examples.... It's still hard to believe (527).

IV

Honor, Orrin Knox has told the convention audience, springs from integrity, courage, fortitude, and grace. For most people, crises of honor do not generally occur when one is faced with a clear, coherent decision involving choices between what is obviously "good" and obviously "evil." Crisis of conscience occur, rather, when the identify of the "good" is not completely visible and the identify of the "evil" is somewhat obscured. Additionally, problematic decisions also occur when one is confronted with a choice between that which is good and that which is perhaps more "good" or slightly better. Even more crucial in decisions of conscience, however, are those choices which are forced upon us by circumstances whereby we are forced to make a decision based not upon a dichotomy of good and evil, the less good and the greater good, but rather the choice between that which is less evil and more evil. Such are the most painful choices placed upon man's conscience, because there can be no positive emotional experience when man is confronted with pain and suffering in those instances where one can be viewed as the direct—although unwilling—cause of the pain and suffering viewed as an evil. Painful, then, is the choice that Orrin makes to continue in the political arena as a vice-presidential candidate: for "the greater good" of the body politic, his family must suffer physically and emotionally. This political decision has a significant impact upon the Knox family unit; and Orrin Knox, in addition to being a politician, is also a husband, a father, and in *Capable of Honor*, he is but two months shy of becoming a grandfather. When Crystal Knox suffers her miscarriage—the "thumper" in her womb is a boy of seven months growth. Thus Orrin's emotional bond with Beth, Hal, and Crystal adds another dimension to his personality which enables readers to empathize with his painful family experiences in *Capable*. Politicians, too, must balance goals, time and energy, and responsibilities within the context of God, country, family, and self—whatever the hierarchy of their values.

For Orrin Knox, love of country—the ideal of service to the largest communal unit—is more demanding than love of family. A politician-statesman with Orrin's ability serves the family that he loves by providing stability and vision to the country through engaging in the political process and government service. This is not to negate, but rather to complement, the fact that Orrin Knox has a political personality: he can best fulfill his potential as a human being by active service in the body politic. Significantly, the Knox family unit shares in his political career and actively participates with him in his life of service to the body politic, thereby "rounding" his personality.

In *Advise and Consent* Drury creates a Beth Knox whose love for Orrin enables her to subordinate her life to his political career. Beth not only is his most intimate—and many times most intelligent and politically sophisticated—adviser, but also she is the political confidante who most influences his most critical political decisions. She is also his partner during his political campaigns. However, despite her political role as an adviser, confidante, and campaigner, Drury never permits us to lose sight of Beth as the loving wife of Orrin Knox—his security blanket in times of emotional and political crisis. Nevertheless, we see less of Beth as mother, than we do of Orrin as father. Early in *Advise and Consent* we learn that Hal Knox will be married shortly to Crystal Danta, the daughter of Stanley Danta, Senator from Connecticut. Through short dramatic pieces sparingly woven into the plot of *Advise and Consent*, Drury presents patches of dialogue between Orrin and Hal which enable readers to sense a strong, warm, emotional bond between father and son. Before Hal's wedding to Crystal, one such intimate conversation is presented; this conversation is paralleled with an even more poignant one between Crystal and her widowed father. Both short, dramatic scenes create familiar familial bonds with readers and Drury's techniques of interspersing short, domestic scenes within the main plot lines is effectively continued in *Capable of Honor* and contributes to our image of Orrin Knox as a loving and loved father of an expanding family.

In *Advise* Orrin seeks Beth's advice and loving, sympathetic companionship when he is confronted with the opportunity to receive the President's support for his presidential campaign in exchange for withdrawing opposition to the Leffingwell nomination; in *Capable*, as we have seen, Beth similarly serves when he is disappointed in the President's ambivalence about his presidential ambitions. Beth's response is unambiguous: "When do we hit the road?" (69). When the President informs Orrin that he will seek election, Beth is again a loving, sympathetic, counseling helpmate. Not surprisingly, once Hal is established in the legal profession he also becomes a member of the familial political council. While seriously considering becoming a candidate for the State Legislature of Illinois, he attends the nominating convention to help his father campaign for the vice-presidential nomination. Beth, Hal, Crystal, and Stanley Danta all offer political advice at the convention and Hal's blunt advice sometimes takes on ironic, comic overtones. The son is much like his father in temperament and values, but he lacks his father's maturing experience. Hal advises his father to be much more aggressive in confronting the slanting tactics of the press and the ambivalence of his supporters. For this, Orrin dubs his son, "Hotspur;" however, the Secretary of State continues to solicit his advice and continues to have him perform as his surrogate in determining the pulse of the convention delegates. When the newspapers label the violence at the convention a "Knox riot" and Hal, Stanley, Beth, and Crystal advise Orrin to defend himself, Hal characterizes Ted Jason with language that corresponds to the intensity of his emotions: "That twisting son of a bitch...that slimy, shifting, two-faced son of a bitch" (390). As the violence becomes more threatening, Hal accurately senses the spirit of the age. He warns his pregnant wife to be careful. Lamenting the hypocrisy which seems to be necessary to succeed in politics, Hal suggests to Crystal that he will reject politics as a profession. Just as her mother-in-law did, Crystal offers excellent advice to her husband, advice which contains the rationale for the Knox family's participation in politics:

> But you don't want to get out of it, she said quietly. And you don't really want him to. Because, now, suppose: suppose all the people like the Knoxes and the Dantas and the rest of us did get driven out by the hypocrites. What kind of world would it be if we all stopped fighting—if we all stopped insisting on what the truth is, even when they shout us down and write us down—if we all gave up because it's just too hard to fight and we're too tired and disheartened and too occupied with other things? That's what they're counting on. But what kind of world would that leave for—and she gave herself an impatient pat on the stomach—him—or her—or—more lightly—whoever you are, in there? (397).

When "thumper" is stillborn, Hal also undergoes trauma, and this trauma will evolve into a central theme and climactic moment in *Preserve and Protect*, the fourth book in Drury's political series. *In Preserve*, as with the previous books, Orrin's intimate relationship with his wife, his son, and the daughter-in-law continues to contribute to his "roundness" of character.

Chapter VII
"Pure" Political Fiction as
Anatomy and Romance: *Preserve and Protect*

Before commenting upon *Preserve and Protect* and the role of Orrin Knox in this fourth book of the political series, let us remember for a moment *Advise and Consent, A Shade of Difference*, and *Capable of Honor* as we have viewed them within the context of Frye's *Anatomy of Criticism* and his "four forms of fiction,"*Advise and Consent*, we have suggested, is essentially a novel: real characters presented in the real world; *A Shade of Difference* is primarily romance and anatomy: idealized characters whose heroism and success threaten the bounds of credibility, partly because they also function as mouthpieces or vehicles for the promulgation of Drury's views concerning the state of the nation and the effect of "liberals" and "conservatives" in formulating America's character. *Capable of Honor* is primarily an anatomy which continues Drury's dissection of the body politic and the state of the union when America is confronted with Communist imperialism in the form of a "war of liberation" in a third world country. Although *Capable of Honor* is primarily an anatomy with a persuasive satirical thrust at the "liberal" temperament, *Capable of Honor*, like *Advise and Consent* which also possesses characteristics of the anatomy, presents real people in a real world; that is, readers can easily identify with the political and journalistic protagonists because of the history of the sixties.

Preserve and Protect functions as a culminating, connecting, and transitional book in Drury's political series and, as we have indicated, when this series is viewed as an aesthetic whole, it is primarily an anatomy: a dissection of the body politic and a report of the political and moral health of America constructed in the form of fiction. *Preserve and Protect*, because it continues the ideological struggle between those who tend to be more tolerant of Soviet intentions and those who tend to be firm is primarily an anatomy which sets the scene for *The Promise of Joy* when Orrin Knox survives an assassination attempt, becomes President, and is able to implement his conservative philosophy from the Oval Office.

Preserve and Protect—a title which indicates the conservative thrust of the text—is divided into three books. "The Speaker's Book" continues the character of Bill Abbott, the Speaker of the House, and presents the high point of his political career: he becomes President after President Hudson is killed in the crash of Air Force One. The second book—"Bob Leffingwell's Book—continues the evolution of Leffingwell's philosophical and

142

temperamental transition from liberal to conservative, a transition which Drury artfully began to develop in *Capable of Honor*. The third book, titled "Preserve and Protect," like the final book in *Capable of Honor*, might also be aptly titled Orrin Knox's book, since Orrin Knox finally achieves his political ambition: he receives his party's nomination for President. Although *Preserve and Protect* is a very readable book, the pace becomes flawed because of the repetition of nomination speeches at the Special Committee meeting to nominate a presidential candidate, the tedious debate over adding an amendment to an amendment, and formal arguments before the Supreme Court generated by a petition which requests that the Court declare the Special Committee process void in its nomination proceedings because of the necessity of convening a national convention in order to determine the party's presidential nominee. In the "real" political world, tedious attention to parliamentary debates and detail is absolutely essential for the health of the body politic; in political fiction, as we have suggested in our discussion of *A Shade of Difference*, it tends to be boring. Within this context, all too frequently Drury's art, when he presents the parliamentary process in the United Nations, the Senate, Congress, the nominating conventions, and the Special Committee, is an imitation of life, an imitation which loses its capacity to entertain in proportion to its frequency and quantity. Be this as it may, *Preserve and Protect* entertained many readers: it was a best seller for twenty-eight weeks (September, 1968-April, 1969).

Within the context of an anatomy, Bill Abbott, the Speaker of the House who becomes a "Caretaker President," is what one might expect on the basis of his previous appearances in Drury fiction: he is a one-dimensional character (the flattest of Drury's major characters), who functions as a mouthpiece for one of Drury's significant themes: the violence which permeates the sixties, a violence which is generated or tolerated by "professional liberals," is intrinsically evil and possesses the capacity to destroy American politics and institutions, as well as America itself. Although President Abbott knows that violence begets violence, the former Speaker of the House, who becomes President after President Hudson is killed in the crash of Air Force One, also realizes—paradoxically—that sometimes, if America is to survive, violence must be met with violence because the appetite for aggression, once awakened, has the potential to be insatiable. Consequently, President Abbott successfully unleashes additional American military power in Gorotoland (in the jargon of the Vietnam War, "a protective reaction strike"), when American intelligence discovers that the Communist "Liberation Army" plans a major offensive against American troops, and he also threatens to blockade the Panama Canal as a means of weakening Communist supplied and instigated Panamanian forces who are attempting to drive American forces from the Canal Zone in order to declare the Canal a Panamanian possession. Within America, there is violent opposition—

mass demonstrations and riots—to this logical extension of the Hudson-Knox policy of responding with firmness and courage to Communist acts of aggression. President Abbott's response to the protest against his foreign policy is predictable. In order to protect the party's National Committee when it convenes to nominate a presidential candidate to replace President Hudson on the party ticket, President Abbott, as Commander-in-Chief, orders American troops to Washington and issues "shoot to kill orders"[1] if necessary in order to protect the members of the National Committee and the democratic process which provides that Committee with the authority to either reconvene the National Convention or to select the presidential and vice-presidential candidates according to the majority wish of the Committee. To prevent anarchy which becomes more and more threatening as a result of protests against American foreign policy, the "Caretaker President" sends to Congress an Anti-Riot Bill (A Bill to Further Curb Acts against Public Order and Welfare) which prohibits the gathering of two or more people "if there is obvious intent to cause civil disturbance or riot."[2] The President's Bill is overwritten and overstates the needs of the country since the President believes that in the normal political and legislative process the House and the Senate will amend the original Bill so that it does not contain any constitutional violations. He is mistaken.

Although the President is perceptive in his understanding of the dangers which threaten to undermine the political process and the foundation of foreign policy, he demonstrates a lack of judgment and prudence in his drafting and sponsoring of the Anti-Riot Bill. Such judgmental flaws generate vitality in Drury fiction, for they serve as vehicles which remind us that everyone has a flawed political vision from time to time because the realities of the political process, the body politic, the constitutional bodies, and human nature are extremely complex and always in a state of flux, a flux which can dramatically alter direction as a result of several, simultaneous causes or as a result of one final stroke of fate beyond the control of the suffering participants within the body politic. Drury suggests that it is in the nature of reality that what would have happened if action were or were not taken can never be known for certain because of the chain reaction of events in the real world.

To shape, to control, to influence the spirit of the age or the temper of the times are motivating factors which suggest to President Abbott the necessity of anti-riot legislation. Violence, mindless violence, threatens to destroy America which is being contaminated by "a sick atmosphere, a savage atmosphere" and which suggests to citizens "that anything, no matter how extreme might happen" (189). The "sick atmosphere" reflects a conflict with religious significance: the conflict between conservatives and "professional liberals" who are identified with "the New Left" is for "The soul of America—that is the prize. Whoever captures that captures the fulcrum with which to move the world" (326). President Abbott can be serenely confident in his order to American troops to shoot American citizens, if necessary (238), because he identifies Ted Jason with Lucifer. His "liberal" opponent, championed by the "liberal" media, suggests to the President "Lucifer incarnate," and the contest for the presidential nomination between Orrin Knox, the conservative, and Ted Jason, the "liberal," is perceived "as though it were some medieval battle between absolute good and absolute evil" (190). Again and again, through the character of Ted Jason, the sterotyped political equivocator, and the agents of violence who champion the "liberal cause," there are echoes of William Yeats' "The Second Coming" which prophesizes the disintegration of Christianity in a world where "The best lack all conviction" and "the worst are full of passionate intensity." In Drury fiction, as in President Reagan's rhetoric, we are on the brink of an apocalypse; therefore, right decisions *must* be made *now* or there will be no future for the United States or mankind in this world.

President Abbott is one of the many "conservatives" in Drury political fiction—President Hudson, Orrin Knox, Seab Cooley, Bob Munson, Brigham Anderson, Cullee Hamilton are others—who firmly believe in God and who are totally convinced that Communist imperialism poses both an internal and external threat to American survival. William Abbott is a "rock" whose fundamental values (duty, honor, country) are not subject to change; and because of this, his character is colorless and static ("Billy's a rock," "Bill Abbott's a rock," and "The Speaker's a rock") (19-20). As we have already attempted to indicate, some characters in Drury Fiction, unlike the personality of Bill Abbott, do evolve and become multi-dimensional: Robert Leffingwell is among those who undergo dynamic transitions.

In *Advise and Consent* Bob Leffingwell is a "liberal" who conceals his youthful flirtation with the Communist party because of his ambition to become Secretary of State. As a result of his "lie" to the Senate, Brigham Anderson is blackmailed and commits suicide rather than live with the humiliation of being exposed as a one-time homosexual. In *A Shade of Difference*, Bob Leffingwell remains a one-dimensional character; however, he has a substantial existence in Drury fiction. He remains in government as Director of the President's Commission on Labor Reform because President Hudson recognizes that he is an intelligent, dedicated, highly capable American who has much to contribute to his country despite his youthful indiscretions and his moral collapse before the interrogation of the Senate Foreign Relations Committee. In *Capable of Honor*, Drury begins to put flesh on the skeleton of the Leffingwell personality. Because of his loyalty to President Hudson for giving him the opportunity to remain in government service in a responsible position, the "liberal" Leffingwell does not immediately support the candidacy of the "liberal" Ted Jason as he jockeys for his party's presidential nomination. However, when the President does declare that he is a candidate for the presidency and explicitly invites an open contest for the vice-presidential nomination between "conservative" Orrin Knox and "liberal" Ted Jason in order to determine if his party and the country will endorse the President's commitment of American troops in Gorotoland and Panama, Bob Leffingwell is able to become the "liberal," "anti-war" Governor's vice-presidential campaign manager and advisor; however, Leffingwell perceives that Ted Jason, as a "professional liberal," poses a threat to the country that Leffingwell deeply loves and conscientiously serves.

A conversation with Justice Davis indicates that Leffingwell possesses more independence of mind than one might have expected from someone who had been a "liberal" hero and the champion of the "liberal" media, a media shaped by "Wonderful Walter" and the executives of highly popular publications and radio and television stations. When Justice Davis requests that he publicly endorse the candidacy of Ted Jason for the presidency, despite the "liberal" pressure, Bob Leffingwell expresses doubt concerning the "anti-war" posture of the "liberals" and suggests to the politically active Supreme Court Justice that perhaps the President and the Secretary of State, Orrin Knox, may be correct in their military reaction to the Communist wars of liberation occurring in Panama and Gorotoland. The perception and moral strength of Leffingwell become apparent in San Francisco in the contest for the presidential and vice-presidential nominations. When Leffingwell is publicly called a liar in a committee meeting, he gracefully accepts the epithet and does not disrupt the committee process because he recognizes the truth of the assertion; he knows that he acted as "a damned fool" before the Foreign Relations Committee. The former nominee for Secretary of State, however, is troubled by the undercurrent of violence at the convention, and sensing that Ted Jason will be unable to control the agents of violence who support him, he cautions and warns the "liberal" Governor of the impending danger. Despite his advice, the Governor accepts the support of KEEP, COMFORT and DEFY; and when "liberal" violence erupts, the Governor refuses to repudiate the actions of his supporters because their intimidating actions enhance his presidential ambitions. In his advice to the Governor, Leffingwell expresses his beliefs in language which explicitly articulates values frequently identified in the sixties with a "conservative" temperament: "I think you are the one man who has it in his power to decide which way this convention will go. It's a sad cliche with sad consequences, but the world is watching what we do in San Francisco, and we have some duty to help preserve certain things in America if we can— those old fashioned things...that Walter Dobius and his friends have such a good time making fun of all the time, like *decency* and integrity and*kindness* and *honor* and being half-way fair to other people even if you are opposing them" (*Capable* 390). Such sentiments generate an irreconcilable breach between the "liberal" candidate and his campaign manager. In *Capable of Honor*, because a repudiation of tactics would jeopardize Jason's support from "wild-eyed Negroes," "half-assed liberals," and "crazy conservative kooks," the Governor either equivocates or remains silent when questioned about the intimidating tactics of his supporters. Consequently, Leffingwell serves his responsibilities to the Governor's campaign and transfers his support to the President when Ted Jason opportunistically decides to challenge the President for their party's presidential nomination. Leffingwell's transfer to loyalty from the "liberal" to the "conservative" segment of the party is unequivocal: he places President Hudson's name in nomination for re-election and in his nominating speech he characterizes Governor Jason as a man without honor. Leffingwell's nominating speech serves as a catalyst, generating support for President Hudson and insuring his party's nomination; it also provides Leffingwell with the satisfaction of knowing "that he had regained permanently an honor that he had lost a year ago in his attempt to win Senate confirmation as Secretary of State" (486); nevertheless, his moral and political victory is not without blemish. In an anti-conservative tirade, "liberals" Frankly Unctuous and "Wonderful Walter" label his support of the President and the President's foreign policy as a "strange apostasy" caused by presidential pressure upon a weak character whose political support is always negotiable if the "price" is right: "a soft, high-paying government job" as Director of the President's Commission on Labor Reform (483-484).

In *Preserve and Protect* the Leffingwell character continues to evolve and undergo a transformation from a "liberal" to a conservative. On an intellectual or cerebral level, Leffingwell becomes a "defector" from the "liberal" camp in *Capable of Honor*; in *Preserve and Protect*, time, experience, and perception about the weakness, sterility, and destructiveness of the "liberal" message and political tactics of NAWAC re-enforce his inclination to support the "conservative" elements within his party. Before the transition from "liberal" to "conservative" can be total, the Leffingwell psyche must first understand completely the depth of his ambition to become Secretary of State and accept complete responsibility for his actions before the Senate Foreign Relations Committee. This he does. In a moment of retrospection he offers a rationale that amplifies his character beyond that of being just another person corrupted by power: "His desire to become Secretary of State,...was far more than ambition for the office. He honestly did believe that he could negotiate with the Communists in such a way as to encourage peace—or whatever that uneasy state of non-fighting accommodation might be that the world could accept as peace in that unhappy country. He honestly did feel that he could help to save America from disasters he believed a more belligerent policy would bring about" (51). The Leffingwell rationale for his actions includes the belief that "almost all men...would lie under oath at some point," and "out of that lie," in retrospect, for him, ironically had come "regeneration" (138, 139). The Leffingwell "regeneration" is not without a painful price.

In order to better understand his thoughts and feelings concerning his political convictions and loyalties, following the advice of Helen-Anne Carew and Ceil Jason, Leffingwell initiates a meeting with Orrin Knox. In their frank exchange, Leffingwell freely admits to his bitter opponent of his Senate Confirmation hearings that although the Senator from Illinois did everything that he could to destroy his attempt to become Secretary of State, the damage that occurred was fully Leffingwell's responsibility since he categorically lied to the committee of his own free will. This meeting of the minds, however, is only partial. Just as Leffingwell resists pressure from Justice Davis to publicly support Ted Jason during his early bid for the vice-presidency, he maintains his independence from the conservative branch of the party because he does not know for certain whether he can sincerely support Orrin Knox and his foreign policy: "I don't know yet," Bob says slowly in reply to Orrin Knox's request for support, "I honestly don't. About my views, however—they can change too, you know. They're no longer what you're trying to say they are, and they aren't with yours, either. There's an in-between, you know. Everything doesn't always have to be absolute" (74). The difference, it seems, is not in the substance of policy. The difference occurs, rather, when "absolute" decisions have to be made concerning the immediacy and danger of Communist imperialism. "Harley and I say—said—,"Orrin Knox explains, "that it was at point A, and you and Ted and the others said it was point B. Ours was earlier than yours and thereby hangs the difference" (74-75).

At the conclusion of *Preserve and Protect*, the rhetoric of events has persuaded Leffingwell to support Orrin Knox for President. Leffingwell's response is negative when Ted Jason, as a bribe, offers his former campaign manager the position of Secretary of State if he will support his candidacy for the presidency. Leffingwell is also discouraged when, despite Leffingwell's warning that he must disassociate himself from his supporters in NAWAC— a composite of "anti-war, black-racist, neo-isolationists" who have met in secret with the Soviet Ambassador to the UN and with the top KGB operative in America—Jason does not do so. When Leffingwell witnesses the political assassination of Helen-Anne Carew who has threatened to print in her column the report of the meeting between the Communists and the leaders of NAWAC, the group that Jason was instrumental in forming from COMFORT, KEEP, and DEFY, Bob Leffingwell, as a patriotic American has no alternative except that of opposing the Jason "liberal" bid for the presidency. Even before such reservations, however, Leffingwell has passed judgement on "professional liberals"—people who work at being "liberal" and "for whom there was an unending, intolerant, relentless war against all differing opinion, for whom everything was always my-my and terribly-terribly, even as they too rose to being three martini and wall to wall" (138). Through experience he learns that once, he, too, had suffered "from the liberal syndrome of the twentieth century, which said that all knowledge, justice and purity lay on the left and all evil, intolerance and reaction on the right. He had learned that nothing on earth can be so intolerant and reactionary as a professional liberal, and he understands now as he never did before that out of intolerance and reaction only evil, in the long run, can come" (132). His wife, who leaves him because of his support of President Hudson, was, and continues to be such a liberal: emotional, impulsive, dramatic, with a penchant for causes and actions which generate newspaper headlines and television exposure. Leffingwell is thankful to God that "He had strayed close to," but never became one with, "what came in time to be described as 'The New Left"—that phrase so beloved of certain segments of the mass media, which really described the same Old Left with a new generation of stooges to manipulate for its own imperialistic Commufascist purposes" (136). The high point of Leffingwell's regeneration occurs at the conclusion of *Preserve and Protect* when, after he has freely pledged his support to Orrin Knox, the presidential candidate asks him to serve as his Secretary of State in the event that his former adversary becomes President.

One of the flaws of Drury's political fiction is his tiresome habit of repetition both in his anti-liberal rhetoric and in his plot. This flaw is understandable when we consider that several of Drury's characters extend their lives over all six books of his political anatomy and that many readers will not have read previous books. For those readers who read only one or two of Drury's novels, past histories of characters and events must be presented in order to establish context so that "a willing suspension of disbelief" can be induced. Even for previous Drury readers, since Drury's series is almost encyclopedic in scope, reviews of past events are helpful to jog the memory, especially in those instances where a relationship between characters evolves over an extended period of time and significantly reflects the growth of a personality or character. Such an instance is the Knox-Leffingwell relationship. In *Advise and Consent* Orrin Knox bitterly opposes Bob Leffingwell's nomination for Secretary of State. When Leffingwell appears before the foreign relations committee, Orrin attacks the nominee because of his ambivalence and equivocation concerning his attitude and his future policy toward the Soviet Union in the event that he was to become the Secretary of State. After the death of his close friend Senator Anderson, Orrin swears to defeat the Leffingwell nomination, and he does. Because of the kindness and astute judgement of President Hudson, Leffingwell's career is salvaged. During the events of *A Shade of Difference*, Leffingwell regains respectability because of his responsible chairmanship of a presidential committee, a respectability he lost when he lied to the Foreign

Relations Committee by denying that he had once been a member of a Communist cell group while he was teaching at the University of Chicago. In *Capable of Honor*, the Leffingwell-Knox adversary relationship begins to thaw when Leffingwell is invited to dinner with the Knoxes, the Jasons, and Helen-Anne Carew by Walter Dobius whose intent is to embarrass and attack Orrin Knox. After Orrin and Bob exchange a friendly greeting and Walter begins his attack upon Orrin Knox and the Administration's policy, Leffingwell expresses dismay at the vehemence of the Walter Dobius anti-Gorotoland posture since he believes that "more can be accomplished by maintaining perspective and balance than by indiscriminate attacks on the leaders of the country" (221). When Walter's attack against Orrin continues, Leffingwell withdraws his agreement to introduce Walter at the soon-to-come Jason award dinner. After the dinner party, Orrin and Bob part amicably and Orrin suggests that Bob visit and exchange ideas with him. Leffingwell is receptive of the invitation. At the nominating convention, Orrin again manifests a "softening" position towards Leffingwell when he learns that Mary Baffleburg has embarrassed Leffingwell by publicly calling him a liar. Although Orrin was extremely adamant about Leffingwell's lie fifteen months earlier, Orrin has mellowed. "I am not as adamant about it as I was then," he explains to Stanley Danta, "I can understand it better, maybe. We're all human—we're none of us perfect—who knows what we might do—and so on" (357). As time and people change, Orrin Knox—since he is a successful man and a dynamic leader—is also capable of changing. At the conclusion of *Capable of Honor*, a grateful Bob Leffingwell nominates Harley Hudson for President. After the President's death in *Preserve and Protect*, a maturing Orrin Knox, while ruminating about the violence in America, about "the beast" that has been "let loose" in an America that has become divided into "two cities" (69) and about the events surrounding the Leffingwell nomination, is visited by Bob Leffingwell. In a friendly, frank, blunt, but sometimes hostile exchange, both evaluate their past histories and the spirit of the age. Orrin does not apologize for his opposition to Leffingwell but he reaches out to build a bridge of friendship which will enable him to solicit Leffingwell's support for his presidential bid: "I don't apologize for it. But people change—opinions change—certainties change. You've changed.... I like to think maybe I have, too. I don't know." Bob responds in the affirmative; however, he is not ready to offer his total support to the Knox presidential bid. Parting company, Leffingwell has learned that he can have a constructive conversation with his once sworn enemy. On the other hand, although Leffingwell has not committed himself to support Orrin, as a politician, Orrin knows that Leffingwell's visit has not been "a wasted evening" (71-75). The fruits of that meeting are reaped by both Knox and Leffingwell after Orrin receives his party's nomination for president and he invites Leffingwell to visit with him.

During the meeting, a tactful, generous Orrin Knox emerges. After Orrin asks Leffingwell to help him to construct a conciliatory acceptance speech, at Leffingwell's invitation he presents "the real reason" for their meeting, an attempt to once and forever put behind them their traumatic experience of confrontation during Leffingwell's confirmation hearings. With a shrewd, friendly eye and kind words, Orrin allows both Leffingwell and himself enough psychic space so that the past may be forgotten and a new bridge of respect and partnership, as well as affection, may be built:

'I wanted to close the books on something, Bob. It may have been a matter of misunderstanding—it may have been a matter of timing—it may have been just one of those things that happen, now and again, in this town. I happen to think it was probably a matter of conviction, for both of us and as such, each of us did what his principles impelled him to do, and neither of us need be ashamed of that.... I won't say,' he remarked thoughtfully, 'that I regret opposing you for Secretary of State a year and a half ago, any more than you regret making the run for it. I just want to say that if any ghosts are still walking from that episode in your mind, I consider them buried in mine. OK?' (384).

An agreeable Leffingwell is not pressed for political support during the campaign. Later, however, Orrin asks a shocked and pleased Leffingwell to serve in his Administration—as Secretary of State. After a year and three months, Leffingwell's political fortunes have turned full circle as a result of Orrin Knox's ability to recognize change in a one time adversary and to be open to growth within himself.

Change is also a keynote in Orrin's relationship with his son Hal. Surprisingly, in the conflict between Orrin and his son, Hal's judgment appears to be more perceptive than that of his father. When Orrin is lobbying to obtain the presidential nomination from the National Committee, Hal expresses a cynicism about the political process which causes a momentary friction between Hal and his mother. When Hal ominously asks, in a foreshadowing of future events, "what kind of deals" his father will have to make in order to win the nomination, Beth Knox defensively asks "do you doubt" the judgment and integrity of your father? Hal does not. This dramatically changes however when his father wins the nomination and seems inclined to choose Governor Jason as his running mate. In a highly emotional father-son confrontation, Hal demands to know why his father would choose as his running mate the man who is either directly or indirectly responsible for killing his son and Orrin's grandson? Orrin's defense is weak. "Politics offers cruel choices," Orrin had previously attempted to explain, "and sometimes even with the best will in the world, one gets caught in them" (349). But the Secretary of State's explanation does not convince his son who is idealistic, angry, resentful, hurt, and afraid because Hal believes that Jason "is a bad man and a dangerous man," a man who, if he becomes

Vice-President, will change his father and then, consequently, all of the Knox suffering and the country's suffering will be pointless. All that the forces of violence need, Hal believes, is one opening; and to Hal's mind, that opening could be the office of the Vice-President. To select Jason as his vice-presidential partner could be "the first step—the only step he needs— they need." Once "they...get him in there beside you," Hal argues, "they'll be inside, then, and you won't be able to control them, anymore than he can" (353). Despite Hal's anger and highly emotional outburst, Orrin's reasoning prevails. Jason is not a bad or evil man, the father explains. Jason shares with all power seekers in Drury fiction the same beliefs: Jason "is sincerely convinced that he has a better answer for the country than I do," Orrin explains. "I think he really believes that if he could be elected President, things would somehow straighten themselves out and he could bring peace to the world at large, and to us domestically: (350). Jason has made mistakes, Orrin explains, but these mistakes have occurred because "he's in that curious state of mind in which ambition really does dominate all. It dominates so much that everything is related to it. Everything becomes possible to it. Everything seems right to it. Everything can be fitted in...and everything that feeds it can be justified" (350). Orrin believes that Jason is essentially "a decent and well-meaning man" who will break away from his violent supporters as soon as he recognizes them for what they are—and, of course, Orrin will help him to see his "liberal," anti-Gorotoland backers clearly. An unpersuaded Hal believes that if Jason does gain the vice-presidential nomination, it will be because of "some deal." That his father would put a "murderer" on the ticket brings out the worst in Hal—or perhaps it brings out his best instincts, depending upon perspective and future events. Unsuccessfully, Orrin attempts to explain that Ted is not "a murderer." Or, that if he is responsible for the death of "thumper" and the other violence it is only in the sense that all politicians are murderers, including Orrin, who "let things slide to a point where—things like that—can happen.... It was the climate, but maybe I'm as responsible as he is for the climate.... Maybe all men who can't deny the ambition for power when they catch a glimpse of where it can lead are guilty" (351-352). Finally, Orrin suggests the most compelling reason for an alliance with Ted. He argues that the country is badly divided and that he defeated Jason by only a narrow margin. Consequently, Orrin needs the support of the Jason faction if he hopes to be elected: "I've denied him the top spot by a very narrow margin, and many of those people are not going to be satisfied unless they see him beside me—unless they can feel that he is offering some moderating influence on my policies, which they think are so horrible" (351). The Orrin Knox of *Preserve and Protect* is no longer absolutely certain that he has all of the answers, that his position is the only correct position. He has learned that change is the law of life and that there are subtleties in reality that he had not previously perceived. Times change, people change, and perspectives change:

> I'm not anywhere near the positive soul I was in the Senate a year and a half ago, you know. I've been close to the center of the machine for a while, and I know it isn't so easy. It isn't all black and white and cut and dried; it's a sort of horrible gray, like fighting your way through a dirty fog where everything is hazy and blurred and you're not even sure that the light ahead *is* a light: it may be just a—just a mirage.... No, I've changed, and I like to think for the better. And so can he. So *will* he, if I have anything to say about it. And I think I will.... So, he has good qualities—he wants to do what's right for the country, I think—he just needs to be shown. And he does command an enormous popular support—(352-353).

This is the reasoning process, then, which persuades Orrin Knox to compromise and to offer the vice-presidential nomination to Jason. Is the overwhelming persuasive point the fact that without Jason on the ticket, Orrin Knox cannot be elected, and therefore Jason must be offered the vice-presidential slot? At bottom, this would seem to be so. Consequently, Hal's idealistic instincts are frustrated by his father's decision. Hal instinctively knows, as we have seen, such a compromise could easily be a first step in the corrupting influence of power. Even Orrin knows that the compromise is a gamble. In a conversation with Crystal, Beth Knox establishes the political context which describes Orrin's painful dilemma: "I don't think that Orrin really has a choice. He couldn't maneuver if he wanted to, really. The need for unity is too great." For Ted Jason, she feels pity: "You know," Beth says, "in a way I feel sorriest of all for him. Because he actually thinks he's controlling the forces of history...and all the time, they're controlling him" (365-366). Because Hal loves and respects his father and because he trusts his father's judgment more than he trusts his own instincts, he eventually graciously accepts his father's political decision, thereby restoring their warm, familial bond. In *Come Nineveh, Come Tyre*, Drury creates a scenario which vindicates Hal's original judgment: Orrin Knox is assassinated; he, rather than Ted Jason, is controlled by the forces of history, and Ted Jason becomes President.

After Orrin's adverserial conversation with his son in *Preserve*, Drury abruptly shifts the scene to a meeting between Orrin and his political advisers—Bob Munson, Bob Leffingwell, and the President—and Ted Jason where he communicates to Jason Hal's criticism of his political style and actions. Jason regrets Hal's evaluation of his political character and their differences concerning the determination of the causes and effects of the violence that seems to permeate the age. After Jason states what Hal had already expressed to his father, namely, that Orrin needs him on the ticket if he hopes to be elected and that Knox's desire to compromise in order to become President indicates a defect in his political and moral character,

Orrin confronts him with the notes of Helen-Anne Carew which provide evidence that the supporters of NAWAC have secretly met with the Soviet Ambassador and a lieutenant general in the KGB, the commander of the Soviet intelligence network in the eastern sector of the United States, immediately after the NAWAC leaders had met with Jason to discuss political strategy and shortly before Helen-Anne's murder. During the meeting, Helen-Anne's notes reveal, LeGage Shelby said "we're planning to burn down the whole country if necessary to get our man in the White House" (358). Despite such evidence of Jason's association with radical elements who discuss strategy with the KGB, Orrin offers Jason the vice-presidential slot on the ticket if Jason will unequivocally reject his NAWAC supporters and the use of violence as a political weapon. If Jason refuses to sever his connection with the NAWAC elements, Orrin is prepared to choose a different vice-presidential candidate even if this means he will lose the presidential election since the Secretary of State does not "want to win and preside over the dissolution of the democracy" or "to administer the graveyard of the republic" (356). Still, Orrin Knox's open-mindedness permits him to perceive that many sincere people sympathize with Jason's anti-war position, the value of their protest, the need for protest within a democracy, and his evaluation of the Knox personality. Yet during their conversation, Jason has vigorously articulated a troubling perspective of the Hudson-Knox response to protest and Knox's political *Hubris*:

How strange a concept you have of the legitimate forces of protest that disapprove of your policies! I have a few things to say, too, on that score. How much longer are you going to continue to regard legitimate protest and dissent as being traitorous and subversive? How much longer are you going to try to maintain that opposition to your policies *must* be subversive, *must* be hostile to democracy, *must* be inspired by a desire to destroy America? Don't you make any allowance for honest dissent? How am I supposed to feel, when I contemplate running with a man possessed by such—such dangerous egomania-and self-righteousness? What must I sacrifice of my integrity and beliefs to accept the Vice Presidency, when you imply you must sacrifice so much of yours to offer it to me? (356).

At some point, Orrin Knox and his conservative advisers and friends believe, toleration must end and reason must "take up arms against unreason' (361) because the nation "can't have a democracy without stability" (362). Jason believes that the danger against America is not so immediate and desperate. Stability, Jason believes, has not yet been shattered enough to jeopardize democracy. Therein lies the difference between the Knox-Jason, conservative and liberal factions, in *Preserve and Protect*.

While Jason ponders his decision, Orrin reflects upon the cruel choices which make politics a difficult profession. Orrin realizes that he is engaging in "a gamble" and that he may be making "the greatest mistake of his lifetime" (372). If unity is not restored to America, and he believes that only he—with Jason as his Vice-President—is capable of bringing peace and harmony to America, then America is doomed: it will become a "graveyard" (371). Orrin's "cruel choice" becomes even more difficult when Jason tells Knox that he will repudiate violence and NAWAC, but then in a speech he again equivocates. His equivocation is so masterful, however, that both the conservative and the liberal factions of the party are able to believe that Jason favors their position although such is not simultaneously possible. "I am absolutely and unequivocally opposed to the use of violence to express dissent, or to settle political or social problems in the country," Jason declares to the National Committee. But then he declares that he is in agreement with Orrin in that when dissent occurs, it "must be within the law, and the protest must be within the bounds of the law and common decency...Therefore *if* in the organization known as NAWAC or in any of its member organizations such as COMFORT, DEFY, KEEP or any of the others—there *be* any whose purposes are not within the law and within common decency—then I repudiate them here and now and declare that I wish their support of me to cease forthwith" (378 Italics added.). With such equivocation, Jason is able to maintain and expand his power base, and Orrin is confronted with the choice of whether taking half a loaf is better than no bread at all. Orrin chooses to take half a loaf, because at the bottom he believes that Jason is decent, intelligent, patriotic, and open to change toward the conservative spectrum and that an "Era of Reconciliation" is in the process of becoming a reality (385-386). As *Preserve and Protect* nears conclusion, even Hal concedes in a gesture of friendly reconciliation that his father "probably" did the right thing. For a brief period of time, Orrin Knox approaches euphoric joy as he reports the day's events to Beth:

> 'Everything's all right, all right, all RIGHT! We're going to run a great campaign, and we're going to have a national unity, and we're going to have a great Administration and we're going to do such great things for America, and the world. We are, we are, we ARE! I'm going to win, hey, *hey* and it's going to be GREAT, and everything's going to be *all right*! Do you hear me?' he demanded striking a dramatic pose. 'All *right*, I said, woman! ALL right!' (389)

Beth's response is to invite her husband to bed so they can "bubble together." Orrin's experience of joy is short lived. After he and Jason exchange pledges of trust when they appear on the platform to make their acceptance speeches to the Special Committee's convention, an assassination occurs. In *Come Nineveh, Come Tyre* we learn that Orrin Knox and Ceil Jason have been killed. In *A Promise of Joy*, however, Drury has constructed an alternate conclusion. In *Promise* we learn that Orrin Knox has survived to become President; Ted Jason and Beth Knox, rather than Ceil Jason and Orrin Knox, have been killed.

Chapter VIII
"Pure" Political Fiction as
Romance and Anatomy: *A Promise of Joy*

The Promise of Joy, like *Preserve and Protect*, is predominately a political anatomy which continues to present Drury's major themes, his political and historical perception of the temper of the times, and the spirit of the age in the sixties and seventies. As in *Preserve*, the plot of *Promise* is episodic and functions as an illustration of the dangers which threaten contemporary America. In *The Promise* Drury creates a romantic scenario of what would happen if a "true conservative" were elected president. Although *Promise* consists of five books, there are two separate but loosely related narrative movements: the first narrative section focuses upon Knox's ability to remain firm under extreme pressure and the second illustrates Knox's ability to change policy when there is a potentially dangerous shift in the international balance of power.

As *The Promise* begins Orrin Knox is recovering from an attempted assassination which wounded him and Ceil Jason and killed his wife Beth and Ted Jason, the party's vice-presidential candidate. Consistent with Drury's thematic thrust in previous fiction, the "liberal" press infers that Knox supporters may have been responsible for the death of the peace or "dove" candidate. Shrewdly, to heal party wounds, Knox nominates Ceil Jason to be his running mate. When Ceil Jason rejects the opportunity to be the first woman vice-presidential candidate in history, Knox selects Cullee Hamilton, a black, "hawk" Congressman from California as his vice-presidential partner, thereby illustrating that "true conservatives" are not prejudiced against black people and that "true conservatives" are able to respond flexibly to social and political changes in the body politic.

The "liberal" press and anti-war demonstrations are unsuccessful in preventing the election of Orrin Knox. In his inaugural speech, the President, reminiscent of President Johnson's and President Nixon's Vietnam policy, offers a carrot and a stick: he extends an invitation to Russia and China to meet with him in Geneva to negotiate peace in Gorotoland and Panama, but the newly elected President also requests Congress to allocate ten billion dollars to bolster the weakened military resources of the United States. Communist reaction is swift and negative. Before the inauguration day has ended, Communist offensives are launched in Gorotoland and Panama. The President's response is consistent with his personality: he orders counter-offensives and the blockade of the Panama Canal.

156

The "true conservative" response appears to be disaster. Neither the Congress nor the United Nations approves the President's response to increased Communist aggression. Despite increasingly intense pressure from the media and after much consultation, study, and contemplation, the President chooses to continue his "hawk" policy. Directly, so that the biased press cannot distort the message, the President advises Americans in a televised speech that the situation is serious and might lead to atomic war; nevertheless, Orrin informs the public that American forces will remain in Gorotoland and Panama because

counter pressure must be maintained if meaningful negotiations are to come about. Past history, in Vietnam and elsewhere, shows that such negotiations only happen when the Communists face matching strength. They never happen when the Communists face weakness—the negotiations mean nothing but camouflaged surrender to the Communist position (174).

Despite his attempt to win support for his foreign policy, strong opposition to the President's "hawk" policy continues. After the *Post* publishes a psychological profile titled "Orrin Knox: Achieving the Unbalance of Power," and American war casualties continue to increase, even intimate conservative presidential advisors suggest that the President should attempt to reopen negotiations. To compound his adversity, anti-war radicals kidnap his son Hal and his wife Crystal in order to coerce the President into reversing his "hawk" policies in Gorotoland and Panama. America's future appears dim. When the Soviet Chairman confronts the President in a secret conference,—a conference which parallels President Hudson's conference at the conclusion of *Advise and Consent* and contrasts with Ted Jason's conference in *Come Nineveh, Come Tyre*—he demands that America accept Russian "peace terms" or else suffer the consequences: total destruction by Communist forces. Instead of withdrawing from Panama and Gorotoland as Premier Tashikov requests, President Knox orders an American offensive which exhausts all American men and supplies, even though such an exhaustion will leave America completely vulnerable to a Russian attack. Providentially, just as America is at the brink of defeat, war spontaneously erupts between Russian and Chinese forces in Gorotoland. When Russia unleashes an atomic war and China retaliates with an atomic attack, both countries petition President Knox to negotiate a peace between the two countries. For a brief time, President Knox is highly praised by the press since the media recognizes that Orrin Knox's superb political intelligence and courage have resulted in a major military and diplomatic victory.

Thus the first section of the narrative depicts a conservative President who possesses the courage to remain firm when his policy and principles are challenged by the majority; the second narrative movement demonstrates that the conservative President also possesses the flexibility to react constructively when a dramatic change of policy is required by new political realities. As *The Promise* moves toward a conclusion, Orrin Knox evolves as a tough, shrewd, determined, but unsuccessful negotiator. The President realizes that Russia, China, and the world are fearful of renewed and extended warfare, and he surmises that if a permanent peace is to be maintained, this peace must be established within ten days before world leaders become acclimated to the current level of fear and anxiety. To make possible a lasting peace, President Knox presents ten demands to Russia and China, and he visits those countries in an attempt to negotiate with their leaders. Both countries fear that their sovereignty will be endangered by at least three of the President's demands or proposals: an international peacekeeping force on the Russian-Chinese border, a significant reduction in military personnel and weapons, and a rejection of an "expansionist" policy. Despite personal appeals to the Russian and Chinese leaders, the President's proposals are rejected; consequently, in order to protect the world from renewed atomic warfare and to establish a balance of power which is vital to world peace, the President requests that the United Nations send military forces to the Russian-Chinese conflict to impose a peace on the belligerent, warring countries. Predictably in Drury fiction, the United Nations reacts negatively to the United States resolution, and the fickle media begins once again to question the political wisdom of Orrin Knox.

Near panic erupts in America when atomic warfare is renewed. Ironically, those groups in America who had formally and sometimes violently urged the withdrawal of American forces from Gorotoland and Panama reverse their thinking and urge the President to commit American troops to defend Russia from the Chinese army. In the words of "liberal" Fred Ackerman who had previously urged an isolationist policy for the United States, "America must save the civilization of the West from the Godless yellow hordes of Asia" (369). Even when Congress passes legislation sanctioning U.S. intervention and aid to Russia, the President remains firm; he exercises his veto so that a militarily strong America will be able to restore order and maintain peace after Russia and China have battled to a mutual exhaustion. However, as China clearly demonstrates military superiority and appears on the brink of a convincing victory, President Knox realizes that non-intervention is no longer a viable policy: a balance of power must be preserved in order to protect the interests of the United States. In a televised speech, the President announces his reversal of policy to his countrymen, but not before functioning one final time as a mouthpiece for Drury's conservative themes. Although America's social conscience has responded responsibly to much of the pain and suffering in the world, the President reminds America, too many Americans have fallen short of the moral ideal of the conservative conscience. This ideal has been challenged by the intellectual community, he explains, a community dominated by the liberal media, a media which "has consistently denigrated, downgraded, vilified and sabotaged every worthwhile impulse and effort of its country" (439). This decline in patriotism is also manifest in some churches, in schools, and in the courts which have been besieged by "a steady campaign to weaken, destroy, and subvert the laws necessary to maintain in our society" the balance and order necessary for America's survival (440). It is in order to insure that survival that the President announces American intervention in the Sino-Soviet war, an intervention that will be successful because America is strong because God, the preserver of America, will respond generously to America's prayers. Somewhat paradoxically, through this military intervention, the President believes, lies the road to a permanent peace, a peace that will be based upon American strength and the balance of power which take "into account the endless deviousness and boundless treachery of the human animal." President Knox believes that though "men try to be good,...too many are not good" and for this reason men need restraints; unless men "know they will be punished when they break the law, they will break it with impunity" (438). The President concludes his speech with a rhetorical ploy which will promote understanding and sympathy for the much maligned President (and help Americans to understand the tremendous pressures placed upon President Johnson and President Nixon during the Vietnam War). As President Knox announces American intervention, he challenges American citizens with a series of questions: "What would you do, my friends, you who applaud and you who condemn? How would you handle it?" (443-444) Each citizen, then, is left to ponder the time and the place, as well as the military and political strategy, which must be determined before American troops set foot on Russian soil. To maintain balance of power favorable to the United States it would seem that China must be prevented from overwhelming Russia, but both the sovereignty of China and Russia must be maintained to divert their military energies from a focus upon America. Equally important, Americans must strive to develop empathy with political leaders, especially presidents, who are sometimes confronted with complex problems that cannot be solved without pain, suffering, and sacrifice if the republic is to be preserved and protected.

II

Like the anatomy, the romance also presents stylized characters and episodic plots; in addition, the romance deals primarily with an "idealized" rather than a "real" world. Although there are romantic strains in *A Shade of Difference*, *Capable of Honor* and *Preserve and Protect*, it is not until *Promise of Joy* that the romantic strain reaches its full fruition and we find a pure political romance. In the romance there is a major adventure which takes the form of a quest, and one of the central forms of the quest-romance is the St. George and the Dragon myth where a knight (good) slays a dragon (evil).[1] The political career of Orrin Knox presents an obvious parallel. In *Advise and Consent* Orrin, no longer young but still virtuous, continues his quest for the presidency despite serious opposition. In *A Shade of Difference, Capable of Honor,* and *Preserve and Protect* he continues his quest in accordance with the traditions and rituals of nominating conventions and presidential elections. Although Orrin is wounded in an assassination attempt, he continues his quest; he is a symbolic conservative knight dedicated to doing good deeds in the body politic. After he is elected President he successfully battles evil as it is manifested in Russian imperialistic Communism. Through his wisdom and courage in confrontational negotiations with the Russians and Chinese, nuclear catastrophe is avoided for America and the world. The political adventures of Orrin Knox also reflect the stages of the quest-romance: "perilous adventures" on a "perilous journey," "a crucial struggle," and "an exaltation of the hero" (186-189). For conservative readers, *The Promise of Joy* is wish-fulfilment. (*Come Nineveh, Come Tyre,* which provides an alternate, negative conclusion to Drury's political series, is a political nightmare.) Orrin Knox is an ideal public servant who personifies conservative values in both public and private life. Despite potentially destructive military and political threats, Knox remains faithful to his vision of right and justice, even though fidelity to the vision may claim the life of his son and daughter-in-law, the destruction of his political career, and perhaps even the destruction of America and the world. One would expect a man to be plagued with doubt, to frantically search for alternatives, and perhaps even to waver and change policy in such a circumstance. Or, a "real man" in a "real world," as we would find in a novel as contrasted with a romance, might suffer severe depression or have a heart attack under the strain of such multiple pressures. Such is not the case with Orrin Knox who steadfastly maintains his faith in his God, his country, and himself as he performs his duty flawlessly despite traumatic personal and political problems.

Quite obviously, the rendering of events and the conclusion of *The Promise* contain strong romantic characteristics and overtones. Although Drury does provide a few small hints that there is potentially a rift in Sino-Soviet relations, Russia's atomic aggression is unexpected and improbable; it is a *deus ex machina* which provides a fortuitous conclusion prophetically illustrating the folly of America's flirtation with the "peaceful intentions" of imperialistic Communist countries who support and wage "wars of liberation." The romantic tendencies of *The Promise* are again underscored by President Knox who reflects that

He was saved by the bell—not by an effort of the American President, not by any recognition of the world of America's decent purposes, not by any triumph of American principles or American courage or American strength—but simply because two ravenous *beasts* (italics added) of history's jungle had...turned on another... (236 Italics added.)

in mutual hatred.

"Saved by the bell," however, must be placed within the context of the President's religious faith. To Orrin Knox, God was "basically impersonal, impartial, and generally uncaring of ordinary mortals," but Orrin Knox was not an ordinary mortal; he believes that God was concerned about and interested in him (34). In moments of crisis, Orrin prayed to God, petitioning that God to give him the strength and the courage to put into practice his firm conviction that if America responds with courage and does right, right and humanity will prevail. By doing right, that is, by reacting aggressively to the Communist military incursions in Gorotoland and Panama, the Lord will take "some interest in America" (209). Twice in *The Promise* the President directly appeals to the religious faith of the American people. When he announces that America will not intervene in the Sino-Soviet conflict and again when he reverses himself and declares that America will indeed intervene, he appeals to the American people with the same sentiments and the same language:

The Lord has preserved us through many perils, for some purpose. We must be confident that He will continue to do so. I make no pretense to you whatsoever that it will be easy. But I call to you to join me in meeting whatever the future holds, with courage, with determination, with unity and with faith in ourselves, our traditions and our purposes (369).

In the peroration of his final speech in *The Promise*, he adds

We are doing the best we can, and we are doing it selflessly, generously and, we hope, helpfully for all mankind. The event rests in the hands of God, but you and I, his servants, bring to it the best that is in us. I am confident He will accept our offering, and to it gives His blessing and success (442).

In the context of *Promise*, then, America is not "saved by the bell." It is saved by the courageous actions of a president who retains his faith in God during a time that tries men's souls, and that faith and courage is rewarded by Divine Providence. Let us look more at Knox's character.

Orrin Knox in *The Promise* continues to be a firm but evolving character. As we have observed, because of international developments, the president is compelled to change his policy of non-intervention. This evolution is consistent with his character as it is presented in *Advise and Consent, A Shade of Difference, Capable of Honor*, and *Preserve and Protect*. After Beth

Knox's assassination, President Abbott reflects upon Orrin's changing character. While reflecting on Knox's political career, Abbott remembers the unique romantic, domestic, and political partnership that the Secretary of State has shared with his wife, their "uncompromising integrity" and their "uncompromising opposition" to the attitudes and trends which weakened America. As a result of this "uncompromising opposition," President Abbott recalls, Beth and Orrin had received much hostility from the media, as well as from "the academic, religious, and professional worlds." Despite criticism from liberals, his "lively temper" and "a tongue sometimes too willing to be tart and impatient," Orrin had experienced a successful career in the Senate. In a different position of power, as Secretary of State, President Abbott observes, Orrin had curbed his abruptness and had become "a much more moderate and diplomatic soul...more willing to compromise, a little less certain he had all the answers to everything." As a presidential candidate, Abbott notes, Orrin is mature in a way he "had never really been mature before" (39-40). Through the trauma of his twice shattered presidential ambitions, the death of Harley Hudson, his narrow victory at the nominating convention, and his acceptance of Ted Jason as his Vice-Presidential candidate, the steel of the Knox moral and political character had been tempered. As we have observed in the earlier fiction, this maturity has not evolved without the conscious effort of Orrin.

Although Knox is a dynamic, strong president in *Promise*, the characterization of Knox is less effective than in earlier Drury fiction. True, Orrin Knox experiences a wide range of emotions in *The Promise*—anguish, anger, rage, grief, anxiety, frustration, fear, despair, faith, hope, love, and joy—but these emotions are communicated more by narration rather than by dramatic scene which makes a more vivid and lasting impact upon the reader. An effective emotional scene does occur, however, after the President has ordered the American offensives in Gorotoland and Panama despite the Russian warning that if America persists in the war, America will suffer severe consequences. As the dispirited President ponders his gamble, Senator Lafe Smith visits his office to share some good news: The Senator from Iowa announces his engagement to Mable Anderson, and he joyfully informs the President that Jimmy Frye, the brain-damaged son of Hal Frye, has finally begun to speak in the environment of love provided for him by Lafe, Mable, and six year old Pidge Anderson. This scene, though much narrated by Lafe Smith, effectively conveys with pertinent details the shifting emotions—anxiety, joy, anguish, despair—of a President who awaits the results of a decision that may cause the destruction of the United States and the death of his kidnapped son.

Although much of the characterization in *The Promise* tends to be two dimensional rather than "round" or "full", within the context of the romance and anatomy as forms of fiction, the characterization is effective and Knox as a conservative President makes a vivid impact upon the reader. As Senator, as Secretary of State, and as President, Knox is an unforgettable political creation. Perhaps some of the success of the Knox character in *The Promise of Joy* results because he is a fully developed personality in the context of the earlier political narratives and a "recognition factor" operates upon those readers already introduced to Drury's fictional world. In much the same way, except for *Advise and Consent*, the success of the Knox characterization may be viewed within the context of the political action of the series, keeping in mind Drury's analytical thrust and his attempt to delineate the spirit of the age and the temper of the times from a conservative perspective.

Chapter IX
Liberals, Conservatives, and
Drury's Political Spectrum

As we have examined Drury fiction as political anatomy, we have focused more upon conservative characters and conservative ideology rather than upon liberals and liberalism. Before we examine *Come Nineveh, Come Tyre* as an anatomy-romance, let us look at Drury's use of the terms *liberal* and *liberalism*, his major liberal characters, his political spectrum which includes both a far left and a far right, and the historical roots of the Communist conspiracy theory which is central to much of Drury's fiction. These combined elements undoubtedly contribute to the creation of the spirit of the age in Drury fiction, a creation which is essential for evoking "a willing suspension of disbelief" in pure and serious political fiction.

In mid-century America, the terms *liberal* and *liberalism* were in a process of semantic deterioration, a process of evolving connotation which still continues.[1] This is not surprising since the term liberal possesses different meanings in different time frames, cultures, countries, and academic disciplines, such as economics, political science, philosophy, and theology. Although one may be a theological conservative, one may also adopt some "liberal" economic principles or concepts. Semantic confusion has also evolved because the term *liberal* has been used in politics as both a "slur" word and a "purr" word. When individuals identify themselves and their friends as *liberals*, it is a "purr" word with highly favorable connotations. On the other hand, sometimes when some conservatives, such as Spiro Agnew or Barry Goldwater, have used the term in the political forum, it was definately a "slur" word. What is true of the words *liberal* and *liberalism* is also true of the terms *conservative* and *conservatism*: ideological friends use them as "purr" words; ideological adversaries use them as "slur" words. In 1953, four years before Allen Drury began writing *Advise and Consent*, Lawrence Sears had perceptively examined the need for denotative definitions in an article titled "Liberals and Conservatives" which was published in *The Antioch Review*. In the article Sears reported a "growing concern with the meaning of the term political conservatism and a dissatisfaction with the way that term is popularly used." He then suggested that "to a large degree both 'liberal' and 'conservative' are today little more than honorific terms used to give a comfortable glow of satisfaction, or else epithets designed to destroy the influence of those with whom we disagree." As a result, as

164

early as 1953 the terms "liberal" and "conservative" had already become "blurred." Along with the blurring came a polarization: both those who viewed themselves as "liberals" and those who viewed themselves as "conservatives" believed that they "held the truth" in a right versus wrong confrontation and that each side must be ready to do battle for their beliefs. Sears then identified a goal: "...it is one of the urgent tasks of our time to get these terms sharply defined" (361-370). Drury's political fiction reflects and continues the polarization between "liberals" and "conservatives;" in Drury, there is no middle ground. "Conservatives" are presented as being "right" in their stance against Communism; and "liberals" are presented as being categorically wrong.

In Drury fiction there are three kinds of liberals: one kind are those liberals who are sensitive and intelligent but who must be shown the truth ("the true American way") through experience and example. Such liberals possess courage and are "capable of honor," but it takes time. In fact, for such characters as Tommy Davis, Walter Dobius, and Bob Leffingwell, it takes thousands of pages. A second type of liberal is a well-meaning pseudo-intellectual who is a dupe of "the far left" who does not realize that his idealistic actions harmonize with and foster the Communist goal of world domination. Such naive liberals find it difficult to perceive any action of America in a positive perspective. In Drury fiction, most members of the media, including publishers and editors, are in this category. With them, also, in Drury fiction, are students and college professors, as well as some Senators and Congressmen. Congressman Bronson Bernard is a symbolic representative of this group that might be termed "professional liberals." A third category of liberals consists of those on the far or radical left. This group is comprised of COMFORT and DEFY who unite with KEEP, an ultra-right organization, to form NAWAC; Senator Van Ackerman exemplifies this third category of liberals in Drury fiction. Such liberals are unable to perceive any positive value in America or its history, and they believe that peace with Russia must be achieved at any price even if that price requires the participation of Soviet officials in the American political process. NAWAC manipulates the "liberal press" through intimidation and violence.

Too late in Drury fiction, Walter Dobius and Tommy Davis realize that they have misunderstood the nature and threat of Communism. When Dobius and Davis are faced with the potential demise of America, they comment upon the shifting values and definitions of *liberal* and *liberalism* which now dictate a desperate need for distinctions in the term *liberal* ("genuine liberal," "true liberal," "professional liberal") because as a blanket term in Drury's created political world, the term liberal now possesses a pejorative connotation. In *Come Nineveh, Come Tyre* when Dobius and Davis realize that President Jason is being intimidated by the tactics of

NAWAC, Davis states his and Walter's alliance with liberalism as it is reflected in the values and actions of NAWAC:

"We have to remember that NAWAC *does* represent what you and I believe basically. It is against war, and it is for peaceful accommodation with the Russians, and it does support the President, who is trying to keep the world at peace. We have to remember all these things, Walter. It does represent the liberal point of view basically" (247).

In reply, Walter—a far different Walter than we have seen in *Capable of Honor*—disassociates himself from NAWAC. "It doesn't represnt my kind of liberalism," he tells Tommy, continuing:

Not yours, either really. We don't believe for instance, in killing our opponents. I may write harsh columns and you may hand down tough decisions, but we do it in the context of this democracy, not in the way this NAWAC crowd is doing this. We give the Conservatives hell and they give us hell, but there's a basic compromise, a basic *compassion*, if you like, for each other's views. At least we're fair-minded" (247-248).

Both Walter and Tommy evolve; courageously, they come to understand that they have not been fair-minded and that, as a result, they have significantly contributed to the deterioration of America. When the fate of America seems almost beyond the control of patriotic Americans and Supreme Court Justice Davis must rule upon the constitutionality of the repressive Help America Bill passed by Congress in *Come Nineveh, Come Tyre*, Davis muses upon the corruption of the word *liberal* and the transition of values associated with that term:

Tommy had seen many things besides water pass under the bridge, particularly the meaning of the word "liberal." When he began "liberal" had meant *real liberalism*, with all its passionate, impatient, but still basically tolerant devotion to the common weal. Now that he was in the final years of his life and service, liberal had come to mean the rigid, ruthless, intolerant and unyielding orthodoxy that had finally and inevitably produced the mood, the spirit and the fact of a "Help America" Act [a Dictatorship Bill] (397 Italics added.).

Conservative Bob Munson, the former Senate Majority Leader, also is concerned about the word "liberal," especially since Senator Van Ackerman has been able to adopt this term as a virtue or "purr word" and use "liberalism" to create a power block that will perhaps thrust him into the presidency. In order to protect Lacey Pollard's position as President Pro Tem in the Senate, Senator Munson—a conservative in Drury fiction—unexpectedly associates himself with the values of liberalism in a statement that he hopes will destroy Van Ackerman's heretofore successful attempt to polarize "liberals" and "conservatives" against each other:

There are some of us, I say for the information of the Senator from Oregon, who were 'liberals' while the Senator from Wyoming was in nursery school. *Real liberals. Genuine ones.* People who favored social progress and worked for it, fought for programs, put laws on the books—really made liberalism mean something. And at the same time remembered that personal liberty makes for social progress and not the other way around; and that when there has to be a choice, personal liberty has to come first, or the whole thing goes under. That's the kind of liberals we are, I will say to the Senator from Oregon. His friend is far from that (418 Italics added.).

In addition to Tommy Davis and Walter Dobius, Bob Leffingwell is another "liberal" who examines his liberal ideology and then adopts a more "conservative" value system. Robert Leffingwell in *Advise and Consent* is as the name suggests—*well to the left* of the center of the spectrum. However, in *Come Nineveh, Come Tyre*, Leffingwell is a conservative. This change is not sudden and dramatic; it evolves through *A Shade of Difference, Capable of Honor*, and *Preserve and Protect*. Leffingwell moves from the far left as a young man—he is a member of a Communist cell group at the University of Chicago, and as a "liberal" candidate for Secretary of State he was "soft on Communism"—to the far right as Secretary of State in *Come Nineveh*, where, ironically, given the events in *Advise*, he counsels a military response to Russian aggression and permits conversation about the assassination of a "peace" President. In *Preserve and Protect* Leffingwell undergoes disenchantment with the "liberals" after he views the violence of the left and Ted Jason's unwillingness to repudiate such political intimidation. While contemplating his life and values, Leffingwell recognizes that

he was suffering from the *liberal syndrome* of the twentieth century, which said that all knowledge, justice and purity lay on the left and all evil, intolerance and reaction lay on the right. He has learned that nothing on earth can be so intolerant and reactionary as a *professional liberal*, and he understands as he never did before that out of intolerance and reaction only evil, in the long run, can come (132 Italics added.).

The one-time "professional liberal" also knows that he once "had strayed close to what came in time to be described as 'The New Left,'—that phrase, so beloved to certain segments of the mass media, which really described the same Old Left with a new generation of stooges to manipulate for its own imperialistic, Communist purposes" (136). Linked in Leffingwell's mind are "professional liberal," "The New Left," "The Old Left," "Communism," and "evil." In Drury political fiction, all of these elements merge and as a result, a Communist conspiracy to conquer America evolves. At the conclusion of *Come Nineveh, Come Tyre*, through the cooperation of "liberal" Senator Van Ackerman, who has presidential ambitions, Russia has subjugated the American President, "liberal" Ted Jason, to its will. As we have suggested, during the fifties and sixties, many highly respected Americans sincerely believed that there was a Communist conspiracy to destroy America and that "liberals" were the dupes of Communist manipulators. In *The Crucial Decade and After 1945-1960* Eric Goldman offers an historical interpretation of Liberalism, Socialism, and Communism which helps to explain why many Americans—Drury's potential reading audience—came to believe in the Communist conspiracy (113-134).

Generally speaking, people who identify themselves as liberals tend to view themselves as being open-minded and temperamentally inclined toward experiment and change. On the other hand, people who identify themselves as conservative tend to view themselves as being more comfortable with existing views, conditions, and institutions and temperamentally less inclined toward change than the liberal. Conservatives view themselves as not being opposed to change that will benefit the country; however, for those of a conservative temperament, there must be very convincing evidence that change is necessary and that the change will improve the quality of life in America before the change can be recommended. Both liberals and conservatives wish to preserve or conserve what is best in American values and institutions; however, the definition of "best" varies in the context of time and circumstance. During the Depression, there were many dramatic proposals for a revision of America's economic and social structure; many of these proposals took the form of laws which were adopted by the Congress. Collectively, these laws which significantly transformed the economic structure of America were identified with the Democratic Administration of Franklin Roosevelt and were labeled "The New Deal." In terms of an economic and political spectrum, this economic and social legislation moved America toward the direction of the economic and social left, that is, in the direction of Socialism, a transitional stage in the Marxist theory between Capitalism and Communism, a stage which is characterized by an unequal distribution of goods and services administered by the government. The Ronald Reagan speech, "Encroaching Control, Keep Government Poor and Remain Free" reflects the fear of change engendered in Roosevelt's New Deal.

In 1948, in his inaugural address, Democratic President Harry Truman added two new terms to the political vocabulary. President Truman introduced the term "Fair Deal." The "Fair Deal" was "an extension of 'The New Deal.'" Both "The New Deal" and "The Fair Deal" mean, Truman explained, "greater economic opportunity for the mass of the people." In "The New Deal" and "The Fair Deal" there are differences, Truman added, "not of principle, but of pace and personnel;" the New Deal, because of the times and its very newness, "was marked by a tempo at times almost frenetic. Now there is a steady pace, without the gyrations of certain early New Dealers." Those certain "New Dealers" the Democratic President dismissed as *"professional liberals"* (Goldman 92).

In a chapter titled "The Great Conspiracy," Goldman reports that "since 1933 millions of people in the United States had been listening sympathetically to speakers who charged that New Dealers were socializing the economy, leading the nation to ruin in foreign affairs, and leaving the whole of American life prey to radical intellectuals," and such thoughts, Goldman continues, "easily slid over into a theory of conspiracy" as a result of fear and anxiety generated by shocking events in 1949 (125-126): the fall of China to Communism, Russia's explosion of an atomic bomb, and the accusations of Whittaker Chambers (a man, like Gelman in *Advise and Consent*, who was accused of mental instability) that Alger Hiss (a man like Leffingwell, a sophisticated liberal with years of government service) was a Communist spy (111-112).

Something of the temper of the times in 1949 was reflected in the volatile anti-Communist rhetoric of a *Chicago Tribune* editorial that characterized liberal Secretary of State Dean Acheson as "another striped pants snob" who "ignores the people of Asia and betrays *true Americanism* to serve as a lackey of Wall Street bankers, British Lords, and Communist radicals from New York" (127-128). According to Goldman's historical interpretation, recent immigrants were concerned with being "100% American" and many immigrants in Chicago and throughout the country listened sympathetically when Catholic clergyman associated "liberal agitations" with Communism. In 1937 Pope Pius XI had spoken bluntly and clearly about the dangers of Communism in his encyclical titled *Atheistic Communism*. "See to it venerable Brethren," the Pope wrote, "that the faithful do not allow themselves to be deceived. Communism is intrinsically wrong, and no one who would serve Christian civilization may collaborate with it in any undertaking whatsoever" (130). After World War II, one of the most influential Catholic spokesmen in America, Cardinal Spellman of New York, warned of a Communist conspiracy in America. Again and again, the nationally influential Cardinal bluntly and publicly declared the dangers of Communism in words that traveled throughout America:

"The fear weighs upon me that we may fail or refuse to realize that Communists, who have put to death thousands of innocent people across the seas, are today digging deep inroads into our own nation."
In "this hour of dreadful, desperate need...Once again while Rome burns, literally and symbolically, the world continues to fiddle. The strings of the fiddle are committees, conferences, conversations, appeasements—to the tune of no action today." Americans "will not be safe 'until every Communist cell is removed from within our own government, our own institutions, not until every democratic country is returned to democratic leadership.' "

"Are we, the American people, the tools and the fools for which the Communists take us?" (130-131)

In Drury's political fiction, Cardinal Spellman's worst fears for America come to pass. *Come Nineveh, Come Tyre* is a prophetic example of what will occur if a "liberal," a man sympathetic to "The Left," a man far to the left on the political spectrum, a leader "soft on Communism," becomes President. In the real world of American politics during and after World War II, the term "Communist" was an effective slur word in many election campaigns.

Much to their dismay, New Deal Democrats were frequently accused of Communist sympathies, and President Roosevelt's attempt to end the Depression was repeatedly associated with the dogmas of Marx and Lenin. In 1944, for example, the Republican Vice-Presidential candidate habitually charged that the Democratic President depended upon the support of "Communist and radical elements" and that the Democratic party had become the "Communist party with Franklin Roosevelt as its front" (Reeves, *The Life and Times of Joe McCarthy* 100). Republican leaders such as Senator Robert H. Taft, House Majority Leader Joseph W. Martin, and New York Governor Thomas E. Dewey publicly linked the Democratic party with Communism. Republican National Chairman B. Carroll Reece charged that "Democratic party policy, as enunciated by its officially chosen spokesman...bears a made-in-Moscow label. That is why I believe I am justified in saying that from a long-range viewpoint the choice which confronts Americans this year is between Communism and Republicanism." During the same campaign a Congressional candidate found "there was no difference between "New Dealism, National Socialism, and Communism" (Reeves 100); and in 1946 the Knights of Columbus "called for an all out attack upon 'infiltration of atheistic Communism into our American life and economy' " (Reeves 101).

Similar anti-Communist fears, fears associated with liberals, permeate Drury fiction. The basic assumption underlying Drury fiction is that totalitarian Communism is intrinsically evil and that Communism's ultimate goal is world domination, an end or goal that Communists will strive to achieve by whatever moral, immoral, or amoral means are expedient, including propaganda, lies, subversion, intimidation, infiltration, betrayal, and violence. A Drury thesis is that in Communism's constant war against American democratic Capitalism, a steady progress is being made. Though President Jason is unable or unwilling to prevent the continuing success of Communism, the "liberal" President in *Come Nineveh* is aware of the erosion of American power and the increase of Russian power. This is one facet of the Soviet plan or conspiracy to enslave America and dominate the world. In a moment of reflection, President Jason's thoughts suggest Matthew

Arnold's poem "Dover Beach" in both its somber mood and brooding pessimism: "He walked again to the open window, stood listening again for a moment to the somber sea before he closed the panes against the now sharply chilly night. Unchanging and unchangeable, the Pacific advanced...withdrew...advanced...withdrew...advanced again, in the eternal, inexorable attack that always takes from the shore and adds to the sea—but does not always, or of necessity, take from the sea and add to the shore" (105). Inexorably, in Drury fiction, as a part of a master plan, Russia has been eroding America's confidence, will, and determination, thereby creating a climate where not only will a conspiracy to topple America become a possibility, but also, because of the erosion of perception and patriotism in America, Americans will not be predisposed to recognize a Communist conspiracy; or if they do recognize a Communist conspiracy, they will lack the power and confidence to do something about it. When the Indian Ambassador joshingly suggests that Senator Lafe Smith believes "that old chestnut about Communist conspiracy in America," the former United Nations Representative provides background to his affirmative reply: "There's been some all right, but basically it's a lot simpler than that K.K. Basically, it's been a conspiracy of *intellectual bias*, arrogance and stupidity conducted by a bunch of closed minds who think they're so superior that they can tell everybody else what's good for them" (201 Italics added.).

As we have already seen, one of the chief architects of the "liberal" intellectual bias has been Walter Dobius; and Walter, after moving from a left-wing bias to a more central position on the political spectrum, moves once again, this time completely to the right when he discovers what has been suggested since the crash of Air Force One in *A Shade of Difference*, namely, that there was in fact a Communist conspiracy to destroy American political leadership. By suggesting a Communist conspiracy in his fiction, but by dramatically withholding damning evidence of it, Drury has been keeping his readers in suspense. At the conclusion of *Come Nineveh*, the suspense is ended when Walter Dobius learns from reliable sources that there has been "a Communist conspiracy" behind the deaths of President Harley Hudson, Secretary of State Orrin Knox, and Mrs. Ceil Jason (*Preserve and Protect*). Leaked official documents also directly link the "Communist conspiracy" with members of the National Anti-War Activities Congress (NAWAC). In a column which demonstrates what even his detractors have always conceded—that he is a very diligent, intelligent, and courageous, although biased, reporter—Walter reports directly to the American people:

The assassinations of Secretary Knox and Mrs. Jason at the Washington Monument Grounds in August were planned and executed by the same group responsible for the death of President Hudson. This group is composed of native American fanatics of the left, some of them in very high positions in the National

Anti-War Activities Congress—NAWAC. These native fanatics of the left are working in close conjunction with members of the Russian secret police, the KGB, posing as staff members of the Soviet Embassy in Washington (437).

By investigating and developing this story, Walter demonstrates that he is worthy of Helen-Anne Carew, his former wife, who suspects links between Communism and NAWAC in *Capable of Honor* and develops the evidence to prove it in *Preserve and Protect*. As with Harley Hudson, Orrin Knox, and Ceil Jason, Helen too is assassinated. Unfortunately, she is assassinated before she is able to fully develop her evidence and publish the story which would have destroyed the career of "liberal" Senator Van Ackerman and the power of NAWAC. Senator Van Ackerman functions as a main character in the Soviet conspiracy which ultimately results in the suicide of President Jason in *Come Nineveh, Come Tyre*. Let us examine the character of Senator Van Ackerman along with other liberals and conservatives as they appear as members of political groups in the political spectrum of Drury fiction.

II

If one views the political spectrum in Drury fiction from *Advise and Consent* to *Come Nineveh* from the center, Senator Van Ackerman is far to the left of the center. At the other extreme of the spectrum—to the far right—is Hal Knox, the son of conservative Orrin Knox; and surprisingly, linked with Congressman Knox on the extreme right at the conclusion of *Come Nineveh* are the Secretaries of State and Defense—Leffingwell and McDougall. At the center of the political spectrum in *Come Nineveh*, prior to Ted Jason's becoming President, is a very troubled Acting President, William Abbott; in a time of crisis, he wishes to conserve the best of America's institutions, traditions, and values by using morally acceptable means to achieve the safe and secure future of America. At the same time, Abbott wishes to assist Jason by assuring an orderly transition between his conservative government and Jason's new "liberal" approach to foreign policy. Ideally, at the center of the political spectrum are patriotic statesmen who may possess either liberal or conservative inclinations or temperaments. The shared values of liberal and conservative statesmen at the center of the political spectrum are three: (1) They believe that the good of the country transcends the benefit of party or political career. (2) They have a desire to preserve what is best in American government, institutions, and values. And (3) they have a disposition to meet the challenges of changing circumstances by making changes or adjustments that will obviously improve and preserve the quality of life in America within the existing framework of institutions and traditions. When differences exist between statesmen— there are "liberal" statesmen and there are "conservative" statesmen—these differences are honest and sincere ones which focus upon the perception of what is "best" for America. Next to the statesmen on the spectrum are responsible liberals on the left and responsible conservatives on the right.

Responsible "liberals" *tend to view the nature of man and government from perspectives which emphasize the potential good in man and the perfectibility of man*: man is viewed as being essentially generous and good, especially when man is provided with a nurturing environment. To *responsible* "liberals," history reflects the evolving perfection of man and governments. Since change has been beneficial to man and society, temperamentally, the responsible "liberal" is very comfortable with change. The *responsible* "liberal's" appetite for change, however, is restrained by native intelligence, a knowledge of history, observation, perception,and immediate experience. *Responsible* "conservatives," on the other hand, *tend to view the nature of man and government from perspectives which emphasize not man's potential good, but rather man's potential to fall short of the ideals of moral or ethical behavior. Responsible* "conservatives" also tend to emphasize the potential impact of moral weakness upon individuals and society. Thus the *responsible* "conservative" tends to view man as being potentially selfish and corruptible; and as a result, the *responsible* "conservative" perceives that balances of power in government and foreign affairs are essential to preserve the fruits of historical progress. Ultimately, to those of a conservative predisposition, coercion (law) rather than persuasion, is necessary to preserve "the status quo." To the *responsible* "conservative," traditional values, processes, and institutions are viewed as "good" and adequate, if not as the "best" in an ideal, rather than "real" world. Nevertheless, the responsible "conservative" is somewhat open to change, but the burden to prove the need for change is paramount. There must be extremely persuasive evidence that a proposed change will be beneficial to individuals, institutions, and society before action for change will be championed.

When the "liberal" Ted Jason is elected President in *Come Nineveh, Come Tyre*, President Abbott and his "conservative" friends gather at a private dinner in the White House where President Abbott toasts the "liberal" Ted Jason: "To the next President of the United States. May God give him the strength he will need to lead us safely in the path he proposes" (124). All present at the dinner—the President, Beth Knox, Lucielle Hudson, Lafe Smith, Mabel Anderson, Sarah Johnson, Elizabeth Adams, Bob and Dolly Munson, Stanley Danta and Crystal Danta—are *responsible* conservatives, except for Hal Knox who refuses to support Ted Jason because, as he has earlier told his wife Crystal and his mother Beth, "I think he is an evil man, and even more fundamental than that, I think he is a fool" (52). As the dinner progresses and political discussion evolves, the President is forced to defend his generous posture of cooperation with the incoming "liberal" president who has not yet categorically repudiated NAWAC, the left-wing, radical organization which supported Jason's peace policy in Gorotoland and Panama and which advocates accommodation with Russia, policies which run counter to the foreign policy of the Hudson-Knox and Abbott Administrations. Reasonably, and then with a touch of exasperation, President Abbott argues with Hal who believes the President is mistaken in his cooperation with Ted Jason:

"Look," the President said, with a certain frustrated annoyance, "let's all remember one thing, shall we? The man *is* about to become President. I haven't been able to ignore that fact, much as I would have liked to. He has had *some* right to say what should be done. I have had to take *some* account of his views, after all."
"You could have told him to go to hell and kept right on with what you were doing until the moment you left this house," Hal Knox said bluntly. "Others have."
"Yes, so they have," the President said with a show of real anger, "and a hell of a mess it's made for their successors and for the country. I sometimes think you young hotheads on our side of it are just as *ruthless, intolerant* and *impractical* as the hotheads on the other side of it.... I have tried to cooperate as much as I could, consistent with my own convictions," he went on more calmly. "That has been my concept of it and that has been my training and tradition, and that is how I have done it. I know some people haven't liked it. I know I haven't liked it myself, sometimes. But I am still enough of a *Christian* and a *gentleman*, I hope, so that I will *do unto others as I would like them to do unto me*, were the situation reversed. I'm not ashamed of it (127 Italics added.).

From the perspective of President Abbott, and in earlier books in the series, from the perspective of his father, Hal Knox is "intolerant and impractical." In the context of Drury fiction, Hal is also right. Hal had advised his father, Secretary of State Orrin Knox, not to accept Ted Jason as his vice-presidential candidate, and despite his father's best efforts, Hal was never completely persuaded that his father had made the right choice. Concerning Ted Jason, NAWAC, and Communism, Hal's vision is very clear. When confronted face to face with political and moral evil, Hal is also "ruthless." Although his wife and his mother attempt to persuade him to be temperate, he remains true to his vision. Early in *Come Nineveh*, his vision is prophetic. Crystal Knox and Beth Knox may be able to "soft-soap" Hal, but they cannot "soft-soap" Ted Jason because as Hal tells his wife and mother:

"he's gone already—long gone. And he isn't coming back, the road he's gone down to get where he is. It's too late to save the country, Mother. He's given it away already, by accepting the support he has. Roger Croy, for God's sake! And Fred Van Ackerman. And LeGage Shelby. And Rufus Kleinfert and George Wattersill and all the terrible elements they represent, of violence at home and weakness abroad." His face contorted with a sudden pain. "It's too late. When they killed Dad, they pulled the plug on everything that held us together. And," he concluded simply, *"I hate them for it. I hate them with all my heart and all my being. And if I have a chance to kill some of them before they kill me, I will"* (53 Italics added.).

As *Come Nineveh* nears conclusion, Hal's worst fears are being realized; ex-President William Abbott, a statesman and conservative, is forced to move from his centrist position to the far right on the political spectrum. Rather than see America be destroyed by the ineptitude of a "liberal" President, the ex-President makes a radical suggestion: assassination. In the context of *Come Nineveh*, the world has been turned topsy-turvy: assassination is not treason; it is an act of patriotism, the only possible alternative if America's government, institutions, and values are to be preserved. Secretary of State Robert Leffingwell and Secretary of Defense Ewan MacDonald agree to discuss this radical alternative. Eventually, they will be imprisoned for conspiracy against the President.

In his fiction Drury has skillfully constructed a tragic "conservative" dilemma: "conservatives" are left with no acceptable options because of the failure of "liberal" political intelligence and courage. "Extremism in defense of virtue" is necessary for American survival, even though that extremism requires that "evil" means be used to achieve "good" ends. "Conservatives" in Drury fiction find it difficult to adapt the ethic that "the end justifies the means," and such thinking puts them at a disadvantage as they struggle with those on the far left of the political spectrum. Senator Lafe Smith reflects upon this reluctance as he contemplates the political power of Senator Van Ackerman and the Soviet aggression against the United States:

And, so what to do? Lafe found himself, like any decent and well-meaning citizen, up against a stone wall when it came to dealing with genuine evil. He had cast his vote in opposition, but once that was done, what else could he do? Fred would be able to do certain things to his opponents, and Lafe had no difficulty at all in imagining what they might be. But Lafe himself could no more imagine himself doing those things to anyone than he could imagine himself flying. Lafe belonged to that great mass of well-meaning people (he suspected, the overwhelming majority of mankind) upon whose hesitant impulses and general inability to recognize and comprehend evil, let alone cope with it, dictators and tyrants build their worlds. He was more sophisticated than many: he could see and believe in the evil. But he was as helpless as they because he could not bring himself to adopt evil's methods to defeat it (425).

Responsible conservatives are burdened and restricted by moral absolutes which influence them to strive to be fair and consistent in their political activities; on the other hand, again and again in *Come Nineveh*, the "liberals" of the far left are unhampered by such ethical considerations. Once Senator Van Ackerman and Governor Croy achieve their goals after exercising their rights of freedom of speech and mass protest demonstrations, they reverse themselves about such freedoms. To the far left there are no absolutes except power: might makes right; the end justifies the means. Confronted by such harsh realities, responsible conservatives move to the far right of the political spectrum and violent action, including presidential assassination, becomes an acceptable means to attain the end or goal of maintaining "the *status quo*" or traditional values of America. In order to preserve freedom and democracy, the most essential political, ethical, and religious rights may be violated. Survival of America justifies politically "evil" acts.

Thus on the right of the political spectrum we have statesmen who have conservative tendencies. Such statesmen blend into responsible conservatives, who in turn blend into some conservatives who become partisan politicians, who in turn blend into a group on the ultra-right, far right, who become reactionaries to all change. In the rhetoric of Drury fiction, those individuals who are on the far right and members of IDF (Individuals in Defense of Freedom) are viewed in very unflattering terms by Drury characters who are on the extreme left of the spectrum. Thus conservatives are sometimes viewed or characterized as "radicals of the right," "Right-wing reactionaries," and fascists of the right, though they are actually patriotic Americans in the context of Drury fiction (51, 243, 250). In Drury fiction conservatives are obviously good guys who wear the white hats.

The bad guys who wear the black hats are those on the far left of the political spectrum. As on the right, factions on the left blend into one another and overlap. There are statesmen who are liberals; there are responsible but partisan liberals; there are liberals who become "rigid and intolerant" and who evolve into irresponsible liberals. Some of the irresponsible liberals blend in with NAWAC which is "the New Left." "The New Left" ideologically and politically blends into "the Old Left" which is identified with Russian totalitarian Communism. Those on the far left of the spectrum are for radical change and they adopt the principle that "the end justifies the means." Their ideology and actions harmonize with the expressed goals of totalitarian Communism, including the economic goal shouted by Premier Khruschev during a temper tantrum at the United Nations as he pounded his shoe on the table: "We will bury you" (America). Such an economic burial from the Communist perspective would inevitably foreshadow the destruction of the American Republic. Consequently, in Drury fiction when NAWAC and Senator Van Ackerman militantly advocate peace with Russia, a peace at any price, they are acting in harmony with expressed Soviet goals of Communist economic and political domination. When Senator Van Ackerman secretly meets with the highest Russian intelligence agent in the United States, Drury explicitly links NAWAC with Soviet plans and policy. In a nasty twist of political rhetoric, Senator Van Ackerman, the most opportunistic, most unprincipled political villain in Drury fiction, a man who has "a psychotic whine" and who is mentally unstable, is linked by juxta position with a Kennedy, presumably Democratic Senator Robert Kennedy, a liberal who was a militant opponent of the Vietnam War and a potential presidential candidate before his assassination by Sirhan-Sirhan. Van Ackerman, during his first Senate Campaign, wins the support of the "liberal" press; and Drury describes the response of the print media:

A DARING YOUNG FIGHTER TAKES ON WYOMING'S CONSERVATIVES, *World* had trumpeted early in his campaign. WYOMING SENDS AN EXCITING NEW LIBERAL TO THE SENATE, *Times* had dutifully announced after it was all over. *VAN ACKERMAN OF WYOMING: A NEW KENNEDY?* wistfully inquired *Newsweek*, ever engaged on the ceaseless quest (*Come Nineveh*, 268 Italics added.).

The support was not limited to newspapers and magazines; Drury continues:

The *Times*, the *Post* and the networks, kit, caboodle and all, had rallied 'round with glowing articles, flattering photographs, sycophantic, interviews, fatherly, approving commentaries and editorials. He had fooled them all, and it was only after he had taken office and begun to reveal his contempt for the traditional customs, and the frayed but still valid decencies, of the national political game, that some began to become a little uneasy (268-269).

A few paragraphs earlier, Drury had already sketched the causes of Van Ackerman's flawed character—a character who was "almost completely amoral," "ruthless," and "almost completely cold and dead inside"—and commented upon his overly generous treatment by a press that did not hesitate to attack conservatives.

Had the nation's politically minded psychiatrists turned their attention to analyzing Fred Van Ackerman with half the zeal with which they publicly analyzed statesmen who they considered more conservative, they would perhaps have harsh explanations for his behavior. Since he had always been on the *Right Side of Things* they had never given him such kindly treatment. Yet, in many ways, the junior Senator from Wyoming was a classic example of all that they alleged, and condemned, in others. And now it appeared that he might be about to get away with it all, at last.

He had come, of course, from a broken home. He had been, of course, a loner as a child and youth. He had not, of course participated in games, achieved with any particular distinction in school, succeeded in acquiring or keeping friends. His attempts at romance had been, of course, sporadic, feeble, unsatisfactory, unfulfilled. At an early age, he, of course, acquired a contempt for authority, a desire to get even with society for all the vaguely defined but terribly hurtful things that seemed to go wrong with his inward life. And he combined all of this, of course, with a brilliant, almost animal, shrewdness in discerning the main chance, and an intelligence limited in scope and compassion but supremely able to seizing upon and profiting from the weaknesses of others (267 Italics added.).

It is Senator Van Ackerman who masterminds the manipulation and intimidation of Ted Jason. However, Van Ackerman pre-dates Ted Jason in Drury fiction.

Senator Van Ackerman makes his first appearance in the early pages of *Advise and Consent* as a flamboyant orator who urges negotiations with Russia to 20,000 Americans during a Madison Square Garden Rally of COMFORT (Committee on Making Further Offers for a Russian Truce). If it means "crawling to Moscow" the Senator tells a highly sympathetic and responsive audience, "I say I had rather crawl to Moscow than perish under a bomb" (28, 147). To his surprise, such sentiments catapult him into national publicity. Shrewdly, he realizes he had "a good thing" which might eventually make him President (193). Van Ackerman is a political opportunist who is not trusted by his senatorial colleagues: there is "a certain animal force" about him, "an almost disturbing note of caged unbalance that might flare up" at any time (194). When a fellow Senator casually suggests that Russians might be behind COMFORT, Van Ackerman expresses his belief that this is not so and indicates his motivation and naivete:

"I don't really think so. I think it's mostly, as I say, big New York money. You know how they are about Causes, and this is just about the biggest Cause there is right now. Oh, if I thought it was a Commie outfit, Stan, I wouldn't have anything to do with it. I think it is just a genuine desire for peace. And if they want me to be a talker, why should I refuse? It gets me plenty of publicity" (195).

When Van Ackerman becomes a militant, partisan supporter of Leffingwell's nomination for Secretary of State, Senator Seab Cooley acutely assesses his character and advises Senate Majority Leader Munson that Ackerman is a danger to the country and that his political career must be destroyed while such destruction is still possible. Senator Cooley's judgment is vindicated when Van Ackerman uses blackmail to force Senator Anderson to withdraw his opposition to the Leffingwell nomination. At a COMFORT rally there is a "savage, animal roar" when the Wyoming Senator announces that the Utah Senator's opposition can be removed because he has documented proof of Anderson's moral corruption that he will present in the Senate. Faced with public disgrace, Senator Anderson commits suicide. However, Senator Van Ackerman does not escape politically unscathed; at the conclusion of *Advise*, he is censured by the Senate.

In *A Shade of Difference* Van Ackerman continues in character. He wishes to "get even" by supporting Ted Jason in his presidential bid against his conservative enemies. In his unsuccessful attempt to recruit Bob Leffingwell in his crusade, Van Ackerman reveals himself to be both opportunist and racist:

"I think you and I and the Jasons and COMFORT and the nigger politicians like LeGage Shelby and Cullee Hamilton can all make common cause on this dustup in the UN. That's what I'm here for. I think it's a great opportunity to co-ordinate all the elements in the country that want a truly progressive approach to world peace and a truly liberal outlook in world affairs. I think we can get terrific backing all over the country. It'll also give us a head start against Orrin in the campaign next year. We can carry it right on into the convention and give Ted Jason terrific backing for the nomination. It's a natural" (211).

As Van Ackerman later tells the black LeGage Shelby, he believes that "all of us *liberals* can get together" (244 Italics added.). In an attempt—a successful attempt—to persuade Shelby to unite the power of DEFY (Defenders of Equality For You) with COMFORT, Van Ackerman argues that a coalition should be formed to "put over the *liberal point of view*." Both Ted Jason and COMFORT are interested, and *The New York Post* and *The Washington Post* will support them. LeGage is persuaded to join with Van Ackerman in "the cause of *true liberalism*." The naive LeGage is unaware at this time that Van Ackerman is a racist who believes that LeGage is "a damned good boy, *for* a nigger" (252-253 Italics added.). The darker side of Van Ackerman's personality is again demonstrated when he forces Senator Cooley to follow the letter of parliamentary law during his filibuster against aid to Gorotoland, a filibuster which extends the energies of Senator Cooley and, ironically, in view of Seab's earlier assessment of Ackerman's character, causes his death.

In *Capable of Honor* the Wyoming Senator continues his opposition to President Hudson and Orrin Knox by opposing their foreign policy. Rufus Kleinfert, the Knight Kommander of KEEP (Konference on Efforts to Encourage Patriotism) is persuaded to join forces with DEFY and COMFORT. As with Van Ackerman, Kleinfert wishes America to withdraw from Gorotoland. Kleinfert, a Texas oil man, believes that the President and the Secretary of State are either Communist agents or Communist dupes and that "our entanglement in Gorotoland is a Communist plot to drain our manpower and resources as they have been drained in so many places in recent decades" (205). Kleinfert does not trust Ted Jason either: the California Governor is perhaps "a dangerous, radical, Communistically oriented liberal" (206). This highly unlikely coalition, which uses political intimidation and violence to support a foreign peace policy, leads Ted Jason to believe that he can win the presidential nomination of his party. When Governor Jason is unable to do so, Senator Van Ackerman demonstrates the power and influence of his political coalition by demanding that Ted Jason attend a pre-convention organizing meeting for the purpose of forming a third party, a "peace" party to oppose the "war" party of the Hudson-Knox presidential ticket.

In *Preserve and Protect* Drury makes a direct link with Communism and the anti-war groups: COMFORT, KEEP, DEFY. Journalist Helen-Anne Carew gathers evidence that conclusively demonstrates that Senator Van Ackerman, along with LeGage Shelby and Rufus Kleinfert, had met with Soviet Ambassador Tashikov and a Lieutenant General of the KGB in order to discuss campaign strategy for the presidential campaign of the pro-peace candidate, Ted Jason. Before the Senator meets with Helen-Anne Carew, he reflects upon his political career and his principles. Van Ackerman rationalizes his blackmailing of Senator Anderson in *Advise and Consent* as "legitimate political hazing" of a "pathetic, little weak sister" whose suicide could not have been foreseen (200). In Van Ackerman's campaign for re-election to the Senate, he perceives his peace platform to be legitimate: "...was there anything wrong in wanting to put a stop to these endless petty wars that were draining away the substance, the unity and purpose of America?" In addition, the Wyoming Senator believes that his support of Bob Leffingwell for Secretary of State is justified, as also are Leffingwell's lies to the Senate sub-committee. To Fred Van Ackerman, ends justify means: "Anybody could lie to protect himself in politics. Fred did it all the time. One little lie or another wasn't going to affect a man's abilities to lead the crusade for final peace" (201). In addition, Fred has no scruples about campaign finances. He does not know where COMFORT's funding originates; however, "he knew it was an invaluable ally and a perfect sounding board for him in the crusade for peace," and peace is the most noble goal possible (201, 202). The rationalization disintegrates when Helen-Anne Carew confronts him with evidence of his meeting with the Russian Ambassador. After a stormy session in which Van Ackerman admits nothing, the Senator places a telephone call that results in Helen-Anne Carew's assassination. Rather than being contrite about his part in the journalist's assassination, Van Ackerman makes a veiled threat to the press during debate over the Riot Control Act (A Bill to Further Curb Acts Against the Public Order and Welfare). When he is asked in the Senate what he knows about Helen-Anne's death, he replies: "I thought she was just a reporter who got into the wrong story. It happens. It's probably going to happen more from now on, if the press gets curious about the wrong things" (277). As *Come Nineveh, Come Tyre* nears conclusion, both Congressman Bronson Bernard of New York and President Jason from California recognize Van Ackerman for what he is by using animal metaphors. As a result of the new Riot Control Bill, the Senator has the power to imprison or to commit to an insane asylum those who disagree with him. Too late, the "liberal" Bronson, the dupe of Van Ackerman, perceives "the awful consequences of a misguided but terribly well-meaning idealism." Because he expresses disagreement with the Senator's repression of the press, Van Ackerman threatens him with commitment to St. Elizabeth's, a mental hospital. "Monster!" "Monster!" Bronson shouts as Van Ackerman grins: "Somebody should have thought of that a long time ago." Fred Van Ackerman views the world as "a jungle" and himself as a "predator" who stalks "with the best" (450-451). When President Jason realizes that the Senator is using the Riot Bill to suppress legitimate speech and dissent, and the President requests his resignation,

Ackerman once again intimidates the President. The President's creation, "a Frankenstein's monster," forces President Jason to back down.

"Oh no, you don't" Fred cried with an exasperated harshness. "Oh, no, you don't! If you want me out of here you'll have to come right out like a big, brave man and fire me, Mr. President. You won't trick me into it. You'll have to *do* it. So, go ahead. Go ahead, and see what that gets you from your true supporters! Why, listen!" he said scornfully, abandoning the ranting tone in one of his typical lightning changes, "do you want NAWAC in the streets in five minutes rioting against *you*? Do you want this country *really* turned into an armed camp? It can be done now, Mr. President, and you know it. *You know it*. So you just tell me how you want it, and I'll be happy to oblige" (461).

In *The Promise of Joy*, the political career of Fred Van Ackerman takes a different turn. Because NAWAC finds the foreign policy of President Knox's Administration unsatisfactory, Van Ackerman, LeGage and Kleinfert approach Vice-President Cullee Hamilton and suggest that the conservative President be assassinated; such a suggestion is a reverse of events in *Come Nineveh* where ex-President Abbott suggests the assassination of liberal President Jason. In *The Promise* the black Vice-President vehemently rejects such a notion, just as President Knox rejects Van Ackerman's and NAWAC's pressure to side with the Russians—the Caucasian race—in the Russian-China atomic war which has racial and cultural overtones and implications. Although Fred Van Ackerman is not labeled an animal or monster in *The Promise*, both ex-President Abbott and President Knox perceive him as a Hitler, a fascist of the left. President Knox believes that Ackerman is an "evil genius;" he is "one of those fortunately rare types who know exactly how to appeal to all the lowest instincts of their fellow beings.... The reason Fred was able to achieve such successes of evil was because they (evil instincts) were hidden there waiting for him, needing only to be called out with the right words and the right timing. His appeal could succeed, as Walter (Dobius) said, *only because it synthesized what many were secretly thinking*" (377 Italics added.). Ex-President Abbott believes much the same: Van Ackerman appeals to "the most ugly and elemental instincts of the human *animal*." Once someone such as Van Ackerman meets with success, there will be a bandwagon, steamroller effect: "Before you know it, the *herd* is on its way, running wild and impossible to control" (371 Italics added.). Unfortunately for Van Ackerman in *A Promise*, his taunting racist comments and arrogant political manipulation bring out the worst human instincts in LeGage Shelby. The chairman of DEFY finally realizes that if Van Ackerman wishes the destruction of the yellow race, once the Chinese are subdued Van Ackerman will probably promote the destruction of blacks. LeGage's anger is intensified by Van Ackerman's desire to assassinate the black Vice-President, Cullee Hamilton, who is LeGage's former best friend.

For the last time, Van Ackerman reveals to LeGage his ideological orientation, an orientation which reveals his sympathies with Russia and which demonstrates his contempt for different religions, races, and ideologies:

Russia's falling and we've got to save her, and the man who stands in the way is going to be wiped out by the people of this country. They'll kill him or they'll impeach him or they'll do something—anyway, they'll sweep over him. And when he's gone, which won't be very many more days or maybe even hours, now, they'll turn to the man who understands them and knows how to appeal to what they *really* want, not all this idealistic crap we've had to feed them in recent years to get them to follow me, after this—except maybe"—his eyes looked oddly tortured for one seeing a vision apparently so attractive to him—"except maybe a few of the damned niggers and the damned kikes and the damned conservatives, and maybe even"—and for a moment a savage humor touched his face—"maybe even a few of these high and mighty *liberals* whose asses I've had to kiss for so long to get where I'm going...(415).

LeGage's response in *A Promise* is to find a knife and murder his "liberal" tormentor. Fred Van Ackerman, like Ted Jason, illustrates the failure of liberals and liberalism to preserve and protect the traditional values of the American body politic. That failure is most pronounced in *Come Nineveh, Come Tyre*.

Chapter X
Come Nineveh, Come Tyre and
The Failure of Liberalism

To give the most sympathetic reading possible to *Come Nineveh, Come Tyre*, it must be read as the conclusion of a series which includes *Advise and Consent, A Shade of Difference, Capable of Honor,* and *Preserve and Protect.* Even within such a comprehensive structure, most critical readers will find it wanting as quality political fiction. Although *Come Nineveh, Come Tyre* might serve as an example of pure, serious, and popular political fiction—in 1973-1974 it was on *The New York Times* Best Seller list for twenty-six weeks—it is flawed by a simplistic, obtrusive, propagandistic thrust, a propagandistic thrust sanctioned by Edmund Speare in his definition of a political novel "where the main purpose of the writer is partly propaganda, or exposition of the lives of personages who maintain government, or the forces which constitute governments" (ix).

Undoubtedly, many readers were intrigued by the possibilities of a plot generated by the question what would happen if a liberal "soft on Communism" became President? Undoubtedly, many conservative readers were vicariously thrilled as they traveled through a fictional world where their worst fears about "professional liberals" were confirmed. On the other hand, many liberal readers found the same *Come Nineveh, Come Tyre* lacking the artistic sophistication necessary for evoking and sustaining in them "a willing suspension of disbelief" even taking into account that *Come Nineveh* is primarily a combination of anatomy and romance rather than a novel. Let us briefly comment upon propaganda, anatomy, and romance, as well as the contrasting characters of Orrin Knox and Ted Jason before we turn to a critical exposition of *Come Nineveh, Come Tyre.*

As we have observed in the previous chapter, Orrin Knox is an ideal conservative who embodies in his thoughts and actions the traditional values capsulized in the words God, country, duty, and honor. Knox's character is consistent with the heroes of romance, the "mythos of literature," as Frye suggests, "concerned primarily with the idealized world" (the world as we would like it to be) and the romance, again in Frye's words, "a fictional mode in which the chief characters live in the world of marvels" or the improbable (*Anatomy of Criticism* 367). Despite potentially destructive and intensive external political pressure, Knox remains true to his conservative vision although a fidelity to ideals and principles may destroy his political career, his family, the United States, and perhaps even the world. In short,

Knox is a dramatic contrast to Ted Jason, the "liberal" who becomes President in *Come Nineveh, Come Tyre*.

In *Come Nineveh, Come Tyre*, Ted Jason is a protagonist who functions as a naive villain in order to illustrate a Drury thesis: as a political philosophy, pure or theoretical liberalism is inadequate to repel the challenge posed by imperialistic Communism as that Communism has evolved in the Soviet Union. Although Jason functions as a villain in *Come Nineveh*, he possesses the capability of evoking sympathy within most readers. Not only is Ted Jason not an evil person, he also sincerely wishes to do good and avoid evil. His failure is one of intelligence and will; he has noble intentions and ideal goals, but he misunderstands the nature of man and the nature of Communism. He totally accepts the theoretical principles of liberals and liberalism without understanding that a discrepancy between theory and practice possesses the potential for disaster. Jason's optimism in *Come Nineveh* is unwarranted, because it is not ground in an emotional and intellectual understanding of Soviet history. As a presidential candidate, as President-elect, and as President, Jason demonstrates in words and actions an inability to perceive the world as it really is: Jason fails to understand man's potential to commit evil acts. Consequently, he is manipulated not only by Senator Ackerman, but also by Chairman Tashikov. For Allen Drury, "liberal" Ted Jason is a "straw man" created and developed as a "foil" to conservative political philosophy; he is created in order to be destroyed, a prophetic example of the ineffectiveness of liberals and liberalism. When Orrin Knox is pressured by the Russians in *The Promise of Joy*, Knox clings to his conservative principles and emerges as a hero. When Ted Jason is pressured by the Russians, Jason clings to his liberal principles, but he emerges as a political villain. Unlike *The Promise* where good triumphs over evil, in *Come Nineveh* the darker side of the psyche prevails. Nevertheless, there are significant and essential romantic parallels in the political careers of Orrin Knox and Ted Jason.

Both Ted Jason and Orrin Knox engage in a major political quest or adventure: the quest for the Presidency. When Ted Jason first appears, he desires to become President for the same reason as Orrin Knox: to do good deeds for America. Gradually, however, readers see Ted Jason become corrupted by his pride, his presidential ambitions, his liberal ideology, and his misunderstanding of the nature of Communism. As a result, in *Come Nineveh, Come Tyre* we have a reversal of the St. George and the Dragon myth: instead of the good knight slaying the evil dragon, the dragon seduces and destroys the knight, a knight who has "perilous adventures" while on "a perilous journey," engages in "a crucial struggle," and experiences "the exaltation of the hero" upon his election as President. Ted Jason's exaltation is short-lived. *Come Nineveh, Come Tyre* does not engage readers as a wish-fulfilment dream but rather as a nightmare which embodies the dangers of Communism and corrupted liberalism in the American body politic; it reinforces conservative fears of liberal philosophy influencing American foreign policy. Such romantic and propagandistic political fiction falls short of generating an *enduring* "willing suspension of disbelief" in most sophisticated readers.

Come Nineveh, Come Tyre combines the strains of anatomy—a dissection of the weakness of liberals and liberalism as it meets the challenge of Soviet imperialism—and romance; it presents an idealized villain in an action or actions which conclude with an unrealistic ending where evil triumphs over good, thereby providing pleasure for those who emotionally identify with conservatism and who believe that "liberalism" has the potential of destroying America. To Drury, "liberals"—Senator Van Ackerman, "Wonderful Walter," the opinion molders of the media and *academia*, and Ted Jason—erode America's traditional values, and weaken the American character. Such a trend, Drury reiterates in *Come Nineveh*, might eventually contribute to the decline and fall of America. Through the thoughts and actions of Bronson Bernard, a newly elected "liberal" Congressman from New York who helps to shape "The New Day" in Congress and the Senate, a day when "liberals" are able to impose their flawed intellectual vision and their will upon America through legislation, the narrator directly states the negative effects of "liberal" education and then the narrator directly identifies the cause:

In the mind of Bronson Bernard certain basic tenets had been implanted by his teachers at every stage from grammar school through college, and nothing was ever going to shake them. The United States of America was no damn good. Its ideals were a mockery. Its history was a fraud. Its purposes were corrupt. Its achievements were empty. Its hopes were a sham and its dreams were a lie. What ever good might have come from it here and there over the years—and that was precious little—had been entirely inadvertent and accidental. It was sinister, hypocritical, imperialistic, racist, worthless, and cruel. It was a mess...(288-289).
So believed Bronnie Bernard and so believed many millions of his generation who had spent their adolescent years passing through American schools, reading American newspapers and magazines, watching American television and listening to American radio, absorbing with rapt and respectful attention the savage attacks and denigrations of American intellectual and cultural leaders (289).

As an anatomy, then, *Come Nineveh* continues Drury's message heralding the potentially destructive consequences of unrestrained, theoretical liberalism (289).

As *Come Nineveh, Come Tyre* begins, Ted Jason is preparing to leave for the convention center to formally accept his party's nomination for Vice-President. Unlike the early pages of *The Promise of Joy* in which Orrin Knox is the center of consciousness, in *Come Nineveh* events are viewed from the mind of Ted Jason. From a different perspective, then, from the perspective of Ted Jason, we see events that have occurred in previous Drury fiction, events that are vividly depicted in previous books and which contribute to the development of an evolving Jason personality. As Jason ruminates over the past, we learn that confrontational meetings between Harley Hudson and Jason, between Orrin Knox and Jason, and between William Abbott and Jason have had some impact on the vice-presidential nominee. From time to time, readers are reminded that despite his public words, Jason has sometimes doubted his "soft" position on Gorotoland and Panama, as well as the wisdom of his continuing alliance with NAWAC, the National Anti-War Activities Congress. Although Jason does realize that his NAWAC supporters may have behaved irresponsibly and reprehensibly, Ted Jason never questions his own motivations. Up to this point in the political series, the vice-presidential nominee perceives himself as being primarily motivated by patriotism and altruism. If Jason were President, his first priority would be not only to end all wars, but also to end the threat of all wars. In order to become President and to achieve this goal, however, he has adopted the premise that "the ends justify the means." In previous books, Jason was an "equivocator"; his slogan was that "conscience must decide the issue," a slogan that permitted him to build political support without ever categorically committing himself to a foreign policy position. While this posture has been politically effective, it reflects Jason's inability to formulate a consistent principle upon which to base his political philosophy. Consequently, in the beginning of *Come Nineveh*, Jason is acting consistent with the character created in earlier books when he accepts Orrin Knox's condition that he repudiate NAWAC in order to become Knox's vice-presidential candidate. Again, there is consistency of character when Jason equivocates successfully on the NAWAC issue. Jason repudiates NAWAC, but only with the provision that *if* they have been as violent and as irresponsible as Orrin Knox and his supporters have charged. Consistently in *Capable* and *Preserve*, the "liberal" Jason has compromised his principles in order to fulfill his presidential ambitions. When there is a double assassination in the opening pages of *Come Nineveh*,—Orrin Knox and Ceil Jason—Ted Jason wins his party's nomination for President.

As the party nominee, as the President-elect, and as the President, Ted Jason makes several mistakes, mistakes that are deeply rooted in the character that Drury has developed in *A Shade of Difference, Capable of Honor*, and *Preserve and Protect*. Although Ted Jason is politically ambitious in *A Shade of Difference*, this ambition has not yet developed negative, egotistical and hubristic tones. Gradually, in Drury's fiction, Jason evolves into an overly ambitious, opportunistic, and insecure politician. The California Governor possesses a strong need to be loved and admired; consequently, he will not repudiate any faction that will support him or any faction that might aid him in achieving his presidential goal, even when, as with NAWAC, he no longer needs their political support to become President. Paradoxically, Jason is also overconfident; he overestimates his ability to control his supporters in NAWAC, just as he overestimates his ability to promote peaceful coexistence with Communist Russia. These *hubristic* tendencies are the result of his misplaced idealism; his belief that human nature is basically good; and his conviction that trust, rather than mistrust, is the desired strategy for promoting peace. Jason believes that it is much better to be loved than feared; unlike Machiavelli, Jason views the world—and human nature— as he would like it to be, rather than as the way it is. Jason believes that a demonstration of meekness rather than a demonstration of strength will lead to peace. Much to his regret in *Come Nineveh, Come Tyre* he learns never "to trust a Communist." When Jason is dramatically confronted by the leaders of NAWAC and by the Communists, he is timid. When he is pressed to action, the "liberal" Governor, who is elected President, succumbs to fear. At root, Ted Jason is a coward.

Shortly after Orrin Knox and Ceil Jason are assassinated and the wounded and grief stricken Jason is nominated for President, he makes his first major mistake. He permits his irresponsible political supporters—Senator Van Ackerman, LeGage Shelby, Rufus Kleinfert, and Roger Croy—to participate in the discussion of potential vice-presidential choices. From these discussions, which are advisory only, evolves Ted Jason's vice-presidential choice: Governor Croy. Croy is a disastrous choice. When Ted suggests that he might repudiate NAWAC, Croy counsels him that he should not do so because these elements may be needed to control "the radicals of the right" (51). Later, despite this counsel, after Jason is elected President and he perceives the essential reason why he has been unable to categorically repudiate NAWAC, namely fear of physical violence and political defeat, he determines to repudiate NAWAC; however, he tragically finds that he is unable to do so, and that Orrin Knox, Harley Hudson, and William Abbott were essentially correct in their evaluation of his inability to control his irresponsible supporters. Ironically, Senator Van Ackerman and his followers have understood Jason much better than Jason has understood himself. Rather than meekly accepting their rejection, the NAWAC leaders inform Jason that he will need them to suppress the dissent that will erupt when Jason implements his "peace" policies.

Although Jason is able to accept his own expedient inconsistency, he is unable to accept the inconsistency of his "liberal" supporters: " 'You gentlemen,' he remarks, 'are quite amazing in your consistency. You are really calling, I take it, for a serious attempt to suppress dissent in America, after taking advantage of America's tolerance toward dissent in all these recent months. To say nothing of *my* tolerance, I might add. How do you square that with your proposal now' " (98). Senator Van Ackerman's reply

shocks Jason: "You were tolerant of us *because we helped you get elected.
And that's the only reason.*" Still more, Van Ackerman informs the President
that because of his lack of integrity not only has he lost credibility with
NAWAC, but that he has also lost credibility with much of the thinking
American public: "And don't try to get high and mighty *now* and try to
convince us it was anything else. Because we don't believe you, and neither
does anybody else" (99). Earlier in *Come Nineveh* William Abbott has
indicated that although Ted Jason was politically successful, Ted lacked
self-knowledge; he really did not know who or what he was. Through Ted
Jason's response to Van Ackerman's verbal assault, we see that this is true:
"In what he suddenly realized was a cataclysmic moment, the President-
elect could see that Fred spoke the truth. It was a revelation so profound
in its implications for the future, and for the whole concept of himself,
that for several moments he was unable to reply" (99). Consistent with his
character, Ted retreats from his demand that NAWAC be disbanded. Not
only will Van Ackerman remain as his advisor, Van Ackerman will also
eventually become Chairman of the Riot Control Board, thereby possessing
the power to hospitalize and imprison those who dissent with the President's
peace policy. Equally discrediting to Jason's character is his opportunistic
adoption of a peace platform in order to foster his own political ambitions.
When Ted is elected President and he persuades Bob Leffingwell to accept
the position as Secretary of State, Ted expresses a lack of commitment to
the political policy—unilateral withdrawal from Gorotoland and Panama—
that has vaulted him into the presidency; Jason tells Leffingwell that he
is not "as rabid about it" as some of his supporters, "or even some of my
campaign oratory would lead you to believe." Jason is quite willing to reverse
his foreign policy. Though he may not change his position "180 degrees,"
the change, he tells Leffingwell, will be "more like 90" (119). Upon hearing
this, "liberal" Justice Davis is dismayed; he cannot understand how Jason
can repudiate his anti-war platform since such a reversal would betray the
trust and good faith of Jason's sincere supporters, many of whom are members
of the media. In fact, much of Jason's success is generated by the "liberal"
media, a media which shares with Jason the experience of intimidation.
Again, like Jason, the media succumbs to fear; media leaders, like Jason,
also rationalize their cowardice and their dereliction of professional
responsibility because they share with Jason the idealistic goal of world
peace founded upon trust rather than strength.

After the media reports NAWAC political violence during the
presidential campaign, the media receives threats. When *The Greatest
Publication*, publishes an editorial suggesting that Jason repudiate NAWAC,
their building is bombed, three employees are killed, and printing presses
are ruined. As a result, the executive chairman of *The Greatest Publication*,
Walter Dobius, the general director of *The Post* and the editorial director

of *The Times* hold a conference, and during the conference they admit that, although they received political threats during Jason's campaign for President, they chose not to report this to the public because such reports would reflect negatively upon their "liberal" candidate. During their conference, *The Post* regrets this breach of ethics, and Walter Dobius pinpoints the rationalization behind the press's derelication of its responsibility: "It isn't fun to know you're being a coward—even if you tell yourself it's because you're helping the candidate you like and don't want to hurt or embarrass him by raising a difficult question" (109).

Despite such critical evaluation, the press is still incapable of courageous action; even after Dobius expresses his belief that Jason is "an opportunistic lightweight and a weakling," Dobius and his friends are incapable of publicly confronting NAWAC. Instead of fighting NAWAC, they decide to become "careful, cautious," "to water down" criticism in order to avoid violent retaliations. *The Times* rationalizes: "We do have to protect Jason. He's the only President we've got.... If we aren't going to appeal to him, we'd better forget all this concentration on assuring public support for his peace policies. Those, after all, are a hell of a lot more important than us or our problems" (113). If the press had not supported Ted Jason, he would never have been elected President. The press puffs up his ego and gives him misplaced confidence in his ability. Consequently, the media must take some, if not much, responsibility for the political disaster that occurs in America.

The "liberal" press enthusiastically supports Ted Jason during his campaign when he receives a letter from Chairman Tashikov in which the Russian foresees the withdrawal of American forces from Gorotoland and Panama, an end to the arms race, and an end to mutual suspicion and mistrust; the Russian also writes "I see the start of peace." Tashikov shamelessly, but effectively, flatters the presidential candidate: peace, he writes, can be achieved because Jason is a leader who possesses "great and farseeing wisdom" and "absolute courage and integrity;" peace is possible because Jason is a "man of peace," and because he is also Tashikov's "friend." Jason enthusiastically responds to the letter and when he becomes President, Jason converts his response to action by unilaterally announcing during his inaugural address American concessions to Russian foreign policy. The new President announces the withdrawal of American forces in Gorotoland and Panama, the suspension of U-2 flights and satellite surveillance of Russian territory, and withdrawal of American military personnel and weaponry. There are two significant responses. At home, the President's audience responds with "The Sound"—"a great, rolling, roaring shout...growing and rising, and rising and growing, until it seemed the universe must come asunder" (149). "The Sound" reflects a state of euphoria, the joy and ecstasy of "liberals" when their vision has been realized: a "liberal"

President who has the courage to unilaterally take the steps necessary for peace, a risk which is justified because of the intrinsic goodness of man whether that man be a capitalist or a Communist, an American or a Russian. Although the American "liberals" respond to the challenge of peace with emotions of trust, hope, and euphoria, such is not the case with the Russians who have been shrewdly jockeying the American psyche to their political and military advantage. Unlike Jason, Tashikov believes that when a choice of one or the other must be made, the effective ruler should choose to be feared rather than choose to be loved; consequently, while the Americans are joyfully celebrating the inauguration, while the President is attending parties, Russia takes the political and military offensive. The Soviets intensify aggression in Gorotoland and Panama; they land paratroopers in Alaska; they sink the bulk of the American fishing fleet in the Alaskan waters; and Tashikov "invites" a shocked President Jason to a Moscow conference in order to discuss the elimination of "imperialist U.S. aggression and establish world peace" (153).

At the beginning of Book II when President Jason meets with his advisers in the Situation Room to discuss the nation's response to the Russian belligerence, ex-President Abbott advises a "tough" military response to Communist aggression, but President Jason is not so inclined. The President reflects a lack of will to challenge the Communists, a lack of will that Senator Munson identifies as a deplorable characteristic in the American psyche. Rather than confront Russia directly, Jason's response is timid: U-2 and satellite surveillance will be reinstated and the President will meet with the Russians not in Moscow but in a still to be determined neutral country. Mistakenly, the President perceives Tashikov as a closet dove who is surrounded by hawks, a man who really does not wish to provoke war with America. Although the President characterizes his response as "a whip and a carrot," his response to Soviet aggression is all "carrot" and the Russians will read his response as weakness. Nevertheless, the President has the full support of Congress, a Congress that has dramatically changed as a result of Jason's landslide victory. The President's election and his party's winning of a majority in Congress heralds a "New Day" in America. In the "New Day" the new Congress rejects the gentlemanly traditions of the House and the Senate. When Senator Munson is defeated in his bid for re-election to Senate Majority Leader and Congressman William Abbott is defeated in his bid to reclaim his former position as Speaker of the House, they suffer personal abuse from their colleagues. However, President Jason has little opportunity to become joyful over his congressional support because Chairman Tashikov ignores Jason's mild response to Soviet aggression and demands an immediate Moscow conference with the President and threatens devastating consequences to America if Jason does not comply. Because he is unable to comprehend that men can both desire and perform evil on an international scale, President Jason is unable to respond to Russian aggression:

Everything, in this late hour in the Oval Office, combined to confirm in the mind of the President of the United States the conviction that all would, as Frankly said, come right. How could it, indeed, be otherwise? His decisions had been inspired by sincerity, idealism, and good will. Therefore they simply had to bring good because God was good and He recognized goodness, and therefore He would not abandon America, which was so good, or the President, who was so good (194).

Not surprisingly under the circumstances, America's influence in the United Nations rapidly deteriorates. The French Ambassador reflects the emerging international political realities and places them in a historical context which expresses recurring themes in Drury fiction:

The deed is done, only the *coup de grace* remains. It is immaterial what happens here or anywhere except where American power meets Russian. And this President does not want them to meet. Oh, he will talk, he will meet that way. But to meet strength with strength—no, he prefers to run away, this President.... There will be no real meeting and therefore no turning back and therefore no stopping the Russians. It is already history, it is inevitable. The script was written many years ago when the Americans grew tired and lost their nerve (198).

Although the Security Council passes a Russian resolution condemning United States military activities in Gorotoland and Panama and demanding that the President meet with the Russians at Moscow, the resolution is vetoed by the United Kingdom and France. However, when Russia brings their case before the General Assembly, the United Nations is in sympathy with the Russian allegations and demands. Secretary of State Leffingwell explains the tragic significance of the United Nations' response to President Jason: "The military clique in Moscow now has the official sanction of the world for whatever it has done, is doing and may wish to do" (229).

As anti-Jason elements begin to protest Jason's policies and as the danger of Jason's weak response to Russia becomes apparent, the American press begins to become anxious about America's diminishing prestige and power. Although Secretary of State Leffingwell believes that President Jason misunderstands human nature and the flow of history and that, as a result, he has failed to perceive "The Moment" when a strong response to Russia was necessary, Leffingwell is unable to persuade the President to adopt a more realistic foreign policy. Some of Jason's paralysis is generated because America's armed forces are not equipped and trained well enough to wage a successful conventional war against the Soviets, another Drury theme. The only effective response available against Russian aggression is with nuclear weapons. To the liberal Jason, such a response is unacceptable because he believes that at root the Russian leaders are sane, rational men of good will. Jason rationalizes his restraint by comparing his non-aggressive response to the responses of previous Presidents. Again, Secretary of State Leffingwell has a different perspective:

> I just find one thing missing in your historical equation, and that is that, of all those you named, of all who have sat in this house, *all* of them—you are the very first who came into office and deliberately and immediately began to dismantle America's power and position in the world. And from *that*, it seems to me, flow our present perils and the great trouble we are in. It was not a sudden decision by the Russians to move—until you made it clear to them that they could do so with impunity. And then they moved—and kept moving—and are still moving, because from your very first moments in office you made clear to them that you will not stop them. And the world, which I am afraid is really not a very idealistic place, assesses them accordingly (232).

Such explanatory analysis does not influence Jason because Jason has undergone a transformation of personality; he has succeeded in his search for personal identity by totally accepting the goal of peace as his mission. This peace commitment takes on the character of a messianic complex. The "liberal" President has undergone "an inner change, a reformation almost spiritual, a conversion from politician trying to satisfy a ravening ideological consistency to a man profoundly convinced of his own mission." As a result, Jason feels compelled "to show the world by precept and example that an American President could do what both the honestly idealistic and their cynical and politically motivated leaders demanded of them—offer the world a complete and genuine act of peace, without reservation and without guile" (239). This unrealistic, optimistic mood is shattered as the President leaves for Moscow and observes conservative and right-wing demonstrators carrying placards protesting his "peace" foreign policy. Frequently, such demonstrations have erupted into violence between the members of NAWAC and the "conservative" protesters. Despite NAWAC's repressive actions, Jason still refuses to repudiate them, even though Walter Dobius has warned of a "fascism of the left" in his newspaper columns.

As the second book of *Come Nineveh* concludes, the President and his entourage arrive in Moscow, but only the President meets with the Chairman of the Council of Ministries and participates in diplomatic discussions. Ominously, when the President concludes the conference he looks like "a man coming out of hell" and his entourage, along with the reader, is kept in suspense as to what has happened between the President and the Russians behind closed doors.

Book III continues to present "liberals" in a very unflattering perspective. When the President returns to America, he withdraws from everyone and wallows in a state of fear, indecision, and self-pity. Basically, except for the assassinated Ceil, Jason has always been a loner, a person unable to make or keep good friends. While the President isolates himself in the White House, Senator Ackerman and Congressman Bronson Bernard introduce into the House and the Senate "A Bill to Strengthen the United States Against All Enemies, Foreign and Domestic," a bill that proponents label "the Help America Act" and opponents label as "the dictatorship bill." The bill would establish a "Special Branch" to work with the FBI, IRS, CIA, military intelligence, and all other governmental and private agencies that collect data on American citizens "in order to establish peace and tranquility" (260). The proposed bill would also establish a Domestic Tranquility Board to "advise, suggest and encourage" a positive, constructive, and affirmative approach on the part of all sectors of the nation toward the policies deemed necessary "for solving America's foreign and domestic problems" and violators could be fined $10,000 and imprisoned for five years (261). Predictably, conservatives in America respond vehemently to this threat to personal freedom and the freedom of the press. Beth Knox, Cullee Hamilton, and William Abbott join together to form IDF (In Defense of Freedom), a group whose members will have bloody clashes with NAWAC. Conservative fears about the bill are justified. Van Ackerman, who will be appointed to head the Domestic Tranquility Board, wants to "stop the damned dissenters" against Jason's "peace" policy and thereby "preserve law and order" (277). To Van Ackerman, the bill will be an instrument to keep "lily-livered reactionary right-wing bastards under control;" it will also be an instrument to show "who's boss" (277).

Once the bill is introduced, lively debates are presented in both houses. The level of emotion in the country is intensified when Beth Knox is kidnaped and the kidnapers order Congressman Hal Knox to support the bill or his mother will be "liquidated." Hal does not do so, because he knows that his conservative mother would not want him to do so. Despite continued opposition by the conservatives in Congress who refuse to be intimidated by left-wing political terrorism, the Help America Bill is passed. Although the goal of the kidnappers has ostensibly been achieved, Beth Knox is nevertheless assassinated. The purpose of this political assassination—an act of political terrorism—is elucidated by Frankly Unctuous, who, along with Walter Dobius, is increasingly becoming more closely aligned with the conservative element in America: Beth Knox's assassination is "frightfulness for frightfulness sake—terrorist horror for no other reason than to shake the American people—to put the country into a state of shock." It is also "to precipitate exactly the kind of domestic division and internal turmoil that would justify an immediate appeal to the extremely dangerous provisions of the so-called 'Help America Bill' " (337).

The response of "liberals" to "the Help America Bill" or "the dictatorship bill" and the kidnapping of Beth Knox is highly lamentable. The President maintains silence on the bill and permits Van Ackerman and

Jawbone Swarthman to direct the bill through Congress. Although the President orders the FBI to investigate the Knox kidnapping, he makes only a brief statement about the kidnapping, and he does not explain to his followers the devastating implications of such political terrorism to the future of the republic. The "liberal" Congress of "the New Day" is largely made up of a "new breed" who were elected on the coattails of the "liberal" Jason. The new members of the Congress who are of the younger generation are molded by the same liberal forces that have molded Bronson Bernard. The fruits of "liberal" education are frightening: elected officials, as well as teachers, doctors, and lawyers who are

...absolutely innocent, absolutely earnest, absolutely righteous and absolutely terrifying. They *knew*, because they had never been allowed to know anything else, that they were the children of a rotten country that had to be changed no matter what the change might do to liberty or to human beings. They were without objectivity, compassion, the power to analyze or any points of historical or moral reference because objectivity had been destroyed, compassion had been withheld, the power to analyze had been turned upside down and history and the concept of moral reference had been deliberately and scornfully dismissed (289-290).

Not surprisingly then, the new Congressmen and Senators are easily influenced by "liberal" Senator Van Ackerman. They perceive themselves as being more idealistic, more principled than their predecessors who were corrupted by the "old politics" (288). The older, more conservative members of Congress, though they are unable to defeat "the dictatorship bill" foresee the threat to democracy contained in the legislation and they understand that if the Congress passes the bill, Congress will have sent a clear message to the political terrorists that intimidation is a very effective weapon. After prolonged debate, that is the message that the "New Breed" of Congressmen and Senators send to the far left terrorists. The response of the media is also uninspiring.

The "liberal" press responds to the Knox kidnapping on two levels. Headlines in the *Times* suggest that the kidnapping was not a very serious event: "Survey Shows Political Kidnapping Common for Years in Other Lands, But Bizarre Episode is New for America," and the tone of the following newspaper story "was calm, chatty, informative, reasonable, matter of fact, and even...cheery" (312). In the executive offices, both the "Help America Bill" and the Knox kidnapping are cause for some anxiety and discussion. However, "Wonderful Walter" is unable to persuade the top executives of *The Greatest Publication*, the *Times* and the *Post* that a strong journalistic response to the "Help America Bill" and the Knox kidnapping is necessary. The executives are too blind—or too afraid—to recognize that these events may herald governmental control of the press and the eventual loss of their personal freedom unless they choose, as opinion makers and molders of opinion, to function as a propaganda arm of the government. Despite such a threatening political climate, as Book III concludes, T.V. anchorman Frankly Unctuous courageously reports that there is deep unrest in America, that there are bloody clashes between conservative dissenters and NAWAC, that Americans are worried because of a failure in presidential leadership, and that there is talk of impeachment. As American dissatisfaction and turmoil increases, depressed President Jason reluctantly agrees to meet with Congressional and military leaders to finally inform them of what occurred when he and Chairman Tashikov met behind closed doors in Moscow.

As Jason reports the substance of his meeting with Tashikov, in Book IV of this anatomy-romance, the President personifies the failure of "liberalism" and Chairman Tashikov personifies the "evil" of Communism. After an hour and a half of a political harangue, a tirade that Drury reminds us is not new—Nikita Khruschev delivered a similar verbal attack against John F. Kennedy in Vienna, an attack which sent the American President away "dazed and trembling"—President Jason begins to perceive in a new way the threat of totalitarian Communism. As the Soviet Chairman hurls a pack of monstrous lies at the President, Tashikov appears to be insane and Jason begins to realize that his trust in human nature in general and Chairman Tashikov in particular might have been folly. To his advisors and his critics, who are listening in shocked silence, Jason reports his words to Tashikov: "I said you were a decent and peace-loving man who wanted as much as I to establish a viable and lasting peace. I accepted your statements in good faith—*I believed a Communist*" (350). The results of this misplaced idealism and trust are potentially catastrophic. Graphically, Tashikov privately presents information that indicates Russia can totally destroy America while remaining invulnerable because the Soviets possess a combination of military superiority and cunning which would enable Russia to launch simultaneously atomic, chemical, and biological attacks upon America's major population centers. During the Moscow conference Tashikov persuades Jason that biological and chemical bombs are already in place in American cities and can be exploded at the whim of the Russian leader. Naively, a shocked Jason points out that Russia has violated all of its treaties and agreements with America. Tashikov's response emphasizes the duplicity of Communists, a major theme of Drury's anatomy:

So naive! So wishful! So childish! Treaties! Agreements! Understandings! Did anyone in America *really* think we would honor those things? Why on earth should we, when all we had to do was play upon the ego, the gullibility and the infinite self-delusion of your Presidents, your Congress, your intellectual community and your press? America has *begged* to be betrayed in these recent decades, Mr. President! Even if it had not been our intention, we should have been forced to oblige. How else could we have treated a great power whose controlling minds have had so little understanding of what it takes to *survive* as a great power, in this harsh world?

The race goes to the strong, Mr. President. We were supposed to be in the business of helping weaklings to save themselves? That is not the Communist concept, I assure you" (353-354).

A dazed President Jason expresses the basis of his trust in Communist leaders; he had hoped—believed—that they had changed. Again, Drury presents through the words and actions of a Communist, major themes of *Come Nineveh, Come Tyre*, an anatomy which concludes a political series that is essentially anatomical:

"We will never change. We are educated, trained, Communists. Our methods may change, our goals never. We have never made a secret of this, either in our published statements or our actions, over six decades."
"Why are Americans always so self-deluding about this, Mr. President? We frown, and America becomes hysterical. We smile, and America falls down and rolls at our feet in gratitude. We have 'thaws,' we have 'detentes,' we have 'freezes,' we have whatever other easy, sleazy catchwords your media dreams up for us; but all the time we just go steadily right along, no matter who is in charge here, no matter what apparent outward twists and turns of policy we may find advisable: we still go steadily right along. We are programmed by history, Mr. President: history says the triumph of Communism is inevitable. So why should Communism change, if victory is inevitable? Communism never changes. How ineffably childish, stupid and immature of so many influential Americans, so many fools in the West, to deny all the evidence, all the record of history, to self-delude themselves into the thinking that we do.' " (355-356).

Confronted with what appears to be overwhelming Russian military superiority—America has reduced military expenditures in order to initiate and bolster social programs while Russia has dramatically increased its military budget—and cunning, Jason is unable to respond constructively when Tashikov demands that the President make significant and essential changes in both foreign and domestic policy. While Jason is narrating the facts of his humiliation by Tashikov, some of the Russian demands have already been met: American forces have been beaten in Gorotoland and Panama and all that remains is for the President to recognize the new regimes in those countries; disruptive elements protesting Jason's foreign policy are being curbed; and through the newly legislated Help America Bill the President now has the power to curb "the disruptive and hostile elements" in the media and intellectual community who oppose cooperation with Russia (358).

As Ex-President Abbot, Walter Dobius, and other leaders of America listen to the President relate his tragic, humiliating tale, they realize that Jason's gigantic ego directs him to focus upon *his* personal tragedy, rather than on the fate and welfare of America. When Jason continues to demonstrate a lack of will to confront the Russian threat and an inability to trust in

God, his Congress, and the American people, those present realize that for all practical purposes Jason has chosen to be "red" rather than dead. Jason, they believe, is no longer rational (363).

Unlike the President, Walter Dobius has developed the capability of understanding the Communist threat to America without losing his courage. Walter and William Abbott counsel the President to trust the American people and to make a military response to the Russians, rather than to permit the Russians to win control over America by default. Walter and the conservatives believe that Russia does not want war and will back down if America shows courage and retaliates. War, they believe, despite Tashikov's claimed military superiority, is not in Russia's self interest. A reformed Walter admits his and the media's responsibility in the demise of America's influence and power as he unsuccessfully attempts to persuade the depressed President to act, despite the President's fear that action on his part will precipitate an atomic war: why should Russia want war with us, the former "liberal" asks rhetorically,

"When they've gained so much over so many years because of fools like me? 'Yes!' he repeated angrily, 'fools like me!' Like all of us who excused them and rationalized them and justified them, all those years when they were moving into position to cut us down. Who were always so clever and so biting and so arch and so superior when some of our countrymen tried to warn of the trend of events. Who were always so smug and perfect...smug and perfect! That was us, all right. And now we're caught in the gale of history just like you are, Mr. President. Just like you...(364-365).

Though Jason's conservative advisors counsel dramatic military action, he will not act. Instead he will follow an ineffective plan which is in keeping with his character: equivocal. He will secretly encourage Congress to increase American military power but he will deny public approval to the legislation; as a result of this duplicity Jason will be able to present himself to the Russians as a man who continues to cooperate with their foreign policy when, in fact, such is not the case.

Book V of *Come Nineveh, Come Tyre* is the propagandistic climax of Drury's political fiction. In Book IV, Drury has slipped into his text lines from John Keats' "Ozymandias:" "look on our works, ye mighty and despair," lines which suggest that pride of power is vanity and that great nations will eventually crumble as a result of time (346). Just as Ozymandias' kingdom no longer exists, so also can the American republic disappear. This is the significance of the epigrammatic lines from Rudyard Kipling's "Recessional" which introduce *Come Nineveh, Come Tyre*

Far-called, our navies melt away;
    On dune and headland sinks the fire:

Lo, all our pomp of yesterday
    Is one with Nineveh and Tyre.

Both Nineveh and Tyre were famous capitals of powerful countries that
no longer exist: Assyria and Phoenicia. Kipling's "Recessional" was meant
to serve as a warning to the Victorian English who were excessively proud
of the British Empire. To readers of Drury's anatomy, Kipling's poem suggests
that America, like England, can gradually evolve into a second-rate power.
As *Come Nineveh, Come Tyre* concludes, America does become a second-
rate world power by preparing to withdraw from strategic military positions
around the globe. Kipling's concluding lines of the "Recessional's" third
stanza are a prayer:

Lo, all our pomp of yesterday
    Is one with Nineveh and Tyre!
Judge of the Nations, spare us yet,
    Lest we forget, lest we forget.

In the fourth stanza, Kipling suggests that power has corrupted England
and that the English no longer hold God in awe:

Lord God of hosts, be with us yet.
Lest we forget,—lest we forget.

In *Come Nineveh, Come Tyre*, the gods of fiction, the creator and the narrator,
do not save Ted Jason or America from disaster. A series of events occur
which inexorably lead Jason and Vice-President Croy to commit suicide,
thereby moving the President *Pro Tem* of the Senate, Senator Van Ackerman—
a cooperative sympathizer with Chairman Tashikov—one step closer to the
presidency. Very heavily, too heavy to be aesthetically pleasing, Drury again
explicitly expresses his prophetic message in the concluding lines of the
final page of his political series:

All, all had gone wrong for the President of the United States. And not from evil
intentions. But from good intentions, foolishly applied. And so America in her turn
learned the lesson: Great states are brought down, great nations are humbled, great
dreams are destroyed. It can happen here. No one had really believed it. Until now
(481).

As Book Five begins, the final steps in the destruction of America unfold.
Too late, the press begins to react to the Jason presidency. Ex-President
Abbott and his conservative followers contest the Help America Bill before
the Supreme Court in an attempt to have the bill declared unconstitutional.
A heated debate between the Supreme Court Justices and Counsels ensues
while pro-Jason mobs demonstrate outside the court house. Although Chief

Justice Davis is pressured to withdraw from the case because of his "liberal" bias, he refuses to do so. As Davis deliberates over his decision, he composes a long prayer invoking God's aid for himself and the nation. However, this is not to be. Left-wing radicals pose as law staff members and murder the Supreme Court Justice. As a result, the Supreme Court votes a four-four tie on the constitutionality of the Help America Bill and the Bill is declared constitutional. Attorney General Watterstill's argument is successful: America is "on the brink of revolution" and the Help America Bill is necessary to provide the law and order necessary to save America (380). Still fighting the good fight to save America, Ex-President Abbott brings an impeachment resolution against the President; this too is doomed to fail. The "liberal" opposition, however, is more successful in working its will. Senator Van Ackerman is able to marshal the new members of the Senate to support him in overthrowing the current President *Pro Tem* of the Senate, seventy-two year old Lacy Pollard, a representative of the older generation and a practitioner of "the old politics" and become elected to the position himself, thereby becoming third in line behind the Vice-President and the Speaker of the House to become President. At the conclusion of *Come Nineveh*, after Jason's and Croy's suicide, only the Speaker of the House, Jawbone Swarthman, stands between Van Ackerman and the presidency.

V

As American power and prestige are crumbling in the world and America is torn internally with conflict between "liberals" and "conservatives," the only ones with access to President Jason are his family: his sister, Patsy; Herbert, his uncle; and his aunts, Selena and Valuela. Patsy, Herbert, and Selena are "professional liberals" within the context of Drury fiction and are very supportive and protective of Jason; only Valuela, a one time "liberal," has the perception and the mental toughness to see the world as it really is and to confront the weakness of Ted Jason and the imminent danger to America. Although her family disapproves, Val advises Ted that he should make a "symbolic" gesture as a response to the Russians—"maybe bombing their trawlers in Alaska," and, at the same time, "weed out the trash" around him, namely Senator Van Ackerman. Ted should also ask Congress, Val advises, to repeal the "Help America Bill" and "form a national coalition government" with the conservative leaders in Congress (427). Herbert and Selena vigorously defend President Jason's foreign and domestic policies and his alliance with Senator Van Ackerman. Senator Van Ackerman, Selena argues, is always "on the Right Side" and "backs the Genuine Causes." Although Val thinks that Van Ackerman is a "dangerous" "thug," Patsy is fiercely loyal to the Wyoming Senator. Patsy reminds Val that Senator Van Ackerman has "always been a fighter for the Right Things"; he has always been a REAL liberal," and he was "one of the very first to support Ted for the Presidency" (429).

Jason would very much like to follow Val's advice; however, the President lacks the courage and wisdom to do so. President Jason believes that Val does not fully grasp the complexity of his problems; he believes that she has over-simplified both the problems and the solutions. Through the mind of the "liberal" President, Drury again presents a keynote of his fiction: *the decline and fall of the American empire* as a result of a declining confidence within America and the weakness of "liberals" to meet courageously the challenge of Communism:

Americans had been conditioned over many years by their educators and their opinion formers to doubt themselves, question their motives, hesitate, agonize, temporize— retreat. Americans had been conditioned, in fact, to lose. And now, with the greatest idealism and the best will in the world, he had offered the Russians voluntary concessions that could not be taken back, once the Russians had moved, without blowing up the world. And so, under his Presidency, it at last was beginning to seem almost inevitable that America would lose (432).

Again and again, Drury's theme has been the irresponsibility—in fact, the dereliction of professional duty—of the news media, one of the primary shapers of American values; and, in the last book of the anatomy, Drury depicts the potential consequences of such a failure. When the press finally has the courage to respond to its responsibility, it is too late: the Help America Bill has been passed, a "liberal" President is in office, and a "liberal" Congress supports the President's foreign and domestic policies. Consequently, when "Wonderful Walter" learns through *an unidentified source* that there had been a Communist conspiracy to assassinate President Hudson and Orrin Knox, "Wonderful Walter" patriotically prints this "leaked" information. As a result, the renowned columnist, along with other influential journalists, editors, and publishers, is committed to St. Elizabeth's Hospital, a mental institution, under the provision of the Help America Bill. Their imprisonment has been the logical conclusion to a carefully constructed plot that extends through each of the works in Drury's political series. Underlying that plot is a thesis. The "irresponsible" press consistently reports and interprets news by consciously and unconsciously exercising a "liberal" bias. In doing so, the media will lose respect among the American public, the citizens of America. This "liberal" bias is a trap which will eventually result in an erosion of liberty. As the media irresponsibly creates and shapes news in a "liberal" perspective, the media will lose the credibility of the American people and become impotent in its battle to maintain the freedom of the press. Through all of the fiction in this political series, Drury has presented a very unflattering view of Americans and the American voter: they are dupes of politicians and the media. In the world of fiction, which may or may not parallel the world of fact from time to time, the American public is misled by the media. As a result, an uninformed public unwisely chooses its political leaders—Congressmen, Senators, Presidents. Such pessimism eventually blends with cynicism in Drury fiction. Most Americans, Drury suggests in *Come Nineveh*, will act only when their obvious, immediate self-interest is involved. Such a view of human nature has some parallel with Machiavelli's evaluation of human nature as he expresses it in *The Prince*.

...one must say of men generally that they are ungrateful, mutable, pretenders and dissemblers, prone to avoid danger, thirsty for gain. So long as you benefit them they are all yours; as I said above, they offer you their blood, their lives, their children, when the need for such things is remote. But when need comes upon you, they turn around. So if a prince has relied wholly on their words, and is lacking in other preparations, he falls. For friendships that are gained with money, and not with greatness and nobility of spirit, are deserved but not possessed, and in the nick of time one cannot avail himself of them. Men hesitate less to injure a man who makes himself loved than to injure one who makes himself feared, for their love is held by a chain of obligation, which, because of men's wickedness, is broken on every occasion for the sake of selfish profit; but their fear is secured by a dread of punishment which never fails you (62).

As "Wonderful Walter" and other members of the media are being taken to St. Elizabeth's mental hospital, the narrator comes forward in the text. What would you do, the narrator asks the reader, if you saw the publishers and the journalists of the *Times* and the *Post* being taken to jail by the police because of the expression of views that clashed with the interest of the political office in power? In *Come Nineveh, Come Tyre*, the average American would do nothing:

Would you cry havoc and let slip the dogs of civil rebellion to save your free press?
Why, no, of course you wouldn't.
In the first place, two thirds of you wouldn't even glance up from your busy scurrying down the streets on your own private affairs.
And of the third of you who did notice, perhaps only a handful would be informed enough and sophisticated enough, to have an inkling of what was going on.
And of that handful, half would think, very quickly, Well, it's none of my affair, I'd better get on by just as fast as I can and forget about it. I can't afford to get involved.
And *half again would think*, Oh, dear, they can't do that, but how can I stop them, oh, dear, I might get hurt. I guess I'd better not try to do anything, oh dear.
And of the three or four left, perhaps one or two of you might half start forward— and then as abruptly stop, appalled by the unbelievable occasion, paralyzed by the knowledge of your own unarmed vulnerability, aware that you were almost entirely alone, aware that you might very well instantly be shot down...

And so they would take the *Times* and the *Post*... (442).

When "liberal" Congressman Bronson, the symbolic representative of the "new generation" and "the new politics," realizes that Van Ackerman's implementation of the "Help America Bill" is in fact the destruction of the free press, he is appalled. However, when the naive "liberal" confronts Van Ackerman and Van Ackerman threatens him with confinement in St. Elizabeth's, his only response is to call Van Ackerman a "Monster!" When "liberal" President Jason realizes the consequences of Van Ackerman's enforcement of the Help America Bill, he too ineffectually confronts Van Ackerman. When the President asks for his resignation, Van Ackerman tells him that he will not resign, that the President must fire him. Van Ackerman knows that Jason will not resign because the President needs the Senator's support if he wishes to continue as President. Rhetorically, Van Ackerman asks:

Do you want NAWAC in the streets in five minutes rioting against you? Do you want this country *really* turned into an armed camp? It can be done now Mr. President, and you know it. *You know it.* So just tell me how you want it, and I'll be happy to oblige" (461).

The President does not back down, however, when the Secretary of State, the Secretary of Defense, and the Joint Chiefs of Staff demand that the President resign from office within twenty-four hours. Since the "conservative" element in government will not use "evil" means to attain a "good" end, they are ineffective in opposing the "left-wing liberalism" that President Jason now represents. Though there have been discussions of presidential assassination, this has been rejected; instead, "conservatives" choose to conserve and to follow the traditional processes and procedures dictated by law. Predictably, in the context of *Come Nineveh, Come Tyre*, they are ineffective. When twelve noon arrives, the "conservatives" find themselves in jail by order of the President. Though Jason is unable to act against "left-wing liberals," he is a man of action when it is necessary to conserve his own power.

Devoid of counsel, totally isolated from anyone who could help him to save America and yet remain in office as President, Ted Jason requests an immediate conference with Chairman Tashikov. Naively, "liberal" Ted Jason hopes that his "strength of conviction" and "the idealism of his heart" will enable him to deal honorably with the Russian Chairman. Unrealistically, the "liberal" President believes that he will be able to impose his will upon Tashikov. Such is not to be. During this conference Chairman Tashikov reveals to the startled "liberal" President that unfolding events were part of a plan based upon the personality—the lack of character— of President Jason: For three years now, Chairman Tashikov explains

We have been studying the personality of Edward M. Jason. There is very little about you we do not know—the over-riding ambition, the arrogance of family and mind, the strange erratic, impulsive quirks of what you choose to regard as idealism and sincerity, the willingness to compromise with the violent when political advantage seemed the reward, the inability to suffer opposition without being persuaded to strike back blindly, the fatal tendency to let yourself be backed into corners from which the only escape has been by sacrificing yet more of the few remaining principles of this flimsy and dying democracy—above all the weakness under pressure, the weakness in power, the weakness, the weakness, the weakness! (471)

Forced to perceive the harsh reality of his own personality and his role in the destruction of the American Republic after consulting with and informing Vice-President Croy of his decision, the President does what the honor of a President of the United States demands of him, "accepting at last without reservation or self-protection the full responsibility of his actions." Ted Jason commits suicide. Almost simultaneously, Vice-President Croy has reached the same conclusions about honor and responsibility. He, too, we learn from the narrator, commits suicide. Thus both Jason and Croy, when faced with the reality of having to live under Russian domination, choose to be dead rather than red.

Come Nineveh, Come Tyre is the most troubling of Drury's political fiction. Ted Jason is unable to cope with the problems of the presidency; he consistently places his own political and personal welfare above the welfare of the republic. He is unable to control the violent and subversive political forces within the country that were responsible for his popularity and election. Just as he is unable to cope with the pressures exerted on him by Van Ackerman and NAWAC, Jason is unable to cope with the pressure exerted on him by Tashikov, the leader of totalitarian and imperialistic Communism. Jason, though well intentioned and idealistic, lacks courage and wisdom. As America teeters on the brink of atomic war, the President is emotionally unstable. As we have seen, when the President finally decides to communicate the events of his Moscow conference with the political leaders of the country, an unthinkable thought spontaneously enters the minds of the Congressman and Senators: "The President might no longer be rational." To ex-President Abbott and his conservative friends, "this was a devastating thought." So also is presidential suicide.

To some readers in 1973, such plotting and characterization severely challenged "a willing suspension of disbelief." Today, such a scenario might be considered lacking in terms of quality fiction; however, it would not be quite as challenging to the imagination. After the Watergate break-in, the Watergate cover-up, the Watergate trials, President Nixon's withdrawl from public contact, and his resignation from office, such plotting and characterization as we find in *Come Nineveh, Come Tyre* possesses at least some resonant tones of authenticity. Just as Drury sometimes creates fiction which reads like the truth, so also do Carl Bernstein and Robert Woodward present facts of history which read as if they were fiction. *In The Final Days*, the *Washington Post* journalists who won a Pulitzer Prize for *All the President's Men*, graphically depict the closing days of President Nixon's term in office. *In The Final Days* Woodward and Bernstein creatively reconstruct Alexander Haig's response to the continuing congressional and media attacks upon President Nixon:

Alexander Haig felt the burden of government acutely. It was Wednesday, August 7, and Richard Nixon was on the brink of resigning. General Haig's job as Nixon's Chief of Staff was to prevent a rout. He wanted to smooth the way for the country, for the President and for himself. He could see, hear and feel the erosion. Everything was crumbling at once. This was the last dismal stage of the battle, a defeat of dimensions such as he had never experienced. He had read about defeat; this was what it was—noise, irrationality, collapse on all sides. He was not sure he could deal with Nixon. He was afraid the President might kill himself (403).

Based on the testimony of the Secretary of State and President Nixon's son-in-law, the President that Bernstein and Woodward depict in *The Final Days* appears to have difficulty coping with reality. The President believed, according to Secretary of State Kissinger as reported by Woodward and Bernstein, that a "Jewish cabal" was "out to get" him (169, 377). Understandably, the Secretary was worried about the emotional state of the Commander in Chief. At times, Kissinger thought, "The President is like a madman." Ed Cox, Tricia Nixon's husband, was also extremely worried that "The President might take his own life." In a conversation with Senator Griffin, according to Woodward and Bernstein, Cox reported that the President was not sleeping, he was drinking, and he was "acting irrationally." Last night, the son-in-law worriedly told the Senator, his father-in-law "was up walking the halls...talking to pictures of former Presidents—giving speeches and talking to the pictures on the wall" (395). During the sixties and early seventies, the American body politic was in a time of very severe troubles, and Drury's fiction sometimes inadvertently and painfully reflects the troubled spirit of the age as well as ironic parallels in the world of fact. Significantly, in the context of Drury fiction, one of the major complaints of the Republican (conservative) Nixon Administration was that the liberal media, especially *The New York Times* and the *Washington Post*, treated Nixon unfairly. Such was the spirit of the age in the world of fact in the sixties and the seventies, a time of not only advocacy journalism, but also advocacy fiction.

Chapter XI
Sex, Marriage, and the Role of
Women in Drury Political Fiction

As we have observed in an earlier chapter, there were many reasons why political fiction was a marketing success in the sixties and early seventies, and one contributing factor to this popularity was the integration of sexual content into political fiction. Sex is interesting to most readers, and sexual content contributes to the popular appeal of Drury fiction. When marriage and sexual roles are accurately and realistically presented in political fiction, they add vitality and authenticity to the texture of the spirit of the age. Such is the case in Drury's political series where marriage, sex, and the role of women are blended into political plots and unify the focus upon the exercise of political power within the body politic.

Although Drury is a political conservative, his presentation of sex in his political fiction suggests a moderately progressive or liberal attitude toward sex. Drury presents a broad spectrum of sexual activity, and no sexual experience is categorically rejected as being morally reprehensible or socially unacceptable. When *Advise and Consent* was published in 1959, homosexuality was rarely an experience found at the center of a popular, best-selling novel. In *Advise* Drury tastefully discusses the sex life of Senator Anderson and sympathetically relates Anderson's homosexual experience to an evolving identity. Although Brig Anderson's most memorable sexual experience is a homosexual one, he is a bisexual who sexually enjoyed many women in college and many more when he was a pilot in the South Pacific during World War II. As a college student, the narrator informs us, he had girls "often enough" and "enjoyed them sufficiently enough so that he was pretty sure he didn't want what his (homosexual) fraternity brother wanted." In the army, "women came easy" (286). Through sexual experience Brig found out about himself, learned his identity, and developed a liberal sexual ethic:

He was forthright enough to admit to himself that finding good in what many would consider evil might be all an elaborate rationalization, and yet if it was, both he and society profited from it, so what matter the label that was put upon it? Men, he had observed, believed about themselves what they had to believe to keep going; and matched against the general motley he did not think his method for coming to terms with himself was any worse than anyone else's (295).

Contrasted with the bisexual Anderson in *Advise and Consent* is Senator Lafe Smith, an insatiable womanizer who is very much admired and respected by his male, senatorial colleagues. In a serious conversation, Lafe confides in Brig that "it's getting so I can't travel ten blocks in Washington without passing three places where I made love. It's a hell of a depressing thing when a town gets all filled up with memories of your one night stands" (343). When Majority Leader Munson cautions him to be careful, he responds, "Morals are a professional matter in Washington, you know, and I'm good at my profession" (138). To Lafe Smith, sexual promiscuity is morally, socially, and politically acceptable as long as it is kept secret from the voters. Smith need not have any fear concerning secrecy. In this instance the press in Drury fiction reflects the press in the world of fact in the sixties. As long as sexual experiences do not directly affect the performance of professional duties, the press considers the sex lives of politicians as a purely private and personal matter, even in those instances where sexual activity directly contradicts the carefully constructed image that the politician purposely projects to his constituents in order to be elected and remain in office: an image of a church-going member with conservative sexual values. Even though Lafe Smith has it both ways—he projects a conservative image to his Mormon constituency while secretly practicing an extremely permissive sexual ethic—he is dissatisfied with his promiscuous life and he wishes for something better. Like Lord Byron, Lafe was initiated into sexual experience before he possessed the emotional and intellectual maturity to understand sexual love. "I've never had a chance." He tells Bob Munson, "It started too early and it came too easy. People have been at me since I was eleven years old, all shapes, sizes, and sexes. I never had the opportunity to get started on the right track about sex. They all made it so simple for me. Everybody was so helpful. It's too late now" (120). When Lafe announces plans to marry in *Advise* and asks Brig Anderson to be his best man, he philosophizes about sex and marriage: "After all," he says, "what's sex when you come right down to it? Right time, right place, right mood, right company, there's nothing more wonderful; but how often does that ideal combination of factors come about?... And I imagine that's true even in marriage." Lafe describes marriage with a commercial image. To Lafe, marriage is a bargain: "A bargain between desire and custom, dream and reality, wish and career, sex and society" (343). All men and women, he believes, have to make such bargains and compromises in life. In *A Shade of Difference* we learn that neither Lafe nor his wife received a good "bargain" in their marriage which was terminated after only six months. As Lafe reminisces about his failed marriage with Irene, he realizes that only someone like himself who had slipped out of countless bedrooms would not have recognized that Irene had a sexual history similar to his own, and such experiences suggested that she would be an unfaithful marriage partner.

He was not sure which "had reverted to type first," but to save himself from embarrassment, though knowing he could not find happiness in such promiscuity, he had resumed his prowling (238). Nevertheless, the Senator realized that something very fundamental was missing in his life, that casual sex—hanging "trophies on the wall"—was a sterile existence. As he rationalizes his promiscuity and examines his unhappiness, he appears to understand the core of his inability to have an enduring romantic relationship.

And yet, he thought with a hopeless protest, what had he done to deserve it? Was it really justice? What had he ever done to hurt anybody? Possibly he had, here and there, though he had tried not to. As much as conscious care could prevent it, he had tried to be as kind as possible, to make it pleasant, to keep it light, to be sure that his partners understood that it was in fun and not to be taken too seriously. It was true that there had been a few instances when women had taken him too seriously; it had been clinging and messy, but could that be blamed on him? He had never promised anything, never offered his heart any more than was necessary to achieve his physical objective. Maybe that explained it, he thought forlornly with a rare flash of self-analysis; maybe he never received anything because he had never given anything. But it wasn't that he meant to be hurtful of anybody, he told himself with a bewildered truthfulness. It was just that he meant to be kind (239).

Nevertheless, in *A Shade* Lafe continues the promiscuous life that has won him the admiration of his male political friends and colleagues. After he has casual sex with an Indonesian nurse at the United Nations, she informs him about Hal Frye's illness, although previously she had told Lafe that it would be a breach of professional ethics for her to discuss her patient's medical history with the Senator. Since the UN nurse is helping her husband through medical training in the United States, she agrees to accept money from Lafe in exchange for her sexual love. Lafe is very much impressed with "it." After making love, he is "impressed with the advantages of Indonesian culture." When Lafe becomes depressed, he is very grateful when they resume "it"—their love making (240, 356, 358).

Despite Lafe Smith's sexual promiscuity, he does begin to grow morally and emotionally in *A Shade of Difference.* He has a platonic relationship with Mabel Anderson, Brig Anderson's widow who suffered both guilt and grief because she was unable to live up to the ideal of the feminine mystique. Because Lafe senses that a serious romantic relationship with Mabel might evolve into a permanent, happy, stable marriage, he does not attempt to exploit her sexually. Senator Smith's moral growth is also enhanced by his intimate friendship with Hal Frye, the chief U.S. delegate to the UN. Dying from leukemia, Senator Frye asks Smith to take care of his nineteen-year old son, who has been reduced to a vegetable-like state as a result of brain damage. In future Drury fiction, a sexually reformed Lafe Smith faithfully fulfills this dying request, and this added dimension of responsibility, combined with his romance with Mabel Anderson, provides a positive dimension to the bleakness permeating the final pages of Drury's political fiction. In *A Promise of Joy*, when America is on the brink of defeat in a war with Russia and China, Lafe bolsters the spirit of extremely depressed President Knox when he informs him that Mabel has consented to be his wife and that Jimmy Frye, the widowed Mabel, and her daughter Pidge, have given him faith in the power of love, a faith which motivates President Knox to praise the character of the reformed Washington Romeo:"You have a kind heart, one of the kindest I know, and you've earned this happiness" (227). In *Come Nineveh, Come Tyre*, however, Lafe's generosity and love are not rewarded. Mabel Anderson reverts back to the stereotype of a weak, submissive, passive female; and despite Lafe's attempts to have her renew her faith in politics, America, and the future, she emotionally announces her decision to withdraw from Washington and political life:

> 'It's upsetting me,' Mabel Anderson said with a sudden explosive force, the abrupt release of a shy and indrawn soul assailed beyond endurance. 'I can't take this city any more. I never could. Not even when Brig was here. And then when he—left— I left, and I didn't intend ever to come back. But I did, because I thought—' she stared at Lafe, who looked completely shattered and taken aback—'because I thought there might be some peace and stability here, after all. And maybe there could be if it were just—us. But it isn't just us. It's Ted Jason and Fred Van Ackerman and all the rest of them, and what they're doing to things. It's fear, everywhere. It's what the future holds for all of us who don't agree. It's horrible things about to happen to our country. 'And I can't take it,' she said, beginning to cry in a forlorn, woe-begone, little - girl fashion. 'I just can't take it any more. I'm taking Pidge back to Utah and I'm never coming back. Never, ever, ever!' (455-456)

To Mabel Anderson, politics is evil. In contrast, despite a savage beating and a miscarriage, Crystal Knox refuses to permit her husband to withdraw from politics. Crystal believes that politics is, or can be, an honorable profession and that politicians are *Capable of Honor* and of forming or shaping a better world.

II

Although the life of Senator Smith tastefully interjects sexual material into *Advise and Consent* and *A Shade of Difference*, the most graphic sexual material is generated by the romance and marriage of Cullee Hamilton and Sue-Dan Proctor. When Cullee met Sue-Dan at Howard University, he felt "a desperate sexual urgency" and quickly fell in love with her "clever little fox face" (330). Two weeks after they met, they were lovers. Four months later, they married. In the Hamilton marriage, sex becomes a power game, a game that Cullee experienced before he met Sue-Dan. At Columbia

University, Cullee had participated in the sex games and had been exploited because of a "subtle shade of difference." Although his black friends had warned that whites were patronizing him to satisfy their white consciences, he did not believe them. After a black friend had warned that Cullee would be sexually exploited, and the warning proved to be prophetic, he realized that his black friends were right. The prophecy had been explicit:

'You just wait,' one of them said,... 'One of these days you'll get the final tribute. Some one of these white babes will go to bed with you and you'll think, by God, now I've arrived, she really likes me. But don't kid yourself. She likes black skin and the chance to tell her pals how democratic she is. But as for you, she couldn't care less' (327).

Because of the wise, generous love and teaching of his mother, despite being exploited by a white girl, Cullee does not become hostile to whites. Such is not the case with Sue-Dan who is much more impatient about the injustice that blacks suffer in America; and her confrontational, inflammatory approach frequently clashes with her husband's moderate tendencies. Because Sue-Dan insists that Cullee become more aggressive in promoting equal rights and opportunities for blacks, the Hamilton marriage deteriorates. Because of Cullee's unwillingness to militantly promote the welfare of black Americans, Sue-Dan attacks his identity as a black and as a male. Nevertheless, Cullee remains fundamentally in love with his wife, even when she begins to criticize him for a lack of political ambition. For Cullee, his marital problem is more basic than politics or political ambition:

It is as basic as Sue-Dan Hamilton and what she thinks when she goes to bed with Cullee Hamilton; because while this still happens very often it is beginning to become obvious to one participant, at least, that the other doesn't think too much of it. Certainly not as much as she used to in the first wild months of a union that seemed at the time so inevitable it couldn't be stopped. Now he is beginning to find it possible to think that under certain conditions it *could* be stopped; and the thought terrifies him, for what would life be like without little old Sue-Dan? But even here a basic, ironic honesty still intrudes. You'd get along, boy, his mind tells him; you'd get along. But his body adds instantly, it wouldn't be the same. Oh, no, indeed. It wouldn't be the same (33).

Cullee's confidence is further undermined when he sees that Sue-Dan and "Terrible Terry," the Gorotoland prince, are sexually attracted to each other. When Cullee refuses to help "Terrible Terry" integrate an all-white elementary school in South Carolina, Sue-Dan viciously tongue-lashes her husband because he thinks being smart is "better than being brave;" she tells Terrible Terry and Cullee that she does not know what she married, but she thinks she has "a jelly-fish for a husband." "Where were you when your own people needed you?" she taunts the Congressman. "You let Terry do it! You let a foreigner do it! Someone had to come from Africa and do the job you should have done! And you call yourself a Negro!" (137) Later, Sue-Dan again argues with her husband in the presence of "Terrible Terry," informing terrible Terry that Cullee has been sharing information with Orrin Knox, the white Secretary of State. Tauntingly, she tells Cullee that though she belongs to him, she also belongs "to the colored race.... We wouldn't expect you to understand that, Cullee" (157). When Terry is a Hamilton house guest, Sue-Dan flaunts the possibility of her sexual infidelity before her husband by telling "Terrible Terry" to "be sure you stay in the same bed" (158). Later in *A Shade of Difference*, during a telephone quarrel, Sue-Dan informs her husband that Terry is "a big man" and that she wants to go to New York to help LeGage Shelby open an African Bureau which will link the colored people all over the world. As Sue-Dan defiantly prepares to leave for New York, Cullee quarrels with his best friend LeGage and suggests that LeGage and Sue-Dan are sexually involved. There is a "mighty fine bed upstairs if you want to use it," Cullee tells LeGage. "That little gal's something when you get her in it. Be my guest" (227).

In *A Shade*, LeGage does not betray his friendship with Cullee by becoming sexually involved with his wife; at this point the LeGage-Sue-Dan relationship is a black power, platonic one. However, such is not the case with Sue-Dan's relationship with "Terrible Terry." When Sue-Dan ignores her husband's order and moves to New York to work in the African Bureau, she has a sexual relationship with the Gorotoland Prince. Their love-making is enjoyable, but they harbor ill-feelings toward each other and engage in hostile conversation. "Terrible Terry" taunts Sue-Dan about her failed relationship with her husband, who Sue-Dan admits, has principles. Sue-Dan wishes that "Terrible Terry" would mind his own business and not pry into the Sue-Dan Cullee marriage and sexual relationship. Since he had bedded with Sue-Dan and he believes he is now a member of "the club," he also believes it is appropriate for him to discuss such matters. Just as she hurts her husband by attacking his masculinity, so does she also hurt "Terrible Terry."

'I thought after last night that I was a member of the club. I'm sorry.'
She shrugged.
'Isn't any club. I just wanted to find out what those goatgrease gals in Molobangwe and all those little floozies at the UN see in you. You're not so much.'
An expression of genuine anger shot across his face as he towered above her in his glittering apparel.
'Damned American,' he said with a cold bitterness.
'Damned foreigner,' she said indifferently (406).

To Sue-Dan, sex is a weapon that can be used to her advantage. As Cullee notes,

She always had one advantage, he had often thought bitterly as she had sided increasingly with LeGage in their running battles over race: she could always spread her legs, and he'd come running.... Their arguments did not end in conclusions, but in sex; and that was no ending. Increasingly Sue-Dan, like LeGage, had attempted to control and dominate his thinking, persuade him to change his views, lead him in directions a stubborn steadiness told him he should not go; and she had a weapon LeGage did not have, and used it as cooly and calculatingly as she knew how (340).

There is no doubt that Sue-Dan uses sex as a political weapon or as a means of obtaining influence; on the other hand, Sue-Dan is also used as a sex-object by her husband. For example, on one occasion when Sue-Dan informs her husband that she is too tired for love-making, Cullee persists and resorts to sexual violence.

'Why can't you ever leave me alone?' she demanded angrily, starting to roll out of the other side of the bed; but he reached an arm across and pinned her down with one enormous hand as he reached down with the other, ripping off his shorts, and dropped them on the floor.

'I've got to show you who Cullee's wife really is' he said huskily, stripping back the blankets and clambering over her. 'I think maybe you forgot since the last time.'

'I haven't forgotten anything,' she said through her teeth, struggling fiercely under him.

'Then stop it, he said angrily, his face an inch from hers, his powerfully muscled athlete's body slowly and inexorably crushing down upon her.

'Just stop it. God damn it, do you mean I have to *rape* my own wife?'

Suddenly her struggles ceased as quickly as they had begun, her arms went around him, the world became a place of wild confusion, until at last they cried out together in hoarse, incoherent exclamation and quietness descended.

'Now get off me,' she whispered abruptly with a harshness that broke the mood at once. 'Just get off me, big man. You've proved it, whatever it was you wanted to prove. *Get off me.*'(110-111).

Not surprisingly, the Hamilton marriage does not survive. After Sue-Dan begins working in New York and Cullee realizes that his wife has rejected him, he finds a sexual partner in a bar. His release from misery is only temporary. For happiness, Cullee needs a more meaningful romantic relationship.

In *Capable of Honor* Cullee seriously begins thinking about divorcing Sue-Dan when he becomes romantically and sexually involved with Sarah Johnson, a secretary at the United Nations. The Congressman hesitates about a divorce for two reasons: he still loves his "overclever, overambitious, and waspish" wife and a divorce would negatively influence his political career. Nevertheless, he and Sarah have a very pleasant, comfortable relationship. However, when he and Sarah see Sue-Dan and LeGage Shelby—who is now "jazzing around" with Sue-Dan—participating in a violent demonstration in front of the United Nations, Cullee's reaction is a painful one:

> Staring intently into the sea of insanely contorted faces, Cullee saw at last the two he knew must be there. For a brief instant his wife Sue-Dan and LeGage Shelby stared back at him as though from a cavern in hell. Then they were lost again in the crowd, but not before he knew that they had seen him, too, and not before a terrible pain for a moment wrenched his heart. They were lost to him, lost; yet was not he still lost to them? His face must have said as much, for he became conscious again of Sarah Johnson's hand upon his arm (132).

Despite this emotional relapse, as *Capable* nears conclusion Cullee Hamilton seems to have gotten over his deep emotional attachment to Sue-Dan, and he and Sarah Johnson are planning to marry. It would seem that Cullee is in a maturing process. Sarah is less passionate but more comforting to Cullee than Sue-Dan. Sarah Johnson, the Congressman tells Lafe Smith, gives him "peace of mind" and that

> 'The older I get the more I value that. Didn't used to be very important alongside a couple of hours in bed with nothing else on your mind, but it is now. Sarah's very calm and peaceful and I need that now. I've had enough of the other.' He smiled. 'My brains have been beat in long enough' (270).

Through the experiences of Brig Anderson, Lafe Smith, the Hamiltons and their sexual partners, Drury integrates explicit sexual activity and dialogue into his fiction. There is "a shade of difference" in Drury's rendering of sex. The sex lives of blacks are presented more graphically than that of whites.

Although Drury creates a truly independent female character in Sue-Dan Hamilton, most of the significant female characters in Drury fiction reflect the conservative female model of the housewife-mother, a role which places woman in a subordinate, dependent position to the male. In *The Feminine Mystique* (1963) Betty Friedan rejected such a narrow definition of "The Happy Housewife Heroine" in popular writing because it assumed that woman's nature could not be fully complete unless she became a well-adjusted wife and mother (15-16, 20, 43-44). Though Beth Knox, Dolly Munson, Lucielle Hudson and Ceil Jason have the potential to develop personalities independent of their husband's identities, in most of Drury's fiction their attitudes reflect the happy housewife model that Friedan rejects as being the only model possible for the ideal completion of a woman's nature. Undoubtedly, the overwhelming majority of Americans, both male and female, were intimately familiar with this definition of the role of women during the early sixties, prior to the revitalization and re-emergence of the Feminist Movement in America, a liberal movement that not only raised the conscience and consciousness of men and women, but one which also influenced legislation and court decisions that significantly extended woman's rights in the area of remuneration (Equal Pay Act, 1963), employment opportunities and promotion (Civil Rights Act, 1964), and abortion (Doe V. Bolton; Roe v. Wade, 1973). Although there are independent, successful professional women created in Drury fiction, there are no Feminists. However, two women who are subordinate, traditional wives in the beginning of Drury fiction and who willingly accept that role—Beth Knox and Ceil Jason—do evolve into independent, successful personalities in the male dominated political world of *The Promise of Joy* and *Come Nineveh, Come Tyre*, thereby reflecting changing attitudes toward the capability of women during the sixties and seventies. Surprisingly, it is Ceil Jason in *Capable of Honor* who gives the clearest, female expression of the acceptance of "The Happy Heroine" role. Ceil perceives herself as "a politician's wife" who is "a necessary adjunct of politics" (120). When her political advice is solicited, Ceil politically advises her husband; however, she is passive in this adviser role. Whatever Ted decides, she will go along (119). "I want you to do whatever you think is best," she tells her husband when he is deciding whether he will become a vice-presidential candidate. At this point in Drury fiction, Ceil is totally committed to her husband and his political career without reservation: "I'm your most loyal camp follower, you great big handsome man. Every day after the battle I'll be there to wash your feet and scrub your back and fix a dry martini" (296).

To be a good political wife is a difficult task; the marriages of Ceil Jason, Sue Hamilton, Patsy Laibaiya, Kaye Frye, and Mabel Anderson bear sad witness to that fact. To be sensitive to the moods of their husbands and their problems in Congress and the United Nations, a good, traditional wife must give close attention to the business of the House and Senate, attend Senate and Congressional hearings, host parties, mend wounded egos, and forge and maintain political bonds and alliances, as well as do the housework, shopping and take care of the kids. Good traditional wives are becoming increasingly difficult to find in *A Shade of Difference*. After President Hudson telephones Beth Knox and advises her to take good care of Orrin, who is a very tired and discouraged Secretary of State, the President reminisces. He, Orrin, and Bob Munson have married loyal, loving, devoted women who complement their husband's personalities and help them to achieve their ambitions. Few of the wives of the new generation, the President believes, possess "the secret of wifehood" and can be "helpmates in the old sense." The President thinks—completely unaware that he is metaphorically linking traditional wives with useful, mechanical, inanimate objects—that when it comes to wives, "the older wives seem to be the best models. With the newer ones, something too often seemed to go wrong with the automatic transmissions" (529). The sexist, chauvinistic President feels blessed because his wife Lucielle has given him "a loving heart, a peaceful and comfortable home, two daughters...and the constant strength of her devoted loyalty and encouraging presence" (529). It is the marriage of Beth and Orrin Knox, however, and not the marriage of President Hudson and Lucielle, which serves to most vividly illustrate the ideal traditional marriage in Drury fiction. Beth not only embodies the traditional values of the political wife, she also passes them on to her daughter-in-law Crystal.

III

The romance and marriage of Elizabeth Henry and Orrin Knox represent a romantic ideal of a traditional family. As *Advise and Consent* begins, Beth and Orrin Knox have been married for twenty years. Their courtship and marriage is a romantic ideal; Beth believed her marriage to be "as near perfect as any marriage she knew" (498). After Orrin met Elizabeth Henry (Beth) in college and they fell in love, "he never loved anyone else"; and once Beth fell in love with Orrin "and decided irrevocably that helping him was what she wanted in life," her love never altered (497). Although their courtship and marriage was romantic in the traditional sense, their lives were not without struggle, sorrow, and disappointment. Through their courtship and marriage—a consistent process of growth for Beth—the housewife-mother has a practical, common sense approach to life. When Orrin proposed marriage after their graduation from the University of Illinois, she refused until Orrin graduated from law school. Happily, their marriage was blessed with a boy and a girl; however, when young Elizabeth died of rheumatic fever both husband and wife were extremely stricken with grief. Despite her sorrow, Beth obtains happiness and fulfillment by devoting her life to her son and her husband. When Hal marries, Beth tearfully reflects with satisfaction upon the passage of years and her role as mother and wife:

And there the years went, Beth thought, hurry, hurry, hurry and away with you. Where did they go, and what had you accomplished when they were over? Well for one thing, she brought herself up tartly, you had accomplished this good-looking young male up there at the altar, and that was quite enough to have accomplished. And more than that, you had also helped in a very major way to accomplish this vigorous public servant beside you and that wasn't such a small achievement either. And you had also, not to be too modest about it, accomplished your own place in the world as distinct and recognized, almost as his, and that was a fair triumph too (538-539).

In addition to nurturing Hal to adulthood, Beth nurtures her husband as man, politician, and statesman. In reply to queries about his political success, Orrin publicly acknowledges her nurturing role by telling his constituents "I married Elizabeth Henry" (468). As a politician's wife, Beth dutifully attends bazaars and church meetings and joins with Orrin on the campaign trail. The identification of husband and wife was so complete that campaign signs included Beth's name: "Vote for Orrin and Beth" (469). When personal tragedies occur, such as the Anderson suicide, Beth's wifely role is to create order or a sense of order from chaos. How, she wonders, after Brig Anderson's disastrous marriage and suicide, had she "ever gotten mixed up in politics?"

But even if she hadn't, she decided, things probably wouldn't have been so different. Sooner or later these moments came; it seemed to fall to men to create disasters and to women to come around and mop up after; and even in some other context there might well be a household of unhappy people depending upon her to keep things going while they gradually untangled themselves from the web of sorrow and despair in which they had become entrapped (497).

Beth also receives great satisfaction helping Orrin to understand his prickly personality and the consequences of his impulsive, political acts. When Orrin lost the vice-presidential nomination because of his harsh, negative evaluation of Harley Hudson's character, an evaluation he translated into an angry attack on Hudson despite Beth's warning not to do so, Beth nurtured Orrin's growth: she gradually led him to understand his own responsibility for losing the nomination, thereby helping him to develop the maturity to serve the nation as Senator, Secretary of State and President. Significantly, in *Advise and Consent* when Orrin is forced to decide whether to withdraw his opposition to the Leffingwell nomination in exchange for presidential support for his presidential ambitions, it is to Beth he turns as his final and most important adviser. As always, Beth exercises excellent judgment. She knows, and helps Orrin to understand, that not she, or anyone, can make this decision for Orrin. He must make it himself. As important as Beth is to Orrin, she is, as all women are in Drury fiction, only of secondary importance in the male dominated world.

Although Beth Knox makes infrequent appearances in *Capable*, she continues to be the most vital and memorable of Drury's traditional wives as she functions as both wife and informal political adviser. When Orrin is upset by the "damned hypocrisy" of Walter Dobius and his followers and Orrin plans to continue his policy of aggressive confrontation, Beth restrains him by her observation that Orrin will not change his liberal antagonists by pointing out their hypocrisy; and that, in fact, by pointing out the discrepancy between their words and actions, he will damage his chances of becoming president (73). Later in *Capable*, in order to help his presidential bid, Beth demonstrates initiative by offering Helen-Anne Carew the position of press secretary in Orrin's presidential campaign when she senses that Helen-Anne is sympathetic to Orrin. After President Hudson informs Orrin that he will seek the presidency and encourages Orrin to run for Vice-President, once again Beth offers sympathetic support to her husband, and, by joking with him and philosophizing, she generously conceals the deep emotional anguish that she too suffers because his presidential ambitions are shattered. Beth knows that if she does not control and conceal her emotions, she will be unable to provide the emotional support for Orrin's ego, a support that he desperately needs. Because Beth is a dutiful, generous, heroic wife who places her husband's needs before her own, Orrin does not know the depth of her hurt.

After Crystal's traumatic beating and miscarriage at the nominating convention at the conclusion of *Capable of Honor*, Beth continues as a stable influence on Orrin and the Knox family in *Preserve and Protect*. However, as a result of the verbal and physical abuse inflicted on the Knox family and the death of the President in the mysterious crash of Air Force One, Beth begins to become cynical, though not as much as her son Hal who temporarily rejects his father after Orrin invites Ted Jason to be his vice-presidential partner. Since Beth is politically astute, she knows that Orrin must offer Ted Jason the vice-presidential position in order to unify the party, a necessity if Orrin is to be elected President. Though Beth realizes that Ted Jason may be a dangerous man, she, like her husband, believes that there is no acceptable patriotic alternative because Orrin is the only possible presidential candidate who possesses the potential to save America from destruction. So that there will not be an irreparable breach in the family unit, an irreconcilable rupture between father and son, Beth asks Crystal to persuade Hal to understand Orrin's position and to make peace with his father. Beth knows from experience that Crystal's task is not an easy one:

It isn't always easy, being married to a Knox, is it? They're such combinations of idealism and practicality, bull-headedness and sensitivity. They need one's help a lot more than they let on. Hal will accept this, if you help him. Do you think you can? (365)

Crystal, who possesses the same qualities as Beth and who affectionately calls her "mother," can and will. In *Come Nineveh*, after Orrin Knox is assassinated and Ted Jason becomes President, readers learn that in this instance Hal's intuitive response to Ted Jason's character is much more astute than his parents. However, such is not the scenario in *The Promise of Joy*.

As *The Promise of Joy* begins, readers of *Preserve and Protect* know that both a husband and a wife have been assassinated, but they do not know which ones. Although Beth Knox's character is normally one of cheerful optimism, as she meets with Orrin in the early pages of *Promise*, Beth has a premonition which causes her to be gloomy and apprehensive. As Orrin and Beth prepare to leave for Orrin's acceptance speech, Beth verbalizes what

Orrin knows but does not wish to dwell upon; if Orrin is assassinated, Ted Jason will become president. Beth also speaks Orrin's mind when she reminds him that he cannot simply wish away Communism and political violence since they possess the potential of shaping the future of America. Nevertheless, Orrin reassures and cautions Beth about her pessimism because it gives him the "heebe-jeebies" and the "heebe-jeebies" spoil his political effectiveness. In a tender, affectionate scene, Orrin thanks Beth "for all the kindnesses down through the years" (15). This is their last moment of affection. At the convention center, Beth and Ted Jason are shot by an assassin whose plan goes awry: his true target was Orrin Knox, presidential candidate.

As in earlier Drury fiction, in *Promise* Beth humanizes the political Orrin Knox. Through Beth we perceive Orrin as a husband and father. When doctors forbid Orrin to attend her funeral, he indulges himself in tears of grief in his hospital room—he, too, is wounded by the assassin—before he forces himself to fulfill his responsibilities as Secretary of State and as presidential candidate. During his life-time he knew that "He would always think about her, to the day he dies. She would never leave him. She would always be there, as he knew she was there right now, strong, helpful, companionable, encouraging, just as always, her presence in some ways as real and vivid as though she had never left" (32-33). Weeks later, at a Thanksgiving service at St. John's Episcopal Cathedral, Orrin is again overcome by the sharp pangs of grief and his body shudders with suppressed sobs. The private Orrin Knox is a man of intense feeling who deeply mourns the death of his devoted companion, friend, lover and wife.

Although Beth is a vivid and memorable character, until *Come Nineveh, Come Tyre*, Beth is primarily a static character, a stereotyped ideal political wife whose personality evolves within the context of an expanding family and her husband's political career. However, after Orrin is assassinated at the conclusion of *Preserve*, Beth evolves as an independent personality. Consistent with the patriotic character that Drury has created in the four previous books, Beth's sense of duty compels her to become an activist after Orrin's assassination, even while she is still consumed with grief. Though Beth is still linked with Orrin's identity, clearly Orrin's values are also independently possessed by Beth. In order to continue Orrin's political philosophy and foreign policy, Beth offers herself as a vice-presidential candidate and logically argues that she can unify the conservative and liberal factions of the party. When Jason selects Governor Croy as his running mate, Beth agrees to support the party. She, along with her conservative friends, decides to support Jason and Croy because they believe that their potential influence upon the Jason-Croy administration is in the best interest of the nation. Only Hal dissents at this strategy. He continues to believe that Ted Jason is in the process of destroying America. So vehement are his feelings that he wishes to avoid contact with Jason when he visits the

Knox home to share their grief prior to a visit to the graves of Ceil and Orrin. Hal appears to be a carbon-copy of his father as a young man: impulsive, impetuous, and imprudent, thereby generating a nurturing response in his mother and his wife. Crystal and Beth strive to smooth his rough edges; they persuade him that if he wishes to be successful as a Congressman, if he wishes to be influential, he must be conciliatory and somewhat gracious after suffering a political defeat. Crystal and Beth successfully influence Hal to become more politically prudent and more communicative with Ted Jason than his instincts prompt him to be. Ironically, in this instance, Hal's instincts are correct; his mother's and Crystal's advice, though generally sound in most political circumstances, are disastrous in the context of Ted Jason and his administration. Though Orrin and Beth Knox function as conservative heroes, they are not infallible and this contributes to their credibility.

When Jason becomes President and it appears that a repressive and unconstitutional Help America Bill will be passed by Congress, Beth suggests to her conservative friends and colleagues that they form an organization to counteract the growing threat to freedom in America. As a result, IDF (In Defense of Freedom) is formed and Beth, ex-president Abbott, and Cullee Hamilton agree to serve jointly as chairpersons. Not surprisingly, Beth's life is threatened. In response, Beth calls the president, who sorely needs a confidante and friend, and President Jason agrees to meet with her later in the day. At this meeting Beth intends to inform President Jason of the deteriorating morale in America and to persuade him to take action against the violence of the radical left. Before Beth Knox is able to visit the President as an emissary from the conservative faction in America, she is kidnapped.

The kidnapping of Beth Knox pulls together the plots and themes of Drury's fiction. While the radical kidnappers hope to blackmail Hal into supporting the Help America Bill, their purpose is yet a larger one: to destroy the Knox family in political life because they symbolize conservative values in America. The radical element wishes to prove that Hal Knox "can be forced to do things under duress, that Knox principles are as weak as other men's," and that even the Knoxes can be forced to bow. If Hal can be intimidated, the kidnappers believe, the Knoxes will be destroyed as a political power in America (316). On yet another level, the radical element wishes to prove that terrorism is an effective political weapon. A captor informs Mrs. Knox that fear, horror, and revulsion make people quite powerless, and the captor suggests that this can be seen from the recent experience of terrorism, the bombings, kidnappings, and assassinations that have occurred recently around the globe:

Much can be done with fear, Mrs. Knox. Give people the certainty that nothing is really safe—that nothing save blind luck really holds their world together—that anybody who really wants to can invade and destroy it if he has sufficient ruthlessness and determination—and they become quite reasonable, Mrs. Knox. They forget many fine old democratic loyalties and traditions very fast. They lose their nerve and they become very weak. The foundation crumbles, the certainties go, the safe world collapses. And the strong, the ruthless and the determined take power and lead them" (318).

The heroic Beth Knox, however, will not be terrorized into swerving from her principles and neither will her son Hal. Despite extreme mental anguish, with the advice and support of Crystal, Hal possesses the wisdom and courage to perform his patriotic duty: he publicly opposes the Help America Bill. When Beth hears of Hals' firm rejection of the kidnapper's ultimatum, she is "proud of him" and scornful of her captors whom she knows will kill her. To Beth, the radicals are "the new breed" deserving of pity because they are unable to experience either pity or love; the radicals are "conditioned, cold, intelligent and forever unreachable" (328). Before Beth is shot, she achieves comfort and serenity through prayer. The death of Beth Knox represents and symbolizes the end of an era in Drury fiction. This is especially apparent when we consider the name Orrin Knox (ore in Knox) and Hal's reaction to his mother's death. His instincts told him that "the bright dream was over forever, for the Knoxes" (339). Through the tragedies and the triumphs, Beth Knox emerges as a credible conservative hero both within the context of the feminine mystique and the context of a liberated professional woman.

IV

Beth Knox is only one of a group of traditional wives in Drury fiction, a social-political group that includes Dolly Harrison Munson, Lucielle Hudson, Kitty Maudulayne and Celestine Barre, who "round out" the character development of male figures (Senator Knox, Senator Munson, President Hudson, and to a lesser extent, the English Ambassador and the French Ambassador) and contribute to the texture of the fiction by serving as secondary or background characters in the plots and scenes. Though Beth Knox is a model wife, she does not compare with Dolly Harrison Munson as a hostess. Like Beth Knox, Dolly Harrison is also a political helpmate to the man she loves—Majority Leader Bob Munson. Unlike Beth, however, as *Advise and Consent* begins, the Harrison-Munson sexual relationship has not yet been legitimized by marriage. As the events of *Advise* unfold, we learn that Bob Munson is in no great hurry to make an "honest woman" of Dolly, although he expects that they will marry in "due time" (61-62). For forty-three year old Dolly, this will be her second marriage. After her divorce, the narrator informs us, the millionairess decided to move to

Washington and become a professional hostess even though she knew that people believed that "any bitch with a million bucks, a nice house, a good caterer, and the nerve of a grand larcenist can become a social success in Washington." Dolly is not a "bitch." She is an intelligent and sophisticated woman who knows the formula for becoming a premier party giver in Washington:

You got somebody you know to introduce you to somebody *she* knew and then you gave a small tea or two, and then a small cocktail party or even a small dinner, being careful to include the society editors of the Star, the Post and the News in one or more of them, and you were on your way. Then after the word had begun to get around a little, and you perhaps had been introduced to a Senator or two, and maybe a Cabinet officer and his wife or one of the military, you could sail right into it full steam ahead, set a date, send out invitations broadside to a couple of hundred prominent people, hire yourself the best decorator and caterer you could find, and sit back to await the results. Since official Washington loves nothing as much as drinking somebody else's liquor and eating somebody else's food, the results were all you could hope for, and after that there were no problems. (44-45).

When Dolly planned her appearance on the Washington scene, her one ambition was to become a prominent Washington hostess. After she met and became the lover of Bob Munson, however, her parties deliberately became a political tool, a political instrument to extend the influence of Senator Munson by providing a gracious, social setting. During Dolly's "Spring Party," for instance, a party that consumes a hundred quarts of bourbon, fifty-seven quarts of scotch, and $5,000 worth of hor d'oeuvres, as well as large quantities of ginger ale, soda, turkey, ham, chicken, celery, olives, salad, and marron's glaces, Senator Munson coerces an unwilling Secretary of State to support Bob Leffingwell as his replacement and also lobbies for the support of the Leffingwell nomination with Senators and foreign ambassadors. After the party Senator Munson ostensibly leaves Dolly's home, but later he surreptitiously returns for a night of love with Dolly.

Somewhat predictably, Dolly Harrison becomes a political confidante of the Majority Leader, and she gently chides the Senator for his coercion of Secretary of State Sheppard. Such is the strength of their relationship that Bob Munson asks Dolly to attend Senate Sub-Committee hearings and to function as his political eyes and ears. Dolly also provides him with emotional support during a time of desperate need. After Anderson meets with the President and Munson, and the President demands that Munson give him the documented evidence of Anderson's homosexuality that was given to him by Justice Davis, Dolly comforts him with her sexual love. When the Senator honorably resigns as Majority Leader after the Anderson suicide, Dolly congratulates him on his action and becomes a matrimonial aggressor: "Why don't you marry me?" she asks. "Why don't you ask me?"

he replies. Immediately, Mrs. Harrison does: "All right. I will. I am. I do" (520). Dolly Harrison desires a traditional marriage, and she gets it!

In *Come Nineveh*, after Beth Knox's funeral, Dolly continues her role as Washington hostess by inviting Beth's mourners—Hal, Crystal, Bill Abbott, Bob Leffingwell, Lafe Smith, Mabel Anderson, Krishna Khaleel, Lord Maudulayne and Kitty, Raoul Barre and Celestine—to her fashionable home, the Vagaries,—for food and drink, and the cyclic nature of Drury's plots and the socio-political texture of his fiction become manifest. Regretfully, Celestine Barre speaks what is in the minds of the mourners: that their happy social and political get-togethers will be no more. "How many times," the narrator interjects, "had cars drawn up before those lovely columns, how many times had these same people, and many more besides, stepped forward to enter the all-embracing warmth of the Munson's beautiful home: And would the 'Vagaries' see the likes of those happy days again" (453). Such is not to be again in Drury fiction. Lord Maudulayne underscores the end of the era by commenting upon the derivation of the word "Vagaries" and by reporting a change in British foreign policy. The "Vagaries" is from Latin, he declares, and means "to wander," but "Vagaries" can also mean "a wild fancy, an extravagant notion." Bitterly, he comments upon the current state of affairs in America and the world: "What a wild fancy...that men are, or of right should be, or are capable of being for any great length of time, free! What an extravagant notion!" This, after he had informed his friends that he had been replaced as Washington's Ambassador because

It is felt in Whitehall, in other words, that it is time for us to begin to adapt to the new United States which is suddenly—appallingly—unbelievable—but actually—beginning to emerge. It is believed, he added bleakly, that we must make our peace with the new situation, or, in due course, die. Therefore a new man is needed here. I am considered to have been much too close to the *ancien regime*. I am considered to be too sincere a believer in democracy and too open in my sympathies toward it. The New Day requires new men. Ergo—we bid you farewell, Tuesday week (454).

This restructuring of policy recalls the beginning of Drury's *Advise and Consent* when the President believed that it was time for a restructuring of American foreign policy, that the time was right for detente in Soviet-American relationships, and that in order to implement this change a new, less rigid, Secretary of State was needed. At that time Drury presented the first major social-political party in his fiction as an essential part of the texture whereby politics are discussed, plans are suggested, plots are moved forward, and personalities are inextricably weaved into the political process, even secondary female characters who are peripheral to the political plots.

V

Like Beth Knox, the stunningly beautiful and intelligent Ceil Jason is a traditional wife who metamorphisizes into an independent, successful, public figure at the conclusion of Drury's political fiction. As Beth Knox and Dolly Munson "round out" the characters of their husbands, so also does Ceil Jason illuminate the personality of the Governor who becomes President. As we have observed earlier, Ceil is a devoted wife. It is through her experience, however, that we learn of the erosion of Ted's moral character. *In Capable* after Ted had been governor for a year and developed an "itch for Washington," Ceil advised her husband that he was beginning to lose his "virtue" in the old sense. Though the Governor denies Ceil's allegations, she does force him to confront the issue, and in his heart he realizes that his wife is essentially correct: "his automatic ability to do what was right was atrophying; he was beginning to pause and calculate, now the pragmatic and forceful approach which, linked with integrity, had been invincible, was beginning to give way to a more devious approach. He was beginning to think of dreams ahead in a way that sometimes hurt realities at hand" (330). In response to Ceil's probing observations, Ted becomes aware that "step by step, daily, hourly perhaps, imperceptively beneath the outward show of firmness and determination that remained unchanged, he was becoming more careful, more calculating, more equivocal. In some subtle fashion, that he was partly aware of but seemed powerless to stop, he was no longer the direct and straight forward individual he used to be" (332-331). As the once honorable Ted evolves into an opportunistic, ambitious, dishonorable man, Ceil's life becomes increasingly difficult.

Although the Governor sometimes solicits his wife's advice, he chooses to ignore his wife's wise counsel. When Ted must decide whether or not to clearly express his position on Gorotoland, Ceil advises him not to equivocate, to speak his genuine convictions, whatever they may be. Pragmatically, Ted chooses not to make a statement. Because Ceil deeply loves her husband and knows that he will reject her if she does not support his presidential ambitions, she subtly dispenses unpalatable advice while continuing to express her loyalty. Eventually, however, Ceil is unable to support the politics of her husband. In *Capable of Honor* when Ted refuses to repudiate the political intimidation and violence of his radical supporters, Ceil decides to leave her husband who suffers from *hubris* and "a fatal compulsion to take top prize" (*Preserve* 44).

Although Ceil leaves her husband because of his political ethics, she is too much a traditional wife to seriously contemplate divorce. After Ted loses his bid for the vice-presidential nomination to Orrin Knox, Ceil takes the initiative and telephones her husband. During their friendly, affectionate conversation in *Preserve and Protect*, Ceil honestly, firmly, and in a non-belligerent way expresses her political differences with her husband, explains why she left him, and offers excellent advice which he rejects:

I think you did things you shouldn't have done. I think you permitted things to be done in your name that shouldn't have been done. I didn't approve of them. So I left. I haven't changed my mind about them. They still disturb me, very much. I think what you ought to do now is stay out of it. Orrin has a right to it. The convention decided for the President and Orrin, let Orrin have it. He's the logical choice of the opinion that really, I think, represents a majority of the country. Why should you revive all the bitterness and hatred now? Haven't we had enough of it in the last couple of months? Aren't you satisfied? (44)

Ted isn't; he does not heed Ceil's advice. As a result, Ceil's honor compels her to actively, though in a small way, support the Knox campaign: Ceil advises "liberal" Bob Leffingwell to mend fences with Orrin Knox; she calls the President and offers her moral support to the Hudson-Knox foreign policy; and after the President's assassination, Ceil calls Lucielle Hudson to indicate her approval of Lucielle's political activity against her husband. Such activity, to Ceil, is justifiable: she has witnessed an erosion of integrity in her husband. Ceil's position is a very distressing one, and Drury permits us to enter Ceil's mind and directly perceive her evaluation of her husband, their marriage, and her political relationship:

In her own way, the only way she felt was open to a wife who loved her husband but believed him to be terribly wrong, she had tried to help him; first, by withdrawing to 'Vistazo' in the hope that her leave-taking would jolt him into some fundamental change of direction, and when that failed, by doing what she could to encourage defeat of his ambitions... Since ambition appeared to be taking him down a road whose end, she was convinced, could only be disastrous, then he must be prevented from going down that road. She was beautiful, intelligent and clever, but she was not superhuman: these telephone calls were all she could think of to do, aside from pleading in an open and abject way that would only disclose the full extent of her fear and worry for him. *The end result of that would be to arouse a certain basic masculine contempt and amusement at feminine weakness, compounded by Jason's ego: he would only tell her that he didn't have to worry because he was Ted Jason.___ And so if she pleaded too openly she would lose whatever advantage and influence she might possess (158-159 Italics added.)*.

In a very difficult marital situation, Ceil Jason leads a life of honor; she appreciates her intelligence and possesses enough confidence in her own, independent identity to place her love of honor and country above her love and loyalty to her husband. Ultimately, however, Ceil positions herself in the role of caring, supportive, loving wife because she believes that this is best for both husband and country. Ceil returns to her husband when Orrin Knox selects him to be his vice-presidential partner since she believes that he needs her emotional support and political counsel. As *Preserve* concludes, Ceil assures Ted of her love and informs the vice-presidential candidate that she never believed him to be "a bad man, only a confused one" (389). On the final pages of *Preserve,* one of the candidate's wives is assassinated. In *Come Nineveh,* Ceil and Ted have a happy reunion before the assassination occurs; however, Ceil quickly realizes that there has been no essential change in Ted's political personality.

Although Ted desperately loves and desperately needs Ceil, he will not reveal to her the contents of his acceptance speech. When Ceil pressures him to tell her he will repudiate his radical supporters in NAWAC, Ted shifts the mood from the political to the romantic. With a kiss, Ted stifles her queries and tells her she is "the most beautiful woman in political life today. And the wittiest. And the most intelligent. And the most perceptive. That's what scares me, really—you see through me so" (11). When Ceil and Ted leave for the convention center where Ted will deliver his acceptance speech, Ted sincerely expresses how desperately he needs his wife: "If you were not beside me, I honestly do not know what I would do" (12). However, because the Russians have closely studied the Jason character, the Russians know. At the convention, when Ceil is assassinated, the future president loses his only responsible and trustworthy adviser, an adviser who is the only one capable of providing him with emotional stability. Consequently, Ceil's assassination in *Come Nineveh* is a devastating blow not only to Ted Jason, but also the American body politic.

In *The Promise of Joy,* however, it is Beth Knox, rather than Ceil Jason, who is assassinated. Like Beth Knox in *Come Nineveh,* Ceil Jason evolves into an independent personality who achieves political success after her husband's death. However, in contrast to Beth Knox, Ceil Jason rejects the opportunity to become a vice-presidential candidate after her husband is assassinated. In her speech to the National Committee, Ceil does what her husband Ted was incapable of doing; she rejects NAWAC because she believes this repudiation is necessary for America's welfare and because she hopes that this would have eventually been Ted's course of action.

At the end, I believe he intended to repudiate once and for all the ugly gangs that had gathered behind him under the general banner of the National Anti-War Activities Congress... I repudiate them too, in everything they do and everything they truly stand for, under the pious pretense of peace-loving with which they seek to fool the country (61-62).

Then Ceil demonstrates political sophistication as she explains her withdrawal:

'I know very well,' she said finally, 'that in taking this position I am inviting great hostility from these elements, and that is one of the reasons I am withdrawing from the ticket.' She smiled slightly. 'Secretary Knox has enough burdens without carrying me.' The smile faded. 'If I accepted the support of the violent, I should be a heavy weight upon him. Now that I have repudiated their support, as I must or betray everything I believe in, I should be a heavy weight upon him. I think I can help him better acting independently from outside. This,' she said, and the firmness grew in ᴜer voice, 'I intend to do' (62).

During Knox's successful campaign for president, Ceil demonstrates much courage by introducing Orrin at his campaign appearances. These introductions are sometimes in hostile environments, and although Ceil's life is threatened, she patriotically continues her commitment to Orrin Knox and his foreign and domestic policies. Her loyalty and service are rewarded when Knox is elected: Ceil becomes an Ambassador to the United Nations. As Madame Ambassador, Ceil achieves a prominent, though still subordinate or secondary role in Drury fiction. She makes speeches and introduces resolutions in the United Nations. Ceil is no more nor less successful than her male counterparts, although she does achieve one significant victory: her resolution to abolish the veto in the Security Council is eventually passed. Nevertheless, her formal speeches—though they reveal intelligence and firmness—are essentially no different than other formal speeches by the United States delegates to the United Nations. All formal speeches in Drury fiction merge into one style, whatever their substance. Consequently, Ceil's independent public and political character, despite her ability to tactfully return insult for insult, takes on a blandness which replaces the vitality that has characterized her personality in previous Drury fiction.

VI

Though both Ceil Jason and Beth Knox evolve as independent personalities who are successful without the help of their husbands, they are not as feisty as the less successful Sue-Dan Hamilton. Helen-Anne Carew, a journalistic heroine that Drury introduces in *A Shade of Difference*, combines the professional competence of Beth and Ceil with the feistiness and spirit of Sue-Dan. In *Capable*, Helen-Anne is an extremely successful journalist whose syndicated column is published in three-hundred and twenty papers. Helen-Anne functions as a Drury journalistic model of excellence; she is one of those columnists "who came to Washington determined to tell the straight, unslanted truth" (28); Helen-Anne was not only "Capable of Honor," she also practiced it for many years. Much of Helen-Anne's success is due to her intuition and her ability to establish and maintain lines of communication with all the disparate conservative and liberal political factions in Washington. Even when the President and Secretary of State inform their staffs that they will answer no in-coming phone calls, patriotic Helen-Anne is able to establish communication and offer information and emotional support. Nevertheless, she is not without her detractors. Ted Jason, while recognizing her clout or power as a journalist, unkindly characterizes her in *Preserve and Protect* as "the face that launched a thousand inaccurate columns" (162). Despite Jason's scornful evaluation, readers know from experience that her perceptions are sometimes the most accurate in Washington, Walter Dobius not excepted. Such is the case in *Preserve and Protect* when Helen-Anne's professional curiosity and patriotism influence her to investigate an unpublicized Ted Jason visit to the Hilton hotel. As a result of her courage and initiative, the hard-working and astute journalist learns what others in her profession suspect but are unable to prove, that extreme "left" Senator Van Ackerman, LeGage Shelby, a black activist leader, and Rufus Kleinfert, an extreme right conservative radical, met with the Soviet Ambassador and a Lieutenant General in the KGB immediately after the Jason advisers had met with Ted to plan campaign strategy. Because Helen-Anne recognizes that Senator Ackerman is a part of the "evil" that is in America, "an evil that is a mindless violence...an almost carefree viciousness that in its ultimate form was close to simple anarchy, destruction for destruction's sake" (197), she asks Bob Leffingwell to assist her in confronting Ackerman with evidence of his meeting with the Russians. Although Helen-Anne is intelligent, diligent and patriotic, her judgment is faulty. Instead of informing the FBI—and perhaps losing her "scoop"— Helen-Anne uses her information to threaten the "liberal" Senator. She advises him that though she has not yet "spread any rumors" she is "sure as hell going to spread a story" unless Ackerman calls "off the things" that he has planned with the Russians (204). During their angry confrontation, Helen-Anne courageously responds to the Senator's attempt to physically intimidate her. After the journalist and the Senator leave, Ackerman makes a telephone call that triggers her assassination, along with that of her busboy informant. Because Helen-Anne suspected that she might be assassinated, she wisely entrusted her notes to Bob Leffingwell. Eventually, it is these notes that persuade Justice Davis that Ted Jason and his followers are dangerous to America and therefore no longer deserving of his support in their anti-war efforts.

While Helen-Anne Carew is an interesting and dynamic character in her own right and significant to the plotting of *Capable* and *Preserve*, she also provides insight into the character of Wonderful Walter Dobius—her husband. Their marriage that terminated in a divorce was a pragmatic one: both believed that the marriage would help their journalistic careers. Nevertheless, when they married, Helen-Anne's affection for Walter was sincere, and she possessed a desire to protect Walter who impressed her as being a very vulnerable person. Seven years after their divorce Helen-Anne still feels concern and love for Walter and her caring adds a vital, humanizing dimension to her character and provides insight into Walter's egoistic, chauvinistic personality. To Walter, being a conservative is a terrible sin, and Helen-Anne compounds that sin by favoring conservative Orrin Knox (if he receives the presidential nomination, she will take a journalistic leave of absence to become his press secretary) rather that liberal Ted Jason. When Walter calls her a "conservative" in a contemptuous tone, Helen-Anne defends her "conservative" temperament and provides a warning that her former husband will reject:

You can terrify a lot of our friends in press and television by calling them conservative, but not me. I don't give a damn. I'm interested in what a man is, not in the label you and your pals manage to hang on him. Now: I'm just telling you, and—her tone became noticeably dry—in my own small way, Walter, boy, I'm just as infallible as you are—that you'll be making a mistake if you go too far out on a limb for Edward Jason. It's a screwball family, in more ways than one, and having several hundred million just means that it's several hundred million times more screwball. I'd go slow, if I were you. That's all (Capable 32-33).

As we have observed earlier, after the beating and miscarriage of Crystal Knox, Helen-Anne functions as a mouthpiece for Drury's assault against the liberals in a very vivid and memorable scene which combines the comic with the pathetic. Though Walter has had a love-hate relationship with Helen-Anne, he always respects her intelligence and journalistic ability. However, it is male chauvinism and professional jealousy that destroys their marriage. Walter married with a very clearly conceived notion of a woman's role in marriage in general and Helen-Anne's in particular. This he reveals as he reflects on their relationship after her assassination as he experiences an emotion that is not quite love and not quite grief:

It was not that he still loved her, for all that if it ever really existed, had been destroyed by her obvious hostility—and her raucous sarcasm about his own position in the world. He could see now that she had always intended to have her own column, she had never been able to understand that one famous member was all a Washington marriage could stand. She had never realized that Walter Dobius' wife must love, serve and respect Walter Dobius (*Preserve* 228).

From Walter's perspective, if Helen-Anne had been a more understanding person, less egotistical, less competitive, their marriage might have been successful. Ironically, if Walter had been a better journalist, more competitive than Helen-Anne, he might have "scooped" Helen-Anne on the story that caused her assassination. The "liberal" philosopher-journalist had received a hint of the Jason meeting at the Hilton, but he did not follow the lead. As Walter ponders Helen-Anne's death and speculates about what might have caused her assassination, we see a "liberal" who is a cowardly, hypocritical professional failure:

What was it [that she might have discovered]? He had already considered and rejected a number of possibilities. His own reportorial instinct, which was among the three or four best in the capital, had not told him yet that he had found the right one.

He knew already that if it did—when it did—he would not pursue it further. For he knew that it must be something very dangerous, and he suspected it might lead into areas of the Jason campaign where he did not wish to go. To do so might be to throw into question his entire support for that campaign, and this would not be right. He considered Ted's success absolutely imperative for the country. If there was some reason why the Governor should be defeated that even he could accept as valid, he did not want to know. It could mean political disaster for Ted; and the knowledge of it could even mean for Walter what it had meant for Helen-Anne (229).

Walter sends flowers to his ex-wife's funeral but he does not attend. When Tommy Davis suggests that Walter visit Helen-Anne's grave, Walter breaks down and asks Tommy Davis to stop the car, and the philosopher-journalist pleads to be left out. A visit to the grave would be too traumatic for Walter; it would force him to confront the knowledge that he, "Wonderful Walter" had been wrong. Justice Davis leaves "Wonderful Walter," "his body quivering and shaking with sobs, infinitely pathetic, terribly alone" (305). The Dobius-Carew relationship adds a humanizing and emotional dimension to Drury's political fiction.

VII

As Beth Knox, Ceil Jason, and Helen-Anne Carew evolve through Drury's fiction, they become independent and heroic personalities who achieve success in male dominated professions: politics and journalism. They become doers who actively and directly influence the course of political events, and because of their achievements without the emotional and professional support of husbands, they earn the admiration of their political peers. In *Capable of Honor* Drury introduces a group of women, a group we might identify as the Baffleburg group, (Baffleburg) who do not receive the respect and admiration of the Knox-Munson social-political group. The Baffleburg group, the National Committee Woman representatives at the nominating conventions, are neither full-time wives nor full-time politicians. Though these women sometimes function effectively on the platform and the credential committees, they are frequently comic figures who are projected as being inferior to males as they experience limited power at the nominating conventions in *Capable* and *Preserve*. Their names have descriptive overtones which suggest unflattering characteristics: Mrs. Mary Buttner Baffleburg (Butt, Baffle), Miss Lizzie Hanson McWharter (Handsome, whart), Esme Harbellow Stryke (Strike, Har(d), Bellow), Anna Hooper Bigelow (Hoope, big, low). Mary Baffleburg is short and fat with many rings of flesh around her eyes; Lizzie McWharter is tall and bony; and when Anna Hooper Bigelow presides over the convention, her dress is ostentatious and garish: "her bony frame" was "clad in a mustard-green sheath"; she wore "a purple toque topped by ostrich feathers pinned with an enormous rhinestone buckle, while she exercised the office of glory she had held for three conventions" (Capable 422), that is, the office of secretary. When the Speaker has urgent business, he thrusts the role of Chairman (sic) upon her; though she performs adequately, she is quite nervous. When the convention appears on the verge of getting out of control, the Speaker reassumes the chair because he believes a firmer grip is needed. Nevertheless, the female delegates are independent, partisan spirits who assert themselves, and their participation causes difficulties for their male colleagues. Mary Baffleburg, for instance, calls Bob Leffingwell a liar when they clash on the credentials committee. Only because Leffingwell graciously defuses the confrontation is an impasse avoided. Later, in order to boost the morale of Leffingwell, Ceil Jason unflatteringly characterizes Mary Baffleburg and the part-time female politicians at the convention:

'Don't feel so badly,' she said softly, 'You know Mary Baffleburg. She's one of the characters of these conventions. It's a special type you see in politics Mary Buttner Baffleburg, Lizzie Hanson McWharter, Ann Hooper Bigelow, and—God help us here in California—Esme Harbellow Stryke. The old biddies—or in our case, the young ones—who have the time and the money to make politics their hobby and finally reach the National Committee, there to appear at convention after convention, four years older and four times more irascible each time you see them. I wouldn't worry about her too much' (358).

Despite such a disparaging evaluation, these women participate actively in the convention process and they constitute a minor power faction that must be recognized or there will be distasteful consequences.

Though Drury does not develop any of these women in depth, the National Committee Women add an amusing and vitalizing dimension to the scenes which depict the meetings of the credentials and platform committees, meetings which have a tendency to be dull in fiction as well as in the real, political world. The subordinate role of the Baffleburg group in fiction is an accurate reflection of the subordinate role women played at national political conventions in the sixties.

The Baffleburg women are not the only females who receive unkind portrayals in Drury fiction. Most women who are "liberals" receive acerbic attention. The most extensive example is Patsy Labaiya, Ted Jason's sister who is married to Felix Labaiya, the Panamanian Ambassador to the United Nations who leads a revolution in Panama in order to drive America from his country. The Labaiya's marriage, like the Dobius-Carew marriage, is basically one of mutual advantage rather than one of deep love and permanent commitment. Felix places his political ambitions and his country above his relationship with Patsy, and Patsy places the political ambitions of her brother Ted above the welfare of her husband and her country. Patsy is very ambitious for her brother, and her ambition borders on arrogance which associates the Jason family with the Kennedy's in their desire to occupy the White House:

The Jason's are no different from the Adamses, the Harrisons, the Roosevelts, the Tafts, the Kennedys. No more numerous than the first, no less ambitious than the last, they too see no reason why one or more of their number should not occupy the fearful seat of power at 1600 Pennsylvania Avenue. Her brother is willing, her cousins are eager to help, her aunts and uncles are prepared to spend as many millions as may be required to win the primaries and add the White House to other family possessions (*A Shade of Difference* 38).

Although Patsy works diligently to help Ted's career—this is her primary mission in life—she is not very successful. Her personality is loud, dramatic, opinionated, aggressive, and confrontational. She does not hesitate to quarrel with both the President and Orrin Knox when they meet at parties. In addition, Patsy possesses a ruthless streak and a weak ethical sense; she appropriates ideas, manipulates and uses people, and has no qualms about using race and anti-American sentiments to foster her brother's political ambitions. Like Beth Knox and Ceil Jason, Patsy serves to "round out" the character of a major male politician and to add vitality and zest to the political background.

VIII

During the Victorian era, George Henry Lewes, the husband of Mary Anne Evans (George Eliot), observed in "The Lady Novelists" that since literature is essentially "the expression of experience and emotion—of what we have seen, felt and thought—only literature which has reality for its base" will be effective, and that its effectiveness will be "in proportion to the depth and breadth of that basis (Showalter, *Woman's Liberation and Literature* 172). Drury presents a wide variety of women in his fiction in a wide variety of roles. Most readers could easily identify with someone such as Beth Knox in her role as a traditional wife who subordinates her identity and her goals to those of her husband. Also easily identifiable in the world of fact were the successful professional women as exemplified by Helen-Anne Carew. In Drury fiction, "strong" women such as Donna Valuela,—Ted Jason's great grandmother—Ceil Jason, and Beth Knox are balanced against women who possess weak, submissive personalities—Mabel Anderson, Kaye Frye and Patsy Laibaiya, women who sometimes take on the character of a negative female stereotype. Again, weak submissive females in Drury fiction had their counterparts in the world of fact. Sue-Dan Hamilton, on the other hand, reflects the emerging sexual values and the radical political activism of some American women during the sixties; Sue-Dan places the progress of black Americans above her marriage to Cullee Hamilton who operates within the white-male dominated power structure.

The Hamilton marriage is only one of several unsuccessful marriages in the novels: the Fryes, the Smiths, the Andersons, the Dobius's, the Jason's, the Laibaiya's. Drury fiction also contains illustrations of happy and enduring marriages: the Knox's, the Hudson's. As we have seen, romance, sex and marriage introduce domestic and personal conflicts into the political plots; and this interesting material significantly contributes to Drury's creation of "a willing suspension of disbelief." It significantly contributes to Drury's best political fiction: *Advise and Consent* and *Capable of Honor*; and it makes Drury's less artistically successful fiction more readable and appealing to the popular audience, an audience that has little interest in ideological conflicts between liberals and conservatives. Such readers acquired a painless exposure to the examination of power in the American body politic, as well as a reminder of the major conflicts in post World War II America.

Notes

Chapter I

[1]One useful definition of the "popular political novel" is *The New York Times* Best Seller list. See the Appendix: Best Sellers in the Sixties.

[2]Howe believes that terms such as "the political novel" and "the psychological novel" are "loose" terms. Such terms "at most,...point to a dominant emphasis, a significant stress in the writer's subject or in his attitude toward it" (18). When asked whether *A Tale of Two Cities* was a political novel, Howe told an audience "that I meant by a political novel any novel I wished to treat as if it were a political novel, though clearly one would not wish to treat most novels in that way" (18). Speaking more directly about his study of *Politics and the Novel* Howe describes how he will use the term "political novel" in his study. The "political novel is used here as a convenient short hand to suggest the kind of novel in which the relation is interesting enough to warrant investigation" (19).

[3]In *The Political Novel* Blotner surveys the political novel as it has been written throughout the world. He views political novels from several perspectives: as political instruments, as history, as mirrors of national character, as group political behavior and as individual political behavior.

[4]In *The Modern American Political Novel* Blotner continues to complicate the problem of definition. He includes in his study John Dos Passos' *Adventures of a Young Man*, Lionel Trilling's *The Middle of the Journey* and Norman Mailer's *Barbary Shore*, novels which "do not deal primarily with politicians in the process of directing campaigns, running for office, or performing duties of elective posts" (9). However, Blotner advises that these novels are included because "they present persons (and phenomena) of intense political seriousness who are prevented from performing most such functions because the avenues of office and power are denied them, beyond this they are intensely concerned with political theory and action" (9). As he did in *The Political Novel* Blotner presents chapters on various kinds of political novels. The categories or divisions are much different from those presented in *The Political Novel*: The Young Knight, The Boss, Corruption, Woman as Guide, The Southern Politician, American Fascism, The Far Right and McCarthyism, Disillusionment and the Intellectual, and American Politics Abroad. Blotner regards the novels that he has studied as "reflections of aspects of American political life as seen by the novelists"; and *The Modern American Political Novel* "includes all the political novels" that "he could find" (14).

[5]In *Obligation and the Body Politic* Joseph Tussman concisely links together three troublesome terms: power, politics, and the political arts. Politics "is the study of the struggle for power or influence, its seizure, organization, growth, dissipation or circulation;" the political arts "are the arts of control, of managing a human herd" (4).

⁶Tussman in *Obligation and the Body Politic* makes a distinction between voluntary and non-voluntary participation in government. A democratic body politic is voluntarily formed by its members who can choose to act either actively (by the vote) or passively (non-voting citizens). A non-voluntary body politic views government or the "sovereign as the 'supreme coercive power'." In this type of body politic the "ruler dominates the scene" through power. Tussman explains that "a body politic, on this view, is simply a group of individuals under the domination of a single power, obeying a common center of command, afraid of the same master" (3-4). The Union of the Soviet Socialist Republic would be an example of a non-voluntary or the "supreme coercive power" body politic—a body politic lacking freedom, held together by power, custom, and habit.

⁷In popular, mainstream political fiction realistic technique and an interesting plot might be enough to create "a willing suspension of disbelief" for unsophisticated readers or for sophisticated readers who are writing primarily for escape or entertainment. Much of the Best Selling political fiction of the sixties was primarily escapist. Though serious ideas and serious subjects were treated in the novel, they were not always presented in a serious or sophisticated manner. An example of an escapist and at times a semi-pornographic or erotic political novel is *Dark Horse* by Fletcher Knebel which appeared 19 weeks on *The New York Times* Best Seller List (July 16, 1972—Nov. 26, 1972).

⁸Two books published in 1984 *The Rise of the Right* and *The Republican Right* chronicle the rise of the conservative movement in America during the last twenty-five years and the reluctance of "liberal" opponents who dominate the media to respond seriously, or to take seriously the conservative ideology that was emerging: David W. Reinherd, *The Republican Right* since 1945 (Lexington: The University of Kentucky Press, 1983) and William A. Rusher, *The Rise of the Right* (New York: William Morrow and Company, Inc. 1984).

⁹As a lecturer, for several years prior to his 1964 speech at the Republican Convention, Ronald Reagan presented one basic speech to audiences throughout the country. The text used for documentation in this study is from the speech titled "Encroaching Government Control: Keep Government Poor and Remain Free" which was presented to The Orange County California Press Club, July 28, 1961 and published in *Vital Speeches*, vol. XXVII, no. 22, September 1, 1961, pp. 677-681.

Chapter II

¹On the tenth anniversary of the Communist takeover of Saigon asn Associated Press news story reported that the Vietnam was "the United States longest, most costly and most divisive war, with 58,020 American dead and more than $150 billion spent in military aid to keep the South Vietnamese government in power" (George Esper, "Broke and shunned, Vietnam faces a joyless anniversary, *"The Louisville Courier Journal*, 14 April 1985 D1, 4).

²Le Duc Tho, the Vietnamese negotiator at the Paris Peace talks, and Secretary of State Henry Kissinger were awarded the Nobel Peace Prize in 1973 for their work in negotiating the Peace Treaty. Tho declined his prize; Kissinger accepted his. Ten years after the collapse of Saigon, recriminations and distortions and different perceptions of the Vietnam negotiations and agreements continue. After the fall of Saigon, "Tho complained of 'misrepresentations' by Kissinger during and since the talks. He criticized Kissinger for accusing Hanoi of violating the treaty in its drive that led to the downfall of Saigon." Tho accused the South Vietnamese government

of violating the Peace Treaty and of underestimating the capacity of the North Vietnamese army and stated that "Kissinger has part of the responsibility (for the defeat of the South)" (Bob Sector, "Vietnamese negotiator claims Kissinger lied," *Louisville Courier Journal*, 2 May 1985, A8).

[3]For example,

Kate Witherspoon was moaning blissfully under the ministrations of Eddie Quinn and was slowly turning herself to another pitch of joy. The laving of the right ear by Eddie's tongue, a minor movement orchestrated to the more stately symphony of the pelvic region, aroused sweet torment... Her ear canal quivered deliciously and sent jubilant telegrams racing from one sensory outpost to another" etc. (Knebel Fletcher, *Dark Horse* 40-41).

Chapter III

[1]To Frye, the term *anatomy* replaces the term *Menippean satire. Anatomy* in Burton's *Anatomy of Melancholy*, Frye tells us, "means a dissection or analysis, and expresses very accurately the intellectualized approach of this form" (311-312). The *anatomy* in "its most concentrated" form "presents us with a vision of the world in terms of a single intellectual pattern" (310), and the anatomist, "dealing with intellectual themes and attitudes, shows his exuberance in intellectual ways, by piling up an enormous mass of erudition about his theme or in overwhelming his pedantic targets with an avalanche of their own jargon" (311).

[2]In the anatomy, "Pedants, bigots, cranks, parvenus, virtuosi, enthusiasts, rapacious and *incompetent professional men* of all kinds are handled in terms of their occupational approach to life as distinct from their social behavior" (309 Italics added.)

[3]Frye warns that anatomies are frequently harshly judged because of this "loose-jointed" structure: "The intellectual structure built up from the story makes for violent dislocations in the customary logic of the narrative, though the appearance of carelessness that results reflects only the carelessness of the reader or his tendency to judge by a novel-centered conception of fiction" (310).

[4]At the conclusion of *Come Nineveh, Come Tyre* Russia is in the process of imposing such control over the United States as a result of a weak "liberal" president, Ted Jason, who commits suicide.

Chapter IV

[1]Senator James Eastland "ranted against the NAACP" at the White Citizen's Council rally where these handbills were distributed. The three Montgomery City Commissioners were members of the White Citizens Council and the rally was held at the Montgomery Coliseum (Oates 91-92).

Chapter V

[1]In 1978, "after a number of conservative senators heatedly opposed relinquishing 'sovereign rights and jurisdiction' over the canal, claiming that it would pose a threat to American security," two United States and Panama treaties were ratified which eliminated the United States Canal Zone, thereby restoring the possession of the land and water to Panama in exchange for America's right to protect and to operate the canal until the year 2000. Supporters of the treaties urged that they would "end an important source of resentment against the United States in Panama, and, indeed, all of Latin America" (Gruber 861-862). The clash between America and Panamanian

rights to control and operate the canal is a recurring one in Drury's political series, as is also the question of Communist influence and revolution in Latin America.

[2]A 1985 *Time* magazine article recalls the bitter conflict between the press and the government during the Vietnam War: "When Dean Rusk was Secretary of State during the Vietnam years, he angered the press by asking a persistent reporter, 'Whose side are you on?' " (Thomas Griffith, "It's News, but Is It Reality," *Time* 27 May 1985, 67). General Westmoreland who unsuccessfully sued CBS for libel because they alleged that he wrongfully reported Communist troop strength prior to the Tet offensive in January, 1968, believed that the American press turned a Vietcong defeat into a Vietcong victory: "After the war, in an angry tirade against the press, General Westmoreland alleged that voluminous, lurid, and distorted newspaper and particularly television reports of the Tet attacks had transformed a devastating Communist defeat in Vietnam into a 'psychological vistory' for the enemy" (Karnow 545). Although General Westmoreland did not win his libel suit against CBS for its documentary "The Uncounted Enemy: A Vietnam Deception," he claimed that his honor was vindicated. As a result of a critical cover story in *TV Guide* about the program which won the Society of Professional Journalists' Distinguished Service Award in Magazine Reporting, CBS initiated an internal investigation of the program. As a result CBS issued a formal statement which "admitted many of the charges" but "basically defended the integrity of the document" (Don Kowet, *A Matter of Honor: General William C. Westmoreland Versus CBS*, inside cover).

Walter Cronkite's final response to the Tet offensive caused President Johnson much anguish. In *Vietnam* Stanley Karnow reports that Cronkite's view on Vietnam up to the Tet offensive "had mostly been balanced, nearly bland," but in February, 1968, he changed his views about the war: "Just back from Saigon, he rejected the official forecasts of victory, predicting instead that it seemed 'more certain than ever that the bloody experience of Vietnam is to end in a stalemate.' The broadcast shocked and depressed Johnson, who assumed that Cronkite's despondent comment would steer public opinion even farther away from support for the war. But Cronkite, like all other journalists, was lagging behind the American public—reflecting rather than shaping its attitudes" (547-548). *Capable of Honor* was completed before the Tet offensive; Drury's depiction of the media conflict was prescient.

Chapter VI

[1]In *The Rise of the Right* William Rusher presents the Sharon Statement in full since he believes that it "succinctly and comprehensively" describes "what modern American conservatism was all about." In addition to the four statements which are quoted in the text, the Sharon Statement declared the following:

In this time of moral and political crisis, it is the responsibility of the youth of America to affirm certain eternal truths.

We, as young conservatives, believe:

That foremost among the transcendent values is the individual's use of his God-given free will, whence derives his right to be free from the restrictions of arbitrary force;

That liberty is indivisible, and that political freedom cannot long exist without economic freedom;

That the purposes of government are to protect these freedoms through the preservation of internal order, the provision of national defense, and the administration of justice;

That when government ventures beyond these rightful functions, it accumulates power which tends to diminish order and liberty;

That the Constitution of the United States is the best arrangement yet devised for empowering government to fulfill its proper role, while restraining it from the concentration and abuse of power;

That the genius of the Constitution—the division of powers—is summed up in the clause which reserves primacy to the several states, or to the people, in those spheres not specifically delegated to the Federal Government;

That the market economy, allocating resources by the free play of supply and demand, is the single economic system compatible with the requirements of personal freedom and constitutional government, and that it is at the same time the most productive supplier of human needs;

That when government interferes with the work of the market economy, it tends to reduce the moral and physical strength of the nation; that when it takes from one many to bestow on another, it diminishes the incentive of the first, the integrity of the second, and the moral autonomy of both; (90, 91).

These beliefs pretty much parallel the beliefs expressed by Russell Kirk which are quoted in the text, and such statements provide the intellectual framework for understanding the Knox character as a reflection of ideas which were a significant part of the spirit of the age when Drury was composing his political fiction.

Chapter VII

[1]After Martin Luther King was assassinated in April, 1968, there were riots in many American cities, including Chicago. When Chicago's West Side ghetto erupted, Daley gave an order to shoot rioters: "I told (police superintendent) Conlisk to issue an order to police to shoot to maim or cripple anyone looting any stores in our city.... I assumed that every police superintendent would issue instructions to shoot an arsonist on sight and to maim or cripple any looters. I found out this morning that such orders had not been given to shoot arsonists. I was disappointed that orders had not been given to shoot arsonists" (O'Connor, *Clout* 201). As we have indicated earlier, racial hostility in Chicago was extremely high, and Mayor Daley, the last of the big city bosses, was unsympathetic to the Civil Rights Movement. When there was a Civil Rights Demonstration in Bridgeport, Mayor Daley's neighborhood, Mike Royko reports that the Mayor gave orders—out of sight—from his home, and police arrested the peaceful demonstrators rather than the egg and rock throwing whites who chanted "Two-four-six-eight, we don't want to integrate" and sang "Oh, I wish I was an Alabama trooper, that is what I really like to be-ee-ee. Cuz if I was an Alabama trooper, I could kill the niggers legally" (*Boss* 140).

The riots in Drury fiction are political riots, and protestors fear that America will become a police state. Again, Daley's Chicago serves as a parallel to the fictional world and adds plausibility to Drury's rendering of the spirit of the age. When 5000 anti-war protestors came to Chicago for the 1968 Democratic Convention, the Illinois National Guard (6000) were activated, 5000 federal troops were brought to Chicago, and 12,000 Chicago police were placed on twelve hour duty (O'Connor 204), and still violence erupted. During one night of the convention, Royko reports, protestors ran through Lincoln Park chanting "kill, kill, kill" and neighborhood residents responded sympathetically to indiscriminate police brutality: "Police beat people many blocks from the park, invaded a couple of homes, sprayed Mace into the shocked faces of residents who leaned out of their windows to look, and proved with their cries of 'kill the motherfuckers' that the hippies had no copyright on gutter language" (183). While demonstrators were being beaten by police on Michigan avenue and Major Daley remained inside the convention center, a delegate asked: "Is there any rule under which Mayor Daley can be compelled to suspend the police state being perpetrated at this minute on kids in front of the Conrad Hilton?" When Senator Ribicoff nominated Senator McGovern for president, he commented: "If we had McGovern, we wouldn't have the Gestapo in the streets of Chicago" (184). The violence on Michigan avenue, as well as the convention comments, were presented on national television.

Daley justified the city's tough response to the demonstrators by citing "reports and intelligence on his desk that certain people planned to assassinate many of the leaders, including himself" (187). On Thursday night Daley packed the convention with his supporters, and they chanted "we love Daley, we love Daley" when he entered the hall. During the evening Daley used his supporters to drown out speakers he opposed and disdained: "the Mayor of Chicago 'turned them on and off like an orchestra conductor' " (188). Such was the spirit of the age in Chicago in 1968; *Preserve and Protect* was written between July, 1967 and April, 1968 before the assassination of King and the Democratic Convention.

²In 1950 Congress passed the McCarran Act which was a tough anticommunist bill which authorized the Attorney General to imprison potential spies and saboteurs in time of war, invasion, or insurrection. Under the McCarran Act all Communist and Communist front organizations were required to register with the Justice Department and to label all of their propaganda as Communist propaganda. Under the law maximum penalties for violations were ten years imprisonment and $10,000 fine. Although an appeal procedure was contained in the McCarran Act, the Attorney General was given the power "to cite at any time organizations which he believes to be Communist or Communist fronts" ("There Is a Danger" and "The Anti-Communist Bill," *Time* 25 September 1950, pp. 21-22). Something of the spirit of the age can also be gleaned from the news story about the McCarran Act published in *U.S. News and World Report* which contained a box titled "Roundup Schedule" which presented four statements: "Communists are not to be put into camps now. Concentration camps await many if war comes. FBI crackdown also awaits some fellow travelers. Early registration is called for under plan approved by Congress" ("About Rules for Communists," *U.S. News and World Report*, 29 September 1950, p. 56). Because of the broad parameters of the Act and the power of the Attorney General, some Civil Rights leaders feared that the McCarren Act would be invoked against them as a result of alleged, and perhaps real, Communist infiltration into the Civil Rights Movement and because of the possibility that urban riots might be labeled insurrections. Major Daley of Chicago, for example, stated that "known Communists" had infiltrated the Civil Rights Movement when they demonstrated in his Bridgeport neighborhood (Royko 142). The McCarran Act lends some credibility to the Help America Bill which President Abbott sends to Congress in *Preserve and Protect* and which is passed in *Come Nineveh, Come Tyre*.

Chapter VIII

[1]In *The Modern Political Novel* Joseph Blotner makes use of archetypes as he divides the political novel into several categories, one of which is titled "The Young Knight" and has its roots in the St. George myth (10-13, 18-20). Blotner cites Frye as well as others in his discussion of myth, archetypes, and literature.

Chapter IX

[1]Reinhold Niebuhr indicates the difficulty of defining liberals and conservatives in an article titled "Liberalism: Illusions and Realities" published in *The New Republic*. Niebuhr traces the historical shifts in the meaning of *liberal and conservative* in Europe and America and comments upon the fact that these terms have not always been mutually exclusive. For example, Niebuhr writes: "The new conservatism about which one hears so much these days may claim a right to the title of "liberalism" on the ground that its promise of gaining justice through economic liberty is actually closer to the old classical economic liberalism than the new liberalism is" (4 July 1955, 11-13).

Bibliography

History, Criticism, and Biography

"About Rules for Communists." *U.S. News & World Report*. 29 September 1950: 56.

"The Anti-Communist Bill." *Time*. 25 September 1950: 22.

Barck, Oscar Theodore Jr., and Nelson Manfred Blake. *Since 1900: A History of the United States*. 5th ed. New York: Macmillan Company, 1962.

Bernstein, Carl and Bob Woodward. *All the President's Men*. New York: Simon and Schuster, 1974.

Bernstein, Carl and Bob Woodward. *The Final Days*. New York: Simon and Schuster, 1976.

Blotner, Joseph Leo. *The Political Novel*, Westport, Connecticut: Greenwood Press, 1955.

— *The Modern American Political Novel, 1900-1960* Austin: University of Texas, 1966.

"CBS Reports: 'The CIA's Secret Army. Narr. Bill Moyers. Prod. Judy Crichton and George Crile. June 10, 1977.

Cheever, John. "Letter to the Editor." *New York Review of Books*. February 3, 1977:44.

Crane, Ronald S. "The Concept of Plot and the Plot of Tom Jones." *Critics and Criticism: Ancient and Modern*. Ed. R.S. Crane. Chicago: The University of Chicago Press, 1952. pp. 616-647.

Dean, John. *Blind Ambition: The White House Years*. New York: Simon and Schuster, 1976.

Esper, George. "Broke and Shunned, Vietnam Faces a Joyless Anniversary." *The Courier Journal (Louisville)*. 14 April 1985, Sec. D:56.

"The Fall of Mr. Law and Order." *Newsweek*. 22 October 1973: 27-36.

Fielding, Henry. "The Preface to Joseph Andrews." *Joseph Andrews*. Ed. Martin C. Battestin. Boston: Houghton, Mifflin Company, Riverside Edition, 1961.

Forster, E.M. *Aspects of the Novel*. New York: Harcourt Brace and Company, 1927.

Friedan, Betty. *The Feminine Mystique*. New York: W.W. Norton and Company, 1963.

Frye, Northrop. *The Anatomy of Criticism*. Princeton, New Jersey: Princeton University Press, 1957.

Goldman, Eric. *The Crucial Decade and After: America, 1945-1960*. New York: Random House, Vintage Books, 1960.

Goldman, Peter and Anthony Marro. "J. Edgar Hoover's Secret Files." *Newsweek*. 10 March 1975: 16-17.

Goleman, Daniel. " 'Powerholics' are flocking to Washington therapists." *Courier Journal (Louisville)* 21 April 1975, Sec. D: 1, 4.

Griffith, Thomas. "It's News, but Is It Reality." *Time*. 27 May 1985: 67.

Gruber, Rebecca Brooks. *An American History.* 3rd ed. Reading, Massachusetts: Addison Publishing Company, 1981.

Harwood, Richard and Walter Pincus. "New Article Alleges More Links Between CIA, Journalists." *The Louisville Courier Journal and Times.* 25 September 1977, Sec. D:3.

Hayes, Carlton J.M., Marshall Whitehead Baldwin, and Charles Woolsey Cole. *History of Western Civilization.* New York: Macmillan Company, 1962.

Howe, Irving. *Politics and the Novel.* Greenwich, Connecticut: Fawcett Publications, 1957.

"Inside Story: Special Edition: Vietnam OP/ED." A Production of the Press and The Public Project, Inc., for PBS, 1985.

James, Henry. *Partial Portraits.* Macmillan and Company, 1888; reprint ed., Westport, Connecticut: Greenwood Press, 1970.

Jaworski, Leon. *The Right and the Power: The Prosecution of Watergate.* New York and Houston: Reader's Digest and Gulf Publishing Company, 1976.

Karnow, Stanley. *Vietnam: A History.* New York: The Viking Press, 1983.

Kirk, Russell. *The Conservative Mind from Burke to Santayana.* Chicago: Henry Regnery Company, 1953.

Kowet, Don. *A Matter of Honor: General Westmoreland Versus CBS.* New York: Macmillan Publishing Company, 1984 and London: Collier Macmillan Publishers, 1984.

Lewes, George Henry. "The Lady Novelists." *Women's Liberation Literature.* Ed. Elaine Showalter. New York: Harcourt Brace, and Jovanovich, Inc., 1971, 171-183.

Machiavelli, Niccolo. *The Chief Works and Others.* Trans. Allan Gilbert. Vol. 1: *The Prince.* Durham, North Carolina: Duke University Press, 1965.

Marchetti, Victor and John Marks. *The CIA and the Cult of Intelligence.* New York: Alfred A. Knopf, 1974.

Milne, Gordon. *The American Political Novel.* Norman, Oklahoma: University of Oklahoma Press, 1955.

"Mitchell's 'White House Horrors.'" *Newsweek,* 23 July 1973: 22.

Niebuhr, Reinhold. "Liberalism: Illusion and Realities." *The New Republic.* 4 July 1955: 11-13.

Oates, Stephen B. *Let the Trumpets Sound. The Life of Martin Luther King, Jr.* New York: Harper and Row, 1982.

O'Connor, Len. *Clout, Mayor Daley and His City.* Chicago: Henry Regnery Company, 1975.

"Point of Disorder." Rev. of *Preserve and Protect. Time,* 20 September 1968: 110.

Reagan, Ronald. "Encroaching Control, Keep Government Poor and Remain Free." *Vital Speeches,* Vol. XXXVII, No. 22 (September 1, 1961): 677-681.

Reeves, Thomas C. *The Life and Times of Joe McCarthy. A Biography.* New York: Stein and Day, 1982.

Reinhard, David W. *The Republican Right Since 1945.* The University Press of Kentucky, 1983.

Rogers, W.C. "Walter Wonderful." *New York Times Book Review,* 11 September 1966: 54.

Rotondaro, Fred. Rev. of *Capable of Honor. Best Sellers,* 15 September 1966; 206.

Royko, Mike. *Boss.* New York: E. Dutton and Company, 1971.

Rusher, William A. *The Rise of the Right*. New York: William Morrow and Company, 1984.

Ruskin, John. *The Works of John Ruskin*. Library Edition. Ed. E.T. Cook and Alexander Wedderburn. Vol. 17; *Unto This Last*. London: George Allen and New York: Longman's Green and Company, 1905.

Sears, Lawrence. "Liberals and Conservatives." *The Antioch Review*, 13, No. 3 (Fall 1953): 361-370.

Seib, Charles. "CIA Still Taints the Press." *Washington Post*. 11 June 1976, Sec. A: 27.

Seib, Charles. "Spies Under Media Cover." *Washington Post*. 14 May 1976, Sec. A: 27.

Sector, Bob. "Vietnamese Negotiator Claims Kissinger Lied." *Courier Journal (Louisville)*. 2 May 1985, Sec. A:8.

Speare, Edmund. *The Political Novel: The Development in England and America*, New York: Russell and Russell, 1966.

"There Is a Danger." *Time*. 25 September 1950: 21-22.

Tussman, Joseph. *Obligation and the Body Politic*. London: Oxford University Press, 1960.

White, Theodore. *America in Search of Herself. The Making of the President, 1956-1980*. New York: Harper and Row, 1982.

Williams, Duncan. *Trousered Apes; Sick Literature in a Sick Society*. New York: Dell Publishing Company, 1971.

Wills, Garry. *The Kennedy Imprisonment*. New York and Boston: Little, Brown and Company, 1981.

Wolfe, Tom and E.W. Johnson. *The New Journalism*. New York: Harper and Row, 1973.

Political Fiction

Burdick, Eugene and Harvey Wheeler. *Fail-Safe*. New York: Mcgraw Hill, 1962.

Burdick, Eugene. *The 480*. New York: Dell Publishing Company, 1964.

Drury, Allen. *Advise and Consent*. Garden City, New York: Doubleday 1959.

Drury, Allen *Capable of Honor*. Garden City, New York: Doubleday, 1967.

Drury, Allen. *Come Nineveh, Come Tyre*. Garden City, New York: Doubleday, 1966.

Drury, Allen. *Preserve and Protect*. Garden City, New York: Doubleday, 1968.

Drury, Allen. *A Promise of Joy*. Garden City, New York: Doubleday, 1975.

Drury, Allen. *A Shade of Difference*. Garden City, New York: Doubleday, 1962.

Knebel, Fletcher. *Dark Horse*. Garden City, New York: Doubleday, 1972.

Knebel, Fletcher. *Night of Camp David*. New York: Harper and Row, 1965.

Knebel, Fletcher and Charles W. Bailey. *Seven Days in May*. New York: Harper and Row, 1962.

Knebel, Fletcher. *Vanished*. Garden City, New York: Doubleday, 1972.

Pearson, Drew. *The President*. Garden City, New York: Doubleday, 1970.

Pearson, Drew. *The Senator*. Garden City, New York: Doubleday, 1968.

Serling, Robert. *The Presidents's Plane is Missing*. Garden City, New York: Doubleday, 1967.

Vidal, Gore. *Washington, D.C.* Boston and Toronto: Little, Brown and Company, 1967.

Wallace, Irving. *The Man*. New York: Simon and Schuster, 1964.

Appendix

Best Selling, Washington Focused
Pre-Watergate Political Fiction (1960-1972)
And Allen Drury's Political Series (1959-1975)

Author	Book	Dates on the *New York Times* Best Seller List	Number of Weeks
Burdick	Fail-Safe	Nov. 4, 1962-June 2, 1963	31
Burdick	The 480	July 12, 1964-Oct. 4, 1964	13
Knebel	Dark Horse	July 16, 1972-Nov. 26, 1972	19
Knebel and Bailey	Seven Days in May	Sept. 23, 1962-Aug. 25, 1963	49
Knebel	Night of Camp David	June 13, 1965-Oct. 24, 1965	16
Knebel	Vanished	Jan. 28, 1968-Sept. 8, 1968	32
Pearson	The Senator	Sept. 15, 1968-Jan. 12, 1969	17
Serling	The President's Plane is Missing	Nov. 26, 1967-April 28, 1968	22
Vidal	Washington, D.C.	May 21, 1967-Oct. 1, 1967	20
Wallace	The Man	Oct. 4, 1964-June 20, 1965	38
		Total Weeks	257
Drury	Advise and Consent	Aug. 15, 1959-July 30, 1961	102
Drury	A Shade of Difference	Oct. 7, 1962-April 7, 1963	26
Drury	Capable of Honor	Oct. 2, 1966-July 16, 1967	41
Drury	Preserve and Protect	Sept. 29, 1968-April 6, 1969	28
Drury	Come Nineveh, Come Tyre	Nov. 25, 1973-May 22, 1974	26
Drury	A Promise of Joy	May 30, 1975-Aug. 3, 1975	19
		Total Weeks	242

Index